# FRENCH KISS

# CHANTAL HÉBERT

# FRENCH KISS

## STEPHEN HARPER'S BLIND DATE WITH QUEBEC

ALFRED A. KNOPF CANADA

PUBLISHED BY ALFRED A. KNOPF CANADA

Copyright © 2007 Chantal Hébert

www.randomhouse.ca


Library and Archives Canada Cataloguing in Publication

Hébert, Chantal, 1954–
    French kiss : Stephen Harper's blind date with Quebec / Chantal
Hébert.

ISBN 978-0-676-97907-7

1. Canada—Politics and government—2006–. 2. Québec (Province)—Politics
and government-2003–. 3. Federal-provincial relations—Québec (Province).
I. Title.

FC640.H42 2006          971.07'3          C2006-905390-1


Text design: CS Richardson

First Edition

Printed and bound in the United States of America

10   9   8   7   6   5   4   3   2   1

*For Micheline and Jean-Raymond*

# CONTENTS

# INTRODUCTION

A book about Stephen Harper's 2006 election and his blind date with Quebec is inevitably a book about two missed rendezvous with history.

One is the realization of the Quebec sovereignty movement's goal for full-fledged statehood for the province; and the other is Paul Martin's fulfilment of his presumed destiny as a great Canadian prime minister.

Both had been forecast, by different seers, to take place around the beginning of the new century. Neither materialized. Reading the tea leaves of Canadian politics to get a glimpse into the future is always a risky business.

In October 1995, the Quebec sovereignty movement looked to be so close to its goal that many pundits doubted that the Canadian federation would cross into the new century in one piece. But more than ten years have come and gone and while the Quebec movement is hardly a spent force, the post-referendum decade has sapped its momentum. Instead of floating down the current of history, Quebec sovereignists have had to row upstream, struggling just to stay in place, and not always succeeding.

Yet this has also been a decade of missed opportunities on the federalist side, capped by the dismal failure of Paul Martin to make good on the early promises of his leadership.

To all appearances, Paul Martin was the Prince Charming who would seal the Liberal Party's fate as Canada's ongoing governing party. He became leader at a time when the stars were aligned for a new Quebec–Canada romance. The charismatic Lucien Bouchard had gone, a pariah to some within his own quarrelsome movement. The Parti Québécois was no longer in power, its score in the 2003 Quebec election its worst since it first won power, under René Lévesque, in 1976.

The last year of Jean Chrétien's era had been his most successful in Quebec. His resolve to keep Canada out of Iraq, his endorsement of the Kyoto Protocol on greenhouse gases, his conversion to a more transparent regime of political financing and his decision to proceed with same-sex marriage had been home runs in his native province. All was apparently set for Paul Martin to march Quebec back to the federalist altar.

But the Martin who showed up at the doorstep was not the friendly face Quebecers remembered from the 1990 Meech Lake debate when the conditions for Quebec to sign on to the constitution came tantalizingly close to being met, or even the finance minister they had admired in the mid-nineties.

His bouquet had wilted. The red family car was splattered with mud, some of it embedded so deeply that years of trips to the car wash might not restore its shine. The shoes Martin had stepped into when he replaced Jean Chrétien were caked with dirt.

Martin himself had grown into the clumsy politician who shot himself in the foot by simplistically predicting, in the 1995 referendum on Quebec sovereignty, that a million jobs would be jeopardized by sovereignty. He seemed unable to lead Quebec through a single waltz without crushing his partner's toes.

Stephen Harper was the federal leader Quebec voters knew the least about, by far—the only one of the four who had never lived in the province. In the end, that only seemed to make him more attractive. Besides, by the time Harper came knocking,

Quebec was all dressed up with nowhere terribly exciting to go. The Conservative surge in Quebec was the big surprise of the 2006 federal election. Decades of conventional wisdom flew out the window that night.

If there was ever a match not made in heaven, this was it. Canada's social-democrat province par excellence had bestowed the princely gift of a national mandate on the most conservative prime minister in modern Canadian history, and certainly the only one to pride himself on not being called progressive.

Since January 2006, Harper has striven to turn his unlikely blind date with Quebec into a lasting relationship. But at what cost to his personality, and that of his party?

A stolen kiss is not necessarily the beginning of a great love affair, but it's better than nothing—just ask the New Democratic Party (NDP)—which has been spurned by Quebec for all of its history.

The Liberals and the New Democrats have scorned each other in the past, but misery loves company. Trapped in opposition, the NDP has not aged well. And the Liberals don't even have the genes of an opposition party. The time may have come for them to consider uniting against the Conservatives.

Paul Martin's rendezvous with history is gone for good—a personal tragedy for a man who spent so many years waiting to claim his place at the top, only to come to an inconclusive end, and a setback for a country that invested much of its hope in his destiny. But Martin could turn out to be only the first of a string of disposable prime ministers. In January 2006, voters replaced a Liberal government on probation with an on-trial Conservative regime. It took a profound malaise to throw Quebec into the unlikely embrace of Stephen Harper. That malaise did not suddenly materialize over the brief life of the last Liberal government. On the left and on the right, in Quebec as in the rest of Canada, the coalitions that saw Canada through the twentieth century have broken down. The next majority government in Canada will belong to whomever is the most adept at reassembling the pieces of the federation before it is broken up for good into irreconcilable blocks.

PART 1

—

# THE STARS ALIGN

—

## CHAPTER ONE

## A PERFECT DAY FOR AN ECLIPSE

I n Canada, the stars align in such a way as to let the
Conservative moon block out the Liberal sun about once
in a generation. If every forecast were to be believed,
January 23, 2006, was going to be such a day.

For weeks, Canada's top pollsters had charted the capricious
course of public opinion, and they all concurred. Change of a
magnitude that few had imagined when Canada's thirty-ninth
federal election had been called, back in November of the previous year, was in the offing. One of Canada's longest electoral
campaigns was poised to deliver an unexpected prime minister,
Stephen Harper, about whom little was known and much was
feared. For weeks, Liberals had been warning voters about an
ominous hidden Conservative agenda and a sharp turn to the
right in federal politics.

With political observers calling for clear blue skies over much
of the country, the Conservatives who converged on the Calgary
Convention Centre to watch the election results were as certain
of victory as they had been in decades.

In the past, episodes of Tory rule had usually been exciting
but unsettling times, periods of uncertain duration ruled primarily by the law of unintended consequences.

The 1979 victory of Conservative prime minister Joe Clark

had turned out to be a short-lived distraction. His minority government never reached its first-year anniversary. It was defeated on its first budget vote a few months after the election. Clark was only in office long enough to allow the Liberals to recoup and Pierre Trudeau to get a second wind. That second wind would sweep the country into an era of dramatic change, as he reshaped the Canadian constitutional landscape according to his own designs, and then retired. "French power will always exist. No Canada can exist without the support of this province," the Liberal prime minister told the Quebec wing of his party in March 1984, only a few months before his retirement.

Trudeau's declaration was a prescient one. While Canadians have not had occasion to find out whether their country can exist without Quebec, they certainly had occasion, after he stepped down, to find that it was next to impossible for a party to make it to power without Quebec's support.

Along with Jean Marchand and Gérard Pelletier, Trudeau had come to Parliament Hill at the invitation of Lester B. Pearson in 1965. Over the decade and a half that he and his fellow recruits spent in federal politics, Quebecers had carved out an unprecedented place in the running of the affairs of the country. They did not let go of the levers of power after Trudeau's departure.

In 1984, voters stunned many observers by taking Trudeau at his word and electing Brian Mulroney, another Quebec leader, albeit one from a different political party. A prime minister from Quebec prevailed in five subsequent elections.

But by January 23, 2006—more than two decades after Brian Mulroney had first demonstrated the truth of Trudeau's prediction, and in the wake of the turbulent reign of Jean Chrétien and the aborted first mandate of Paul Martin, French power had become a faint shadow of the proud dynasty of the sixties. The line of prime ministers from Quebec was expected to run out on that voting day. And many Quebecers were expected to take a willing hand in bypassing two of their own to hand power over to a leader from Alberta.

All weekend, Conservative strategists had crunched their numbers. In their best-case scenario, they would break through to a majority and sail on to four years of unfettered federal power. Their worst-case scenario would leave them about a dozen seats short of the safety zone, with MPs in every province, and in a comfortable enough zone that they could show Canadians their mettle for as long as they needed to make the case for a majority next time.

Except that, over the course of the final weekend of the campaign, clouds moved in on their horizon. Not for the first time in the history of the party, did the Conservative math not add up. Urban and Ontario voters were suspicious of Harper, and the floor that Tory strategists had seen as rock bottom would break under the weight of their residual fears. Were it not for Quebecers, the first Conservative government of the twenty-first century would have been stillborn.

For the first time in decades, the decks were no longer stacked in favour of the Liberals. The most elementary assumptions of the sovereignty movement were found wanting. Sovereignist strategists had never imagined that Quebec voters would punish the Liberals by supporting the Conservatives rather than rallying to the Bloc Québécois. And the Canadian left seemed more dangerously divided than it had ever been. By splitting the progressive vote, the NDP and the Liberals had helped Stephen Harper elect enough MPs to form a government.

Like many of Canada's defining struggles, this battle for the soul of the country would take place primarily on Quebec soil. Unlike previous ones, it would not be fought exclusively between Quebec generals.

Back in the Calgary hall where Conservatives had gathered on election night 2006, Ontario was clearly the party-pooper.

The evening had got off to a fine start. The Quebec Tory break-through that had seemed so improbable at the beginning of the campaign had materialized early. In short order, the party had claimed seats in ridings as diverse as Pontiac in federalist Outaouais, Louis-Saint-Laurent in the provincial capital of Quebec City, Beauce in the entrepreneurial heartland of Quebec and Jonquière–Alma in the nationalist bedrock of the Saguenay.

Six more Quebec seats were to come, for a total of ten, many of them won with the kind of big majorities that usually attend landslide victories. In Beauce, Maxime Bernier, whose father, Gilles, had once presided over Brian Mulroney's Quebec cau-cus, had won 67 percent of the vote. In Jonquière–Alma, Jean-Pierre Blackburn, the Tory MP who had tearfully taken down the Canadian flag from his backyard pole on the day the Meech Lake Accord died in June 1990, was sent back to the federal capital after a thirteen-year absence, by 52 percent of the voters of his nationalist riding. During the interval, Blackburn had paid a steep price for turning down the overtures of the Bloc Québécois and sticking with Mulroney. He had gone down with the Tory ship in 1993, and had then been defeated for mayor of Jonquière in the autumn of the 1995 referendum, a particularly poor time to be a federalist running in any sort of election con-test in the Saguenay.

The magnitude of the breakthrough was not lost on the peo-ple in that hall in Calgary; every time a Quebec Tory was declared elected by one of the television networks, the results were drowned out by loud cheers. That same night, Ontario would elect four times as many Tories as Quebec, but it was the Quebec turnaround that caused the biggest sensation.

Memories are often conveniently short in politics, and to some extent this was a night of selective amnesia for the Conservative movement. In the late eighties, in Alberta halls such as these, many of these same people had applauded the birth of the

Reform Party. Back then, they had invested the breakaway conservative party with their fervent hope that it would free the Canadian right from the tyranny of Quebec influence. In 1984, Conservative prime minister Brian Mulroney had come to power on the basis of a strong Quebec–Alberta coalition. But by 1993, the coalition had imploded under the stress of a series of constitutional failures that pitted Quebec nationalists against the right wing of the federal Progressive Conservative Party.

But the conservative movement's relationship with Quebec was coming full circle in more ways than that. In the 1997 federal election campaign, the Reform Party had run English-only ads to implore Canadian voters to terminate the Quebec federal leadership dynasty by rejecting the parties led by Jean Chrétien and Jean Charest.

The ads backfired and were quickly off the air. In the furor that ensued, few would have dared predict that nine years later francophone Quebecers would take matters into their own hands, one-quarter of them putting the X on their ballots next to the names of candidates led by a co-founder of the Reform Party.

A Harper government would not suffer a lack of representation from Quebec—a concern that Joe Clark had had to contend with over the short life of his 1979 minority regime—but it would have to worry about having the bodies required to survive its first week of Parliament.

On the weekend before the election, when Conservative strategists had looked hard at their prospects and come up with their best-guess estimates, their Quebec numbers had been dead-on. They had expected to win between nine and fourteen seats in the province. Their final result was ten ridings. The Prairies and Alberta also had no big surprises in store for them. The results there did not exceed expectations, but they were on track with the party's forecast.

In Atlantic Canada, New Brunswick premier Bernard Lord's and former federal Tory leader Peter MacKay's Conservative coattails proved to be the length of a miniskirt. Delivering only 9 seats out of 32 ridings, Atlantic Canada had not come through for the party. Nor had British Columbia, where the final score was 5 seats short of best-guess Tory scenarios. But the bad-news story of the evening was Ontario. There, the Conservative score of 40 seats amounted to less than half of the province's 106 ridings, well short of the hopes of Conservative strategists.

Ontario was where Prime Minister Paul Martin's team had decided to make its last stand in the dying days of the campaign, and the returns showed that the red Ontario line had largely held. Fifty-four MPs, more than half the caucus that the Liberals would take into the Opposition, were from that province.

Stephen Harper's last campaign week, complete with intemperate statements implying that he saw the courts and the federal civil service as adjuncts of the Liberal Party, had dampened his party's prospects in Canada's biggest electoral market. Ontario—the province psychologically and geographically closest to the main apparatus of the federal government—was neither amused nor reassured by Harper's utterances.

Canada's biggest cities had also given the Conservatives the cold shoulder. In Montreal, the party trailed the Liberals by twenty-three points; in Toronto, the gap was a whopping twenty-eight points; and in Vancouver, the Conservatives finished twenty points behind the Liberals.

Overall, by the end of the evening, the Conservative score was well below the rock bottom that Tory strategists had forecast for themselves just prior to voting day. It was barely within the limits of a workable minority government.

As the evening wore on, the Conservative lead became so thin that pundits turned their attention to the possibility that Paul Martin might actually refuse the verdict of the election, and invite the NDP to join his party in government.

Between the two of them, the Liberals and the New Democrats had more seats than the Conservatives, although they too would be short of a majority if they were called upon to govern. In such a scenario, the Bloc Québécois would have to decide whether to support a fragile rookie Conservative government, or allow a coalition that was ideologically closer to its left-of-centre philosophy to try its hand at governing.

This was pie-in-the-sky punditry. A denial of the Harper victory could only have had legs—albeit shaky ones—if the Conservatives had failed to capture seats in Quebec. A case could then have been made that a Liberal-NDP mix offered Canada more national representation. And even then, the ploy would have amounted to robbing Western Canada of a rare shot at having one of its own as prime minister, a manoeuvre that would have put great strains on Canadian unity, and that the NDP and the Liberals would have had to spend years trying to live down. In any event, the debate as to which of the parties could most legitimately claim to form a government that was national in scope was largely moot, since the Conservatives had pulled ahead of the other federalist parties in Quebec's popular vote.

Once all the votes were counted, only one in five Quebecers had stuck with Martin. Because that number included the rock-solid Liberal fortresses of anglophone Montreal, it camouflaged a rout of historic proportions in francophone Quebec. On January 23, 2006, Quebec was second only to Alberta in its rejection of the federal Liberal Party.

But for the Conservatives, the Quebec results were the bright spot in a picture that was much darker than expected. As the evening wore on, the festive mood in the hall in Calgary gave way to a feeling of uncertainty. The dream of a Conservative government seemed to be turning into the nightmare of an unmanageable minority.

The mood was also going downhill in the suite where the Conservative leader and his advisers were watching the returns. It looked as though Stephen Harper had secured the bare bones of Brian Mulroney's hard-to-handle Quebec–Alberta coalition, along with Joe Clark's short numbers.

By the time the Conservative leader finally emerged to claim his victory and speak to his supporters—past midnight in Atlantic and Central Canada—Paul Martin had not only conceded the election but announced that he would not lead his team in a rematch. To all intents and purposes, he was abdicating before the Chrétien side of the Liberal clan had time to sharpen its knives and come to seek vengeance for the 2002 coup that Martin had led against his predecessor in one of the final episodes of their enduring rivalry.

That took care of any convoluted scenario that could have seen the Liberals clinging to power. Yes Pierre Trudeau had risen from the ashes of a similar defeat in 1980. But Paul Martin was no Pierre Trudeau. Indeed, Martin soon confirmed that he would not even lead the party in opposition until his successor was chosen.

In the first few days after the election, a number of Liberal ministers banded together in a bid to convince Martin to reconsider that decision. They urged him to hang around at least long enough to see if the Conservative government could survive. But they failed to sway him. Curiously, David Emerson—who would defect from the Liberals and be sworn into Stephen Harper's Cabinet a few weeks later—was one of those who made a call to the defeated prime minister to ask him to lead the Liberals in opposition. Who knows? If Martin's answer had been different, Emerson might still be a Liberal member of Parliament.

In the end, Stephen Harper got a shot at putting together a government after all, and he could expect to run it for at least as long as the Liberals were leaderless. Still, Harper was less than jubilant. Upon winning a minority government eighteen months before, Paul Martin had greeted the results with the glee of a man on death row who has just been handed an unexpected pardon. It was as if Martin had not really noticed that his party had been reduced to a minority.

With the ghost of Joe Clark hovering over his shoulder, Stephen Harper seemed all too conscious of his precarious position as he greeted his supporters. Some left the hall after the speech, fearing that they might once again have produced a government that would only serve as a warm-up act for the next Liberal leader. Victory was officially Stephen Harper's, but there was not much of it in the air of the Calgary Convention Centre in the late hours of that election day.

Harper has not publicly divulged the thoughts that came to his mind as he watched his hopes for a solid government founder in Ontario that night, but over the following weeks and months it became clear that he had drawn two tentative conclusions from the experience. The first was that he would have no rest until he came back to this same hall to preside over the election of a majority Conservative government. The second was that his party would look to the less travelled road of Quebec as an alternative route to the treacherous Ontario path to get there.

For the first non-Quebec federal leader to be elected to office in more than a quarter of a century, this was a bold choice. A Quebec political itinerary would involve travelling without much of a road map, in mostly hostile Bloc and Liberal territory, and possibly under a cloud of suspicion in the rest of Canada. But the Bloc was temporarily without a compass. And when it came to figuring out the lay of the land in francophone Quebec, Stephen Harper was already ahead of many of those who would aspire to replace Paul Martin.

—

## CHAPTER TWO

## LOST LIBERALS

A decade and a half before Stephen Harper surprised the country with his win over Paul Martin, Sheila Copps, then the rising female star in the Parliament of Canada, had a glimpse of a future that would see Quebecers favour a politician from elsewhere over a native son or daughter.

In 1990, Copps ran for the leadership of the Liberal Party against Martin and Jean Chrétien, the strongest tandem of federal leadership candidates Quebec had put forward since Claude Wagner and Brian Mulroney defeated each others' bids for the Tory crown in 1976.

While she didn't come close to winning, Copps attracted a remarkable amount of Quebec support and much positive ink. Joe Clark, John Turner, Ed Broadbent and cohorts of lesser figures from the rest of Canada had not managed to make lasting inroads in the province, but in a matter of months the feisty Copps had succeeded in becoming a household name.

Among those who supported her was Quebec's minister of communications, Lawrence Cannon, the very man who would become the top star in Stephen Harper's low-profile 2006 Quebec lineup. On January 23, Cannon beat long odds to become one of the first Conservative MPs declared elected in Quebec, taking from the Liberals the staunchly federalist

Outaouais riding of Pontiac. Back in 1990 he had been a Robert Bourassa Cabinet member and a fervent supporter of the Meech Lake constitutional accord—and just as willing to look beyond Quebec for a federal leader to his liking as when he signed up for the Harper team fifteen years later.

In contrast with many of his provincial colleagues, Sheila Copps and not Paul Martin was his choice. In time, many of Cannon's fellow Quebecers would come to share his indifferent impression of Martin, but back then, he stood out from the crowd.

The leadership episode and her nascent constituency in Quebec stuck in Sheila Copps's mind. For the remainder of her federal career, she strove to remain a presence in the province. She succeeded, at least to the point of being offered a column in the *Journal de Montréal* after her forced retirement from politics in 2004. That column was another first for a political outsider to Quebec.

Sheila Copps was also a glaring exception in a federal Liberal Party that had become intellectually lazy about Quebec in the post-Trudeau era. That laziness reached its apogee in the 1995 referendum campaign on sovereignty. While federal politicians from Quebec fought in the trenches, those from the rest of Canada largely stayed home.

Taking a cue from Jean Chrétien, Reform Party leader Preston Manning—his French non-existent—was invisible in Quebec for the duration of the campaign. The NDP's Audrey McLaughlin's proficiency in Canada's other official language was only marginally higher than Manning's. In any event, she was in the process of handing over the leadership to a successor. She stayed away from the action, leaving Bob Rae, the former Ontario premier, to be the main NDP presence on the hustings.

Like his Liberal predecessor David Peterson, Rae had spent a large chunk of his tenure at the constitutional table, trying in vain to pre-empt the 1995 showdown. Both of them manned the referendum fort for Ontario while Mike Harris, the non-bilingual premier, stayed at Queen's Park, appearing only as a participant in the huge federalist rally that took place in Montreal at the tail end of the campaign.

Not until the campaign took a turn for the worse did most of Jean Chrétien's non-Quebec ministers become totally engaged in the process. As federalist fortunes declined, the thoughts of many leading politicians from the rest of Canada—including some senior federal ministers—started to turn to their potential roles in picking up the pieces of a broken Canada. The process involved at least equal doses of patriotic abnegation and self-interest.

In a 2005 CBC/Radio-Canada documentary, *Breaking Point*, former Fisheries minister Brian Tobin shed some light on his thinking, and on that of most of his Cabinet colleagues from outside Quebec, in the dying days of the referendum. "We asked ourselves difficult questions such as: Could a prime minister from Quebec represent Canada in negotiations? Could a team from Quebec negotiate on Canada's behalf if the province left Canada?" Tobin told the team that put *Breaking Point* together, adding, "The answer is that they couldn't. The structure of government would have to change dramatically."

The fact was that most non-Quebec politicians could aspire to a greater calling in a Canada without Quebec than in a united one. Indeed, the narrow federalist referendum victory and their limited contribution to the outcome would in time put a lid on the political ambitions of most of the prominent politicians who had sat out the referendum.

The reactive attitude of so many high-profile non-Quebec Liberals to such a defining challenge for the federation was part of a pattern that had its roots in the regimes of Pierre Trudeau and Brian Mulroney. By the time the referendum came around, it had become part of the Canadian political culture to leave to Quebecers whatever heavy lifting was involved in dealing with Quebec.

In 1982, Pierre Trudeau's lieutenants had taken his word for the fact that Quebec would come to embrace the patriated Constitution and its made-in-Canada Charter of Rights. The Quebec National Assembly unanimously opposed patriation, but Canadian politicians were assured that Quebecers would eventually come around to the belief that proceeding without the province's accord had been the right thing to do. In fairness, it is hard to see how many non-Quebec Liberals could have thought otherwise, given that all seventy-four members of the Quebec federal caucus were publicly supportive of patriation.

Brian Mulroney's swift 1984 conquest of the province—he won fifty-eight of Quebec's seventy-five seats—could have shaken the widespread Liberal sense that when it came to Quebec, the Quebecers within their ranks knew best. Instead, the Conservative victory had reinforced it.

Rather than alarming the Liberals and raising new questions as to whether the patriation of the Constitution would leave permanent scars on their brand name in Quebec, the Conservative takeover was seen by many Liberals as a passing fad, a symptom of the province's native-son syndrome and a reflection on John Turner's uncertain leadership. On the contrary; it was the first step of a twenty-year decline of the party in Quebec, a period that the federal Liberal establishment spent largely on indulging in denial.

In the normal course of events, the Liberal Party of Canada tends to be made up of astute political animals. When it comes to Quebec, though, they often leave whatever instincts they have at the province's door.

In 1990, few Liberals seemed to wonder how a leadership candidate such as Jean Chrétien, who so clearly stood on the wrong side of the Meech Lake debate in Quebec, could be winning the battle for delegates from the province. Against all evidence, many chose to conclude that the Meech issue was strictly elite-driven.

In fact, it was the federal Liberal leadership campaign that was taking place outside of the Quebec mainstream.

When Liberal politicians from outside the province took time to travel to Quebec to see for themselves how the Meech debate was playing out, they came away with impressions that were much closer to Sheila Copps's alarmed reading of the situation than to Chrétien's take on it.

After a visit to Montreal at the tail end of the Meech Lake negotiations in spring of 1990, New Brunswick premier Frank McKenna noted with trepidation that many Quebecers had come to see the fate of the constitutional accord as a decisive test of Canada's tolerance of their aspirations. On the streets of Quebec's largest city, that was the message he had heard over and over again. Three years into the process, and with Meech teetering on the brink of failure, that seemed to be something of a revelation to McKenna, although he was one of the key provincial players in the debate. But even at that point, the bulk of the federal Liberal establishment was content to dismiss such findings as self-serving figments of Brian Mulroney's and Robert Bourassa's imaginations.

In time, the Liberal notion that Quebec was best left to the Quebecers in the government became cast in stone, with devastating consequences for the party of Sir Wilfrid Laurier and Pierre Trudeau. The feud between the Chrétien and Martin clans, and the decade-long ground war they engaged in, turned this misconception into a life-threatening disability.

For almost a decade after the referendum, Paul Martin—the leading pretender to the throne, and as minister of finance the second-highest-ranking Quebec figure in the government—stayed out of the unity fray, was seen a lot but never much heard from. In the 2000 election he co-starred with Jean Chrétien in Liberal French-language commercials. But between the referendum and Chrétien's last campaign, Martin was virtually silent on the Clarity Act on Quebec secession, the government's landmark piece of post-referendum legislation, which attempted to set some federal ground rules for future secession referendums. As much as possible, he also avoided publicly wading into most of the many Quebec–Ottawa debates that occupied some of his ministerial colleagues from the province on a full-time basis.

His absence from the Quebec debate was so conspicuous that after Martin Cauchon, a Chrétien loyalist, was appointed Chrétien's Quebec lieutenant, some of Cauchon's aides came to talk of their junior minister as the leading Cabinet member from the province, forgetting that Paul Martin also represented Quebec.

Even if Chrétien would have had it any other way, there was no indication that Martin was burning to be proactive on Quebec issues. Once Martin became prime minister, it was quickly apparent that he had less to contribute to the debate than Pierre Trudeau, Brian Mulroney or Chrétien himself had had. When his Quebec ministers finally pushed him to the wall on his vision of federalism, late in his brief mandate, they discovered that they had little common ground with their leader. Stephen Harper, Martin's main federalist opponent, had clearly given the issue more thought than Martin had, and, oddly, his approach to federalism was often closer to that of the Liberal ministers from Quebec than Martin's was.

Other leading pretenders to the Liberal leadership were similarly disengaged. In the years leading up to Chrétien's resignation, Allan Rock and John Manley spent relatively little public time in Quebec, and kept their noses studiously close to their ministerial grindstones whenever they were there. As for their colleague and rival Brian Tobin, he never mastered enough French to be able to take part freely in a francophone dinner conversation.

Having allowed themselves to be reduced to political tourists in Quebec, Allan Rock, Brian Tobin and John Manley all took a pass on the leadership, privately blaming Paul Martin for taking over the party behind their collective backs.

In the case of Quebec, there had been precious little to take over. The Martinites had not so much flooded the party with Quebec supporters as ensured that newcomers could only trickle in. But it was never as if they had to guard against a massive influx of Rock, Tobin or Manley fans. Only Sheila Copps was left to jump into the fray. But by then she had become a casualty of the federal flag war.

After their close call in Quebec in 1995, Jean Chrétien and his team had decided that a maple-leaf flag was worth a thousand federalist speeches. Rather than venture into francophone Quebec to promote federalism, they set out to plaster it with logos. The plan should have raised red flags in Copps's mind. Most of the Quebec ministers refused to touch the initiative, largely for fear of losing the already modest audience they had in the province to widespread ridicule.

But Sheila Copps's good-soldier instincts apparently prevailed over her good judgment. She embraced the flag initiative with the gusto she brought to most tasks, and quickly became identified with an operation that was seen in Quebec as a needless federal irritant long before the Chrétien visibility campaign grew into the ugly wart of the sponsorship scandal.

By the time Paul Martin became prime minister, the federal Liberals were running Quebec as if it were a distant colony, a place psychologically out of bounds to most non-natives. On the ground, the Liberal Quebec fortress—or whatever was left of it—was, in effect, guarded by a mercenary army.

To make up for their message's lack of appeal, and/or for the shrinking ranks of their messengers, the Liberals were spending government money on a sponsorship program of dubious policy merit.

The twenty-year process of turning the party into an empty shell was virtually complete. With some beyond-the-grave help from Jean Chrétien, it took the new leader only a few months to grind that thin shell into dust.

—

## CHAPTER THREE

## SAYING *NON* TO THE PRIME MINISTER

At a private dinner with the Parliament Hill bureau of Radio-Canada, shortly before his swearing-in as prime minister in the late fall of 2003, Martin was asked point-blank about the relative absence of senior Quebecers in his entourage. With one exception, the upper echelons of the future Prime Minister's Office (PMO) were going to be filled by advisers who had little or no working knowledge of French or of Quebec.

Who could be more senior, Martin replied, pointing to himself, than a prime minister whose home, business network and political base were in Quebec?

The journalists present were too polite to point out that Pierre Trudeau, Brian Mulroney and Jean Chrétien, all of them possibly more Quebec-wise than Martin, had felt that was not enough. None of those prime ministers had tried to operate from a Parliament Hill centre that was insulated from the undercurrents of Quebec politics by a language barrier.

In fact, behind the façade of confidence, Martin was scrambling to recruit more Quebec talent for both his office and his first election team—and he was not doing well. Given that he was riding high in the polls, bringing new talent on board should have been an easy enough task. Indeed, by the time he became leader, many Liberal insiders were convinced that he already had a dream team in the wings. That was just one of many false assumptions made about Martin in the months leading up to his victory.

In reality, during that triumphant period he had become used to people constantly coming to him for positions, not the reverse. But (as is usually the case) few of those doing the asking would have commanded a spot on anyone's short list. Moreover, in the fifteen years between his first leadership bid and his second one, many of Martin's Quebec insiders had lost much of the fire in their bellies. They had more or less been kept out of the federal loop by a wary Chrétien clan. Most of them had moved on, away from active politics, and while they were happy that Martin had reached his goal, they were not as willing to go along for the ride as they would have been a decade and a half before.

Paradoxically, now that Martin was about to take office, his efforts to expand his Quebec team were also doomed by the auspicious circumstances that presided over his virtual coronation as Liberal leader, and the hubris that resulted from it.

When Lester B. Pearson had brought Pierre Trudeau, Jean Marchand and Gérard Pelletier into his government in the sixties, Quebec nationalism had been on the rise. Making room for a new generation of Quebecers under the federal tent had been an absolute priority. For his part, Brian Mulroney had appointed Lucien Bouchard to the Cabinet just prior to the 1988 election, to bind Quebec nationalists to federalism on the heels of the successful negotiation of the Meech Lake Accord, as well as to give his scandal-battered government a fresh shine. And in the mid-nineties, Jean Chrétien had recruited Lucienne Robillard, Pierre Pettigrew and Stéphane Dion to counter the fact that his government was spread dangerously thin in Quebec in the lead-up to and the aftermath of the referendum.

In contrast with Pearson, Mulroney and Chrétien, Paul Martin was facing no clear and imminent danger on the unity front in the fall of 2003. He felt no need for a great design to shore up the federation. The man so many Quebecers saw as the solution to their inconclusive national debate was privately no longer as convinced as he had seemed to be, in 1990, that there was a problem to be fixed.

Since the 1960 Quiet Revolution, when Quebec nationalism had become a force to contend with, every prime minister had found Quebec at the top of his or her files. Paul Martin expected a different scenario. He and his team thought he had the luxury of time to make his mark on other fronts.

In the apparent absence of a crisis, it had never been easier for federalist Quebecers successful in their own chosen careers to say no to a prime minister's proposals. As it turned out, more often than not, Martin and his people were willing to take that no for an answer. Indeed, while the prime minister and his advisers maintained that they had set their hearts on courting Quebec talent, they were actually sending rather mixed signals.

For ten years, the Martinites had paid a price for their loyalty to his leadership ambitions. In the summer and early fall of 2003, they increasingly had their minds on the spoils of power. To many of them, the next election looked like a formality. Convinced that they were in for the long haul, those who planned to go into the Langevin Block with Martin were not all eager to share their influence with newcomers, especially those they had no hope of competing with by virtue of their own ignorance of the Quebec scene. And Martin himself was not keen to rock the boat that had delivered him safely to port.

In Quebec, the popularity of federalist superstars is often a mile wide and an inch deep. That was certainly the experience of former Conservative leader Jean Charest. He had looked like an unbeatable champion when he had jumped onto the provincial ice in 1998 to become Quebec's Liberal leader, but had quickly fallen through into the icy currents of the province's politics. It had taken him five years to raise his head above water, and there were many times when it looked as though he wouldn't make it. Because so many of Martin's confidants were tone-deaf to the Quebec debate, they overestimated his appeal.

Having been kept out of the Quebec loop for most of the Chrétien era, many on Paul Martin's team—including some of the few Quebecers among them—were also blithely unaware of the magnitude of the party's decline in the province, and of the fact that this valuable turf was little more than a patch of scorched earth.

In 1990, broadcaster Jean Lapierre had co-chaired Martin's leadership bid. Upon his defeat and the demise of the Meech Lake Accord, he had slammed the door of the Liberal Party to become a co-founder of the Bloc Québécois. Over the years, though, Lapierre had remained in close touch with Martin, who was then the Liberal finance minister. Lapierre's popularity as a broadcaster and his credentials as a loyalist had earned him a place at the top of Martin's personal headhunting list in Quebec.

But such was the winner-take-all mood of the Martin team in the summer of 2003 that even Lapierre was picking up mixed messages. He got quiet hints that, given the popularity of the soon-to-be prime minister, his services might turn out to be, if not dispensable, at least not totally essential. If Martin had not belatedly stepped in to plead his case in person, Lapierre would not have signed on to his team.

He was not destined to be joined by legions of new recruits. By the time the Martinites realized that they needed a lot more Quebec help than they had assumed—by the time Jean Lapierre himself was on the lookout for talent—the sponsorship affair had cast a pall on Martin's prospects. By then, the Martin team was also well on the way to dismantling most of the fragile infrastructure that, under Jean Chrétien, had allowed the party to at least keep up appearances in Quebec.

Sheila Copps—who had the highest Quebec profile of all Martin's out-of-province ministers—was pushed out of politics as part of a bitter battle for a local nomination.

Stéphane Dion—who had spearheaded the post-referendum battle on Chrétien's behalf—waited in vain for his phone to ring on the eve of the swearing-in of Martin's first Cabinet. As a clear indication that his services were no longer required, he was sent to the back benches. The hope among Martin insiders was that he would get the message and retire. In case he didn't, efforts were under way to recruit another candidate for his Saint-Laurent–Cartierville riding.

In the end, the bad publicity resulting from Sheila Copps's demise saved Dion from an ugly local battle. Her defeat for the Liberal nomination in her Hamilton riding sent shock waves across the party and the country. To avoid another spill of bad blood, Stéphane Dion's nomination opponent was pressured into dropping out of the contest.

Bill Graham, whose international expertise and strong communications skills in French had made him a popular presence in the Quebec media even before he joined the Cabinet at the tail end of the Chrétien reign, was also pressured to retire, to make room for a Martin recruit. When he declined, he was moved from Foreign Affairs to National Defence, a portfolio with a much lower profile in Quebec. As for John Manley and Allan Rock, they were not discouraged from pursuing challenges outside the federal arena.

The pillars of the new regime were to be Ralph Goodale and Anne McLellan, two ministers who spoke no French and who, regardless of their other abilities, were therefore barred from having a strong presence in Quebec. Ken Dryden and Ujjal Dosanjh, Martin's star recruits in the rest of Canada, were equally useless on the French-language front.

On the day after the 2004 election, his Quebec dream team was reduced to one person: Jean Lapierre. After almost two decades of letting Quebecers take care of Quebec, the federal Liberals were about to fly blind into the perfect storm of the sponsorship scandal with only a skeleton crew on board, and endure a barrage of sovereignist flak.

All of that would have been enough to guarantee Paul Martin a rocky ride. But what the Liberals did not foresee, even in their worst nightmares, was that they were about to be outflanked on the federalist side.

Fifteen years after Sheila Copps, and with her former campaign co-chair at his side, Stephen Harper was moving into position on the other side of the sponsorship cloud.

The sponsorship scandal was the poison pill of Paul Martin's prime ministership, but it need not have been fatal. A mouse of an affair got the better of a political elephant. In the months before he became Liberal leader, he towered above his competition. He was expected to lead the Liberals to a historic sweep. Some party strategists had predicted that he would win upward of two hundred seats in his first election.

They were not all Liberals; the prospect of a Liberal steamroller looked real to the Progressive Conservatives and the Canadian Alliance as well. For more than ten years, the two parties had competed to be the voice of the right in Canada. Martin's popularity finally convinced them of the folly of continuing their war of mutual attrition. If Peter MacKay and Stephen Harper kept up their feud, chances were that neither would be around to shed crocodile tears at the other's funeral. Instead, they would lie next to each other in the large section of the political graveyard reserved for Martin casualties.

There is no secret recipe to managing a crisis; the ingredients include equal doses of competence and credibility. For a leader about to walk into his first storm, Paul Martin was in better shape than average. He also had the benefit of a lot of advance notice.

The events that lead to an out-of-control political crisis are usually ones that no one could have foreseen. Surprises like a deadly terrorist incident, a natural disaster or even a sudden change of winds on the eve of a referendum are liable to catch a government without a contingency plan.

But the sponsorship affair hardly fell out of thin air. Auditor General Sheila Fraser had served notice that she was investigating the program as early as 2002. It was more than another year before her conclusions stunned the country.

It was also known that the audit was neither a fishing expedition nor a routine spot check. Fraser had had a look at a handful of contracts given out as part of the sponsorship program and had come up with some hair-raising findings. Concluding that every rule in the book seemed to have been broken, she had referred the file to the police and decided to investigate further.

At first, her report was slated to become public in the fall of 2003. The main consequence of Jean Chrétien's decision to prorogue Parliament just prior to his party's leadership convention was to delay the report until the new year. But Fraser's conclusions had been circulated to various government departments as early as the end of the previous summer to give them a chance to respond prior to its original deadline for publication.

Martin had undoubtedly picked up a lot of informed scuttlebutt through government branches in the months leading up to the 2003 Liberal leadership convention. He and his advisers were fully apprised of the report's contents as part of the transition between the outgoing prime minister and the incoming one, later that same year.

At that point, Martin had a number of options. The first was to hand the report to the police and sit back and let justice take its course. The net of a police investigation is designed to catch criminal offenders, not political abusers. It is hardly as wide as that of a commission of inquiry. If Martin had gone the police route, the sponsorship affair would have been removed from the political stage sooner rather than later.

That's what Jean Chrétien would have done, and while the Opposition and the media would initially have kicked up a storm and accused the government of covering its own tracks, it is safe to assume that, without the oxygen of new facts, the story would eventually have died. One could debate ad nauseam whether that would have served public interest better than appointing, as Martin did, a commission of inquiry to probe some of the darkest corners of the Chrétien administration.

The commission headed by Justice John Gomery dominated the public life of the country, particularly in Quebec, for two full years. At the end of it all, it did not find fault with a single sitting politician, and it rapped the knuckles of a very limited cast of public actors.

In the future, the commission's work might have a dissuasive influence on future politicians. It might make them more wary of attempting to exploit government programs for their partisan purposes. But one of its more immediate results was that a program that the Auditor General took pains to describe as an aberrant exception to the rule was used as a reason to place the federal civil service and those who interact with it—including politicians themselves—in a straitjacket of regulations. In the public's mind, the bad apple of the sponsorship program became the symbol of federal governance.

Still, Paul Martin did not want to start his tenure on the same ethical footing as Jean Chrétien. His clan saw itself as totally distinct from that of the former prime minister, and felt it could deflect the negative repercussions of an inquiry. After all, the Martinites and the Chrétienites had operated for years as if there were two Liberal parties rather than just one. They assumed the public understood the distinction.

At the time, Paul Martin's decision to appoint Justice John Gomery to look into the affair was certainly the more courageous option. Having decided to lead his Liberal Party and his government to the promised land of greater transparency, though, Martin started off his crossing of the desert by kicking a sandstorm up into his own face. From the moment he stepped out of his office to address the Auditor General's report in public, he lost control of his government's message. Like an elephant panicking at the sight of a mouse, he tried to climb any tree in sight, breaking branches at every turn, and generally creating havoc in all directions.

Martin set out by flatly denying that he had had any knowledge of what was happening behind the sponsorship scene. That was a double-edged statement if there ever was one; it invited doubts as to either his sincerity or his political competence as a senior Quebec minister.

In the House of Commons, he blamed a rogue cell of civil servants for twisting the rules behind the government's back. But on that same day he also recalled his former colleague Alfonso Gagliano, the minister who had had political responsibility for the file, from the Canadian embassy in Denmark. That gesture suggested that the prime minister believed something much larger was afoot.

Within a week of publication of the Auditor General's report, Martin had publicly abandoned his rogue-cell theory for one immensely more damaging to the party. He stated categorically that there had to have been a political direction to the scandal. He then went on what came to be known as his mad-as-hell tour of the country, convincing Canadians at every stop along the way that, if they were not sure something terribly rotten had been taking place in the Liberal capital, they should be.

Finally, he fired most of Chrétien's former top associates from their patronage positions, usually for reasons that were unrelated to the sponsorship scandal. If Martin had not been a Liberal himself, he might have been accused of using the sponsorship affair to launch a witch hunt. Instead, having adamantly made the case that under the Liberals Ottawa had sunk to a new ethical low, he set out to convince voters that the Liberals were best qualified to clean up what was, essentially, their own mess.

Once Martin set up the Gomery commission, he was in for the long haul on the sponsorship front. His best chance of riding out the bumps that were bound to come his way lay in securing a majority government at the first opportunity. From that angle, his decision to call a campaign in the late spring of 2004—only months after the reunited Conservative Party had selected a new leader, and long before it could get its act together—made eminent strategic sense.

What made no sense was the ugly settling of scores that continued between Martin and Chrétien loyalists during the spring leading up to Martin's first campaign. In their hour of need, common sense dictated that the Martinites needed all Liberal hands on deck.

The lack of focus of Martin's first campaign was also mind-boggling. Here was a political aspirant who had waited in the wings for a decade to make good on the promise of his vision, and still he seemed to have no clear sense of why he had wanted the job in the first place.

In the spring of 2004, Paul Martin was seeking a fourth consecutive Liberal mandate, something that many voters would have been reluctant to hand to any party anywhere in Canada, even at the best of times. Since Lester B. Pearson, no prime minister had ever managed to successfully pass the torch of power to a successor. The last Liberal mandate had been dominated by a civil war at the highest levels of the government. In his leading role in the hostilities, Martin had encouraged the perception that he did not fully agree with Chrétien's decision to keep Canada out of the war on Iraq, his ratification of the Kyoto Protocol on greenhouse emissions and the legalization of same-sex marriage.

Those issues defined the Liberals versus the Conservatives in the lead-up to the election and Paul Martin was seen as ambiguous on all of them. Moreover, his own chosen battles did not always play to his strengths. His attempts to portray himself as a social champion were offset by the deep cuts he had inflicted on Canada's social programs in his role as minister of finance, and as part of his battle against the deficit. He chose to counter that problem by making outlandish commitments such as fixing medicare for a generation, grand promises that he would have little chance of fulfilling if he was re-elected.

As for his self-appointed crusade to restore integrity to the government, that, of course, was overshadowed by his high-profile role in a regime whose ethics had just been exposed as wanting.

Martin also seemed to say one thing and do another. In a speech in Quebec City in March 2004, he insisted that, on his watch, who one knew in the PMO would no longer be a factor in one's advancement. Yet he had let the dogs loose on Chrétien ministers who had not supported his own leadership bid, and many of his recruits were people whose pedigree was dominated by loyalty to his cause.

For all that, Paul Martin could have survived the sponsorship hit in Quebec, and hung on to his majority, if his lacklustre campaign had not lost him thirty-one seats elsewhere. Twenty-five of those losses were in Ontario—and they constituted more than the difference between the majority that eluded him, and the minority he secured.

If the sponsorship crisis had not brought out the best in Paul Martin, might it be that a minority government would? It had certainly worked that way for Bill Davis, Ontario's premier in the seventies. His two consecutive minority governments had allowed him to inject more vitality into a flagging Ontario Conservative dynasty, and thus extend its life for another decade. Davis had personally come into his own as a leader of national stature over that period, running an activist government at home while playing a pivotal role on the constitutional front.

But while Davis had seemed energized by the minority status of his governments, Paul Martin seemed befuddled. Instead of giving Canadians a chance to look beyond the sponsorship cloud, to glimpse a decisive, visionary prime minister, Martin earned himself the devastating nickname "Mr. Dithers." In its issue of February 19, 2005, the influential British newsmagazine *The Economist* used this sobriquet in the title of a piece that described Martin's first fourteen months in the job of prime minister as indecisive. The epithet clearly reflected the spirit of the times, and it stuck. Shaking it would prove even harder than moving beyond the sponsorship stigma.

Martin's final election campaign would fully justify his nickname. It was more than half over before the Liberals even went through the motions of presenting a platform—and the promise that generated the most coverage was not even part of their original plan.

On the occasion of the last set of leaders' debates during that long campaign, Martin surprised some of his own candidates by vouching to get the notwithstanding clause out of the Constitution. At the time of patriation, in 1982, the clause had been inserted at the insistence of various premiers to provide governments with a temporary escape hatch from the application of some Charter rights. The clause allows governments to shelter their laws from Charter-related court rulings for a renewable period of five years.

Back in 1981–82, some premiers worried about the unintended impact of the equality rights of the Charter on their affirmative-action programs. Others defended the principle that elected officials should have the option of having the last word in the courts on rights-related matters.

No prime minister could remove the notwithstanding clause without opening the Constitution and securing provincial support for an amendment. And since Martin had made it abundantly clear that he had no intention of pursuing a constitutional agenda, his statement rang doubly hollow. Even his commitment that a Liberal federal government would never use the notwithstanding clause was bizarre; only a year before, Martin himself had not ruled out using it to protect churches from a possible Supreme Court order to perform same-sex marriages.

During his time in office, it seemed that Paul Martin rarely encountered a problem that he could not make worse for himself. At his first federal-provincial conference, he introduced the concept of asymmetrical federalism and agreed to a side deal on health care with Quebec. But he lost all credit for it in Quebec, and any chance to sell it to a skeptical populace outside that province, when he failed to defend it on either front. Both sides concluded that, when it came to federalism, Martin was making up his approach as he went along. His subsequent decision to negotiate one-off agreements with some provinces on equalization, the federal program designed to redistribute wealth among the provinces so as to level the playing field between them, proved that they were right.

Even Martin's decision to decline the American invitation to participate in an intercontinental anti-missile shield—which should have been a winner with a Canadian public grown suspicious of anything emanating from George Bush's White House—ended up making him look weaker. The prime minister vacillated for months before taking a definitive position, and finally made up his mind just in time to pre-empt his own party from making it up for him by voting the plan down at a national convention.

This was not the only time Paul Martin seemed to put his standing within the party and the caucus before the country. Mississauga Centre MP Carolyn Parrish had come to the attention of the media back in the days leading up to Jean Chrétien's decision to sit out the Iraq war, when an open microphone caught her saying, "Damn Americans . . . I hate those bastards." The media knew a loose cannon when they heard one. From that day on, Parrish's opinions on Canada–U.S. matters were assiduously sought. Over the course of the debate on missile defence, she re-emerged as a virulent critic of American defence policies. She outdid herself in November 2004, by stomping on a George Bush doll on CBC's *This Hour Has 22 Minutes.* Martin fired her from the caucus after that episode . . . but only after she was reported as saying that she did not wish him well in the next election.

In another case of conflicting messages, the prime minister continually told Canadians that he was mad as hell over the sponsorship affair, and that he wanted the Gomery commission to get to the bottom of it. But after Chrétien used his appearance in front of the commission in January 2005 to mock Justice John Gomery and trivialize the commission, Martin told his caucus how proud he was of his predecessor's performance, and led his MPs in an *in absentia* ovation for their former leader.

The inconsistency of some of Martin's actions as prime minister, his short-view, crisis-style management, and his scattered agenda eventually shattered the reputation as an inspired manager that he had earned and cultivated over his decade as the most successful minister of finance in any of the G8 group of industrialized nations.

It was probably a stroke of luck for all concerned that the sponsorship scandal turned out to be the biggest crisis of Martin's tenure. His uncertain handling of it led to doubts as to how he would meet more serious challenges that might come his way. Some shuddered at the thought that a war like the one in Iraq that Jean Chrétien had declined to join might end up on Martin's plate. Others wondered if he had the "right stuff" to fight and win a Quebec referendum, especially now that his own sponsorship actions seemed to have made a rematch more probable. While it's true that the sponsorship affair was the first thread in the unravelling of Paul Martin, it's probable that, if that had not exposed the fundamental flaws of his style of leadership, some other crisis would have.

As Martin floundered, Stephen Harper resuscitated. The Conservative leader had originally been dismissed by many as a rigid ideologue. The Liberals had savaged him in the 2004 election, and afterwards he had been more or less given up for dead. But the indecisive months of Martin's minority government cast Harper in a more flattering light. Voters found themselves craving a respite from Liberal scandals and disorderly policy conduct. The straitlaced Conservative leader was about to be rediscovered by a weary electorate.

—

## CHAPTER FOUR

## "A GREAT LEADER FOR THE REST OF CANADA"

P aul Martin was not the only leader to be blindsided when Stephen Harper defeated him in January 2006. Gilles Duceppe also never saw Harper coming, at least not until it was too late.

Up until the election, the Bloc Québécois leader was one of Stephen Harper's fans. From the day Paul Martin became prime minister, Duceppe never made much of a secret of the fact that he'd rather do business with the Conservative leader than with his Liberal counterpart. Unlike many other political insiders, he never doubted that Stephen Harper had what it took to be prime minister. In fact, the Bloc leader did not rule out the possibility that he might one day find himself across the table from Harper, negotiating the conditions of Quebec's departure from the federation.

Gilles Duceppe's sense of his relationship with Harper was part of the much larger picture he contemplated when he decided to turn down overtures to follow in Lucien Bouchard's and Jean Charest's footsteps, and declined to seek a leadership future in Quebec's National Assembly.

In the late spring of 2005, Parti Québécois president Bernard Landry abruptly resigned from the leadership of his mercurial party. Although Landry had just secured a 76 percent confidence vote, he did not feel that his score was high enough to see him through the long haul of a few more years in opposition, and another election campaign against Jean Charest, let alone a winning referendum.

At that point, Gilles Duceppe was riding highest of any sovereignist figure in the polls. In the early jostling for position at the PQ leadership gate, he was the first choice of many sovereignist activists. He had been on Parliament Hill for fifteen years. Against the backdrop of the sponsorship scandal, the Bloc seemed to be on an irresistible roll. Over the years, the party had turned into a disciplined and effective force in Parliament, with a well-balanced mix of solid veterans and ambitious up-and-comers on its benches. The notion that his Bloc counterpart would step into his place had been a factor in Landry's impulsive decision to step down. Insiders and outsiders agreed that the time was ripe for Duceppe to move on and leave Parliament Hill.

He begged to differ. His expertise was in opposition and in federal politics. He had grown comfortable on Parliament Hill, and the rest of Canada had in turn grown comfortable with him. The latter fact, Duceppe felt, would be a huge asset for the sovereignty movement in the event of a negotiation with the rest of Canada following a victorious referendum. In the interest of the longer game, his place was in Parliament.

Lucien Bouchard had dominated the 1995 referendum, imposing his conditions on the timing of the campaign and the scope of the question, as well as taking over the lead role on the hustings midway through the campaign. If sovereignty had prevailed, the Bloc leader would have been Quebec's chief negotiator with Canada.

Duceppe remembered those days well. He had cause to believe that, in the event of another referendum, he would play as pivotal a role as Bouchard had. The days when the Parti Québécois leader was alone in the driver's seat of the Yes camp were definitively over. Just as successive Quebec Liberal leaders had found themselves overshadowed by the prime minister of the day in 1980 and 1995, whoever next led the PQ in a campaign to determine Quebec's future would have to share the steering wheel with his Bloc counterpart. Bouchard had demonstrated that while the accelerator was under the foot of the PQ — as there could not be a referendum if it was not in power — it was the Bloc that had control of the brakes.

Gilles Duceppe also knew that, should the sovereignist camp prevail in a referendum held within the five-year horizon that PQ strategists were contemplating, Paul Martin was unlikely to survive as prime minister, or the Liberal Party as the government. When he looked for a possible negotiating partner in the House of Commons, his eyes came to rest on the leader of the official opposition more often than on anyone on the Liberal benches.

Duceppe had actually hinted as much to his Conservative counterpart during the 2004 election campaign. As the two men were leaving the set of the leaders' debate in Ottawa, he complimented Stephen Harper on his performance, telling him that he made "a great leader for the rest of Canada."

The comment was more candid than malicious. Back then, it did not cross Duceppe's mind that he would ever have much to fear from the new Conservative Party, or its leader. For obvious reasons, however, the exchange stuck in Harper's mind. Months after the 2004 election, he was still retelling the story, always with some bemusement.

If Stephen Harper needed an extra incentive to keep investing energy in wooing Quebec, Duceppe provided it. In the eighteen months between the 2004 leaders' debate and the following election campaign, Harper would work hard to prove his Bloc counterpart wrong in his blithe assumption that he would never be a serious player in Quebec.

At the midpoint of the 2004 campaign, though, Gilles Duceppe could well afford to shower Harper with thorny roses. The Bloc Québécois leader was on top of the world and on top of his game. He was the veteran among the federal leaders, and the only native French speaker of the lot. His language skills had allowed him to dominate the French-language debate, while his ready knowledge of every file had served him well in the English-language one.

Duceppe was also a born-again leader, enjoying a providential second life. Six months earlier, he, along with almost everyone else who observed Quebec politics, had thought that his party, and maybe also his lifelong cause of sovereignty, were at death's door. From the time Jean Chrétien set the date for his retirement in the summer of 2002, the polls had shown that Martin was poised to crush the Bloc Québécois at the first electoral opportunity. Some opinion surveys forecast that the Bloc would sink below the twenty-five-seat mark in the next federal election. During his last year in office, it seemed that Chrétien would have no rest until he had dug the Bloc's grave himself, leaving his successor the minor duty of playing undertaker at the sovereignist party's funeral.

Gay marriage, the Kyoto Protocol, a new electoral-financing law tailored according to the regime brought in by Parti Québécois founder René Lévesque in the late seventies, and a plan to liberalize the marijuana laws all came across as nails in the Bloc's coffin.

The decision to keep Canada out of the Iraq war had propelled the Liberals to the top of the pack in Quebec polls. For the first time in the Chrétien decade, Quebecers found more cause to laud than to complain about the soon-to-depart prime minister, or his party.

The sovereignty movement was also on the wrong side of the Quebec political cycle. In April 2003, the Parti Québécois had collected its worst election score since it first came to power in 1976, winning only one in three votes cast. A repeat of that scenario at the federal level in the upcoming election would leave the Bloc mortally wounded.

The expected arrival of a fresh batch of Quebec Liberal MPs on Parliament Hill, Paul Martin's reputation as a less confrontational leader than Jean Chrétien, and the presence of a federalist government in Quebec all threatened to cut off the air supply of the federal sovereignist party. By late 2003, Duceppe, who had been the first MP elected under the Bloc Québécois banner in 1990, faced the possibility of going down in history as its last leader. He had quietly started making plans for a life outside politics, exploring options for volunteer work on a variety of fronts.

And then the sponsorship scandal broke. Overnight, the Bloc captured a lead the size of which it had not seen since the days of the Meech Lake crisis. As a bonus, Paul Martin was hardly turning out to be the giant-killer that voters had expected. And he came across as indecisive on the issues that had belatedly made the Liberal Party popular in Quebec.

No one knew for sure whether, in Chrétien's place, the new Liberal leader would have led Canada into the Iraq war. As well, Martin seemed unable to get his mind around the Charter rights of gay couples. And when Canada had signed the Kyoto Protocol, the Martinites had let it be known that they had serious reservations as to the country's capacity to fulfil the obligations Jean Chrétien was taking on.

The immediate aftermath of Auditor General Sheila Fraser's report on the sponsorship scandal also revealed how unaware Martin was of the thinness of the ice he was skating on in Quebec. Moments after the report became public, the new prime minister solemnly denied any knowledge that all was not well with the program, a statement that would time and again come back to haunt him.

For Gilles Duceppe, the 2004 campaign was the stuff that dreams are made of—a month-long early-summer tour of Quebec at a laid-back pace. Its result, a minority government operating under the permanent cloud of the sponsorship inquiry, was another gift. The Bloc Québécois had won Quebec in 2004 with Auditor General Sheila Fraser in Duceppe's corner; now it could realistically expect to ride to a repeat victory on the back of the Gomery inquiry. In the meantime, the Bloc devoted itself to one overriding purpose: using the devastating findings of the commission to needle an already incensed public opinion. It was one of many ways in which Duceppe and the Bloc set in place some of the winning conditions for Stephen Harper's 2006 Quebec campaign.

The sponsorship scandal was the Bloc Québécois's bread and butter for the duration of Canada's thirty-eighth Parliament. Day in and day out, Gilles Duceppe and his MPs climbed on their parliamentary soapbox to dish out allegations against the Martin government, acting as human megaphones for the findings of the Gomery commission. In the month of April 2005, the Bloc led all but one of its question-period rounds of attack with queries related to the sponsorship affair. The party was back at it in May, and again for the best part of June of that year, and yet again in the final part of the session the next fall.

With the possible exception of the patriation of the Constitution in the early eighties, and the free-trade debate later in the same decade, it is hard to think of another issue that has been pursued so single-mindedly and for so long by a federal party. The Bloc used the sponsorship affair to make that thirty-eighth Parliament a living hell for the Liberals.

Leaving the NDP to take the lead on many of the social issues that were the lifeblood of some of the Bloc's core constituencies, Duceppe and his top lieutenants concentrated on running their federalist Liberal foes into the ground. They hacked relentlessly at the Liberals' reputation and, for the most part, Quebecers cheered them on. By the spring of 2005, the province's all-news networks were into wall-to-wall broadcasting of the Gomery commission proceedings. The ratings for the hearings were setting new daytime television records. Almost overnight, the protagonists became local celebrities.

The bulk of the work of the Gomery commission took place in French, which made it something of a first in francophone Quebec. Language had prevented much of the Quebec public from partaking in the Watergate television experience in the seventies. In the era of all-news television, English had been the dominant language of Canadian federal commissions of inquiry. The CBC's *Newsworld* was born at the time of the Meech Lake debate, but RDI, its French-language counterpart, did not go to air until some years later. Likewise, the National Assembly began live broadcasting some years later than the Parliament of Canada.

Relieved of the tedious business of following a federal story through translation, Quebecers spent the spring of 2005 hooked on the Gomery commission. But Bloc attempts to spread the sponsorship paint over the entire federalist camp—to turn a Liberal misdeed into a federalist evil—were less successful. That would prove to be a costly failure for the sovereignist MPs, and it was one that Stephen Harper played a key part in.

For much of the last half of the thirty-eighth Parliament, Gilles Duceppe found himself standing shoulder to shoulder with the leader of the new Conservative Party as the two joined forces to ensure the demise of the Martin government. The Liberals fought back by portraying Stephen Harper as a man who was willing to put self-interest ahead of the interests of the country by striking an unholy alliance with the separatists. That was exactly the argument Belinda Stronach made when she crossed over to the Liberals to save Paul Martin from defeat in the spring of 2005. From the moment she arrived on the political scene as a Conservative leadership candidate in late 2003, Stronach had been a media magnet. After the 2004 election, she added a rare spark of glitter to the Harper line-up in the House of Commons. Snatching her from the Conservatives' ranks was Martin's biggest political coup, though its impact was short-lived.

For its part, the Bloc revelled in showing off its capacity to punish the government, and hoped privately that this would make up for its inability to replace it. But in the end it was Gilles Duceppe who ended up with cause to regret his association with Stephen Harper, rather than the reverse. As he scrambled to stop the Conservatives in their tracks in Quebec, in the dying days of the 2006 campaign, Duceppe's recent cordial association with Harper blunted the edge of his belated attempts to demonize the Conservatives.

The NDP would not reap much benefit in Quebec for having used its position in a minority Parliament to secure more money for the social-policy envelope in exchange for continuing support of the Martin government. Nevertheless, the Bloc's disengagement from that battle would lead some of its progressive supporters to wonder whether the sovereignist was as essential a voice for the defence of Quebec's larger interests as it claimed to be.

But in the fall of 2005, the Bloc had concerns to attend to outside Parliament Hill. One of the more pressing ones was to upstage the Parti Québécois, for fear that its sister party's leadership campaign would turn the upcoming federal election into a referendum dry run that would allow Paul Martin to rally federalist voters behind his party.

For while the Bloc was relentlessly making the case that the Martin Liberals were no longer fit for power, the Parti Québécois was breathing what it hoped was new life into its core mission. With Bernard Landry out of the picture, and with

Gilles Duceppe otherwise occupied, the first PQ leadership campaign in two decades was in full swing. But those who had thought that a competitive campaign might set the stage for a discussion of the gap between Péquiste orthodoxy and the tepid post-1995 popular demand for a referendum quickly lost their illusions. When it came to the inevitability and desirability of sovereignty, the PQ might as well have lined up a flock of parrots in lieu of candidates.

When the Parti Québécois is in power, it often draws on talent that is primarily motivated by issues other than the quest for sovereignty. The party's social-democrat creed as well as its culture of activism have long acted as magnets to attract political talent. But like every other party, the PQ falls back on its core constituency when it is in opposition. In the PQ's case, that constituency is made up of members who see sovereignty not as a possible means to a better end, but as an end in itself. Questioning the basic tenets of the PQ credo is not the way to the hearts and votes of those faithful supporters, especially when the popular appeal of the cause is apparently on the rise. The PQ leadership campaign unfolded as if Quebec was on a march to one last, decisive referendum.

Support for sovereignty almost always goes up when the PQ is not in power. The period between 2003 and January 2006 was no exception, and the sponsorship scandal undoubtedly gave the secessionist cause an added boost. In hindsight, though, sovereignist strategists should have wondered why their support wasn't higher. Even on the darkest days of the Gomery inquiry, support for sovereignty never came anywhere close to the peak of 65 percent registered in the immediate aftermath of the Meech Lake debacle. Instead it hovered in the grey zone between 50 percent and 53 percent, despite the referendum fever gripping the PQ's militant wing.

Of particular concern for the Bloc was the fact that more

Quebecers were willing to support it than were willing to support sovereignty. Those extra voters made up a fragile fringe of supporters, liable to be particularly wary of the notion that the federal election was the first step towards another referendum, rather than the closing chapter to the sponsorship scandal.

In the spring and fall of 2005, Stephen Harper's own actions went some way to slow the sovereignist momentum. If the Conservative Party had not gone to the barricades with the Bloc to topple the Liberals at a time of record-high indignation, it would have been easier for Gilles Duceppe to make his case that the rest of Canada would shrug off a scandal as long as it was designed primarily to manipulate Quebecers. And so, even as Martin was accusing Harper of undermining federalism by threatening the survival of the government, Harper was more likely protecting the federation.

In any event, in the fall of 2005, nothing could have stopped Parti Québécois candidates from treating their return to power as a *fait accompli*, and regarding the imminence of another referendum as a given.

In Quebec federalist circles, minds started turning uneasily to the notion of Paul Martin leading the No camp in another referendum showdown. The thought did not sit well with most federalists. Even when he had looked like a formidable political force, Martin had not enjoyed the total confidence of the federalist camp. His performance in the 1995 referendum had caused his side more harm than good. His prediction, as minister of finance, that sovereignty would put a million jobs at risk had come across as wildly over the top, costing the federalist camp a pint of credibility at a time when it was already hemorrhaging support.

The issue of Martin's capacity to win a referendum had not come up when he became leader, in part because of his overwhelming polling numbers in Quebec, but also because there was a sense that the unity debate was in a lull that would outlast his tenure. But now that he had lost his patina of credibility in Quebec, his government was seen as generally weaker than that of Jean Chrétien, even aside from the sponsorship scandal. For months, the prime minister had been the butt of widespread skits on Quebec's political satire circuit, usually a fatal sign for a politician desperate for a comeback. In politics, ridicule can kill—or at least, it can in Quebec.

To make matters worse, by the spring of 2005 the Quebec federalist establishment was in complete disarray. Some of the leading champions of the previous rounds were so tarnished by the sponsorship affair that they could never hope to hold a post in the public domain again, let alone campaign effectively in a referendum.

Pierre Trudeau and Claude Ryan—the two leading federalist thinkers of their generation—had both died. Jean Chrétien and Paul Martin could not be on the same stage at the same time, and neither commanded the audience he once had. Brian Mulroney—who was finally undergoing the public rehabilitation he had so actively sought since his retirement in 1993—was a living reminder of the failure of the last formal efforts at national reconciliation. Jean Charest—one of the rare federalist stars of the previous episode—was turning out to be one of Quebec's most unloved premiers, while Lucien Bouchard still lurked in the background, his status enhanced by retirement and his inclinations—as usual—too ambiguous for federalist comfort.

In 1980, the advent of the first referendum had been the final straw that had broken the back of Joe Clark's Conservative minority government. Given a choice, many federalists both in and outside Quebec had not wanted to do battle with René Lévesque under the untried Clark if they could have Pierre Trudeau as their general instead.

Now the same dynamics were operating in reverse, with the Liberals offering what seemed like the weakest champion, the directionless and often inconsistent Paul Martin. Stephen Harper—even if he lacked Quebec credentials—could hardly be less qualified to defend Canada in a referendum, and to deal, if the unthinkable happened, with the aftermath of a defeat. Besides, the close call of the 1995 referendum had focused many minds on the difficulties of waking up, the morning after a Yes vote, with a prime minister whose political base had just voted to secede.

While federalists fretted about their dicey leadership options, a malaise was also in the making within the more traditionalist ranks of the sovereignty movement. In the heavily francophone pockets of Quebec that the Bloc had come to take for granted, voters were feeling increasingly left behind by the developments on both the PQ and the Bloc fronts.

If PQ leader André Boisclair had just one word stamped on his forehead, it would be "Montreal." An openly gay politician, he belonged to a generation at least twice removed from that of the *collèges classiques* graduates who had dominated Quebec politics in general and the Parti Québécois in particular up to that point in time.

In the fall of 2005, many in the rank and file of the PQ were drawn to the differences between Boisclair and his predecessors like moths to a flame. A recurring nightmare of the first generation of sovereignists is that their project will die with them, that it will turn out to have been just another baby-boomer pipe dream. By endorsing Boisclair, who was then not yet forty, many Péquistes were fending off their obsessive fear of leaving no heirs and taking their cause to their grave.

But while the youth vote is essential to achieve a referendum victory, a more qualitative win depends on expanding support for sovereignty beyond the circle of Quebec-born francophones. In 2004, Duceppe had made encouraging inroads on that front. In the thirty-eighth Parliament, the Montreal suburb of Saint-Lambert was represented by Maka Kotto. The Cameroon-born actor became the first Afro-Quebecer to serve in an elected capacity. With the Liberals in trouble in Montreal, the Bloc set out to make its strongest pitch ever to the island's cultural communities.

On the surface, it seemed that the sovereignty movement was on the march again. The PQ had rejuvenated itself and, if the polls were to be believed, the public was as ready as the party had been to overlook Boisclair's status as a college dropout, as well as revelations that he had used hard drugs while in political office, to embrace a leader from a younger generation. Meanwhile, the Bloc was busy changing the homogeneous face of the movement, again with the apparent backing of a growing number of Quebecers.

Both parties, as it turned out, were getting ahead of the voters.

On January 23, 2006, every sovereignist chicken came home to roost—in Stephen Harper's henhouse. Half of the Quebec seats the Conservatives gained were in and around Quebec City, an area that instinctively mistrusts anything that comes from Montreal. In 1995, those same voters had supported sovereignty in lesser numbers than the francophone average, in part because they feared that, in a sovereign Quebec, former federal civil servants from the Outaouais would take over their jobs.

Harper also won seats in some of the more tightly knit francophone areas of the province—ridings like Jonquière–Alma and Beauce, where the Conservative creed echoes local sentiments more clearly than the Bloc's social-democrat quest and its bid to be more inclusive of cultural communities. In general, he scored in the places where voters had fewest reasons to identify with the Boisclair-Duceppe tandem and its strong urban, Montreal aura, places where the PQ-Bloc partnership seemed almost as exotic as Alberta's Stephen Harper.

In a bittersweet footnote, the Bloc did win some of the Liberals' Montreal ethnic fortresses—but only because the cultural communities stayed home on voting day rather than choose between sovereignist candidates and the dishonoured Liberal Party. In those ridings, support for the Bloc remained the same as in 2004, but support for the Liberals went down.

Harper benefited from Duceppe's efforts in one other fundamental way. To no one's surprise, given the rich material it had at its disposal as a result of the Gomery commission, the Bloc made an effective case that the Liberals were no longer fit to govern. And the joint Bloc-Conservative bid to topple Martin had showcased Stephen Harper as the only federalist leader willing to hold the minority government to account for the sponsorship revelations. Unlike Gilles Duceppe, Harper had a shot at becoming prime minister.

Thus the best efforts of Duceppe and the PQ had paved the road for Stephen Harper's surprisingly successful election night in Quebec. In making the Liberals unelectable, the Bloc had unwittingly opened another can of worms. If the only way to change the government was to vote for another national party, did Quebecers really need a sovereignist version of the federal NDP, now that the Conservatives had reunited into a single force? Many of them put their tentative answer on their ballots on January 23, 2006.

—

## CHAPTER FIVE

## A CONSERVATIVE UGLY DUCKLING

On the morning after the election, analysts started to look beyond the anemic Conservative score to examine the fine print. They discovered that there was more to Stephen Harper's ugly duckling of a government than first met the eye. By comparison with past governments, the new one looked scrawny but it had the potential to grow into a respectable force.

Not only had the party captured ten Quebec seats—a goal that would have seemed delusionally ambitious only a month before the election—but it had come second in forty other Quebec ridings. For all intents and purposes, Harper had beat his longest odds so far, and had displaced the Liberals as the default federalist option in francophone Quebec.

The prime minister–elect had certainly not taken all the seats he had hoped for, but he had won the ones he most needed. If the Conservatives had traded each of their ten Quebec ridings for two Ontario seats, their government would have had sturdier legs but would have been missing a vital organ.

In 1979, Joe Clark had brought only two Quebec MPs into government with him. This weakness had to a great extent doomed his short-lived minority regime. Harper's rookie team would have faced the same predicament sooner rather than later, especially with the Parti Québécois on the move in the lead-up to a provincial election.

What made the 2006 Conservative breakthrough even more remarkable was the fact that Stephen Harper had achieved it with little or no public support from the Quebec intelligentsia, and in the absence of even the shadow of a strong Quebec team to back him up.

Jean Chrétien had spent his last campaign in Quebec, in 2000, attached to Paul Martin like a Siamese twin. This strategy was in stark contrast to the bloody civil war that followed, but it resulted in the best Liberal election score in Quebec in two decades. Martin himself had hoped that by giving Jean Lapierre a front-row seat in his government, he would attract more nationalist voters. (He only managed to infuriate many federalists.)

By comparison, Stephen Harper was on his own. His Quebec team included a few familiar faces—notably Jean-Pierre Blackburn, who had served as an MP under Brian Mulroney, in Jonquière, and Lawrence Cannon in Pontiac—but both were political has-beens who had operated only at the local level for more than a decade. In any event, they were facing uphill battles in their respective ridings, and neither could afford to take time out to campaign at the leader's side.

As for Michael Fortier, who had run as a dark horse against Joe Clark for the Progressive Conservative leadership in 1998, and who had been virtually alone in the Quebec Tory establishment in backing Harper in 2004, he had opted to stay on the sidelines, providing advice to the leader but declining to run himself.

Both before and after he became prime minister, Paul Martin had been hounded for his failure to bring high-profile francophones within his inner circle. Throughout his time in office, he had tried and failed to make satisfactory permanent arrangements to shore up the Quebec side of his office.

In the lead-up to his first election campaign, he had begged his friend Francis Fox to stay on in the Langevin Block, at least until Martin had secured a fresh mandate from voters. Fox had agreed, but had made it clear that his commitment to serve as principal secretary was not open-ended. After the election, Martin had had even worse luck bringing senior francophones on board. His minority status certainly didn't help, nor did his unimpressive beginnings as prime minister, or the lingering sponsorship scandal. For lack of an alternative, he ended up appointing former heritage minister Hélène Scherrer, who had lost her Quebec City seat in the election, as principal secretary.

There are times when a fallback choice turns out to have been an inspired one. Jean Chrétien had been lucky that one of his school friends, former Quebec City mayor Jean Pelletier, had failed to get himself elected as an MP in 1993. Pelletier had gone on to run the PMO for Chrétien for the better half of his time in office. He turned out to be immensely more useful to the prime minister in this post than he would have been even in a senior ministerial capacity.

But Scherrer was no Pelletier. She lacked his experience, his extended Quebec network and his influence on the prime minister. At a time when the Chrétien clan in Quebec was screaming for revenge on Paul Martin, she did not have the stature to defend him. Neither the Quebec ministers nor the rest of Martin's tightly knit group had great confidence in her judgment. In time, Paul Martin's chief of staff Tim Murphy would come to rely on Jean Lapierre—by then the transportation minister—to give him an oral morning briefing on the French media output of the day, so that he would not depend totally on Scherrer for a sense of what was going on in Quebec.

Significantly, once Stephen Harper was in office, the issue of the Quebec-savvyness of his entourage did not initially come up. Back in Quebec City, Premier Jean Charest was not complaining.

He had virtually a direct line to the new prime minister. Besides, as a former federal Tory leader, Charest was in more familiar territory than he had ever been in Jean Chrétien's or Paul Martin's Ottawa.

For so long Stephen Harper's Achilles' heel, the Quebec file was suddenly seen, somewhat blithely, as the Conservative leader's forte. The same people who had scoffed when Martin portrayed himself as his own best Quebec adviser did not even blink when Harper applied his very hands-on approach to the same issue.

Who would have dared question it? Stephen Harper may not have been the sole architect of his success; Paul Martin, Jean Chrétien and Gilles Duceppe all had a hand, albeit an involuntary one, in creating an opening for his party in Quebec. And he did not lack advice on Quebec from a range of top insiders, including Brian Mulroney, Jean Charest, Mario Dumont and of course Michael Fortier. But Harper would not have been where he was on January 23 if he had not put energy into pursuing Quebec at a time when many within his party felt it was a waste of his time.

From the start, many Conservative Party insiders saw Harper's determination to gain ground in the province as a quixotic quest, at best an exercise to show Ontario voters that he was going through the motions of wooing Quebec. Quite a few Conservatives felt that Harper's time would be better spent courting Ontario or the Atlantic, two regions where the party at least had a real base, than trekking across the Quebec wasteland in search of unlikely disciples.

Through it all, though, Harper kept going back to Quebec, improving his French, choosing Montreal as the site of the party's founding convention and delivering his first speech in the province as Conservative leader only weeks after taking on the position.

Shortly after his government's first budget, in the spring of 2006, Harper made his first prime-ministerial visit to Montreal. The city's office towers emptied as corporate Quebec converged on the Palais des Congrès. The Board of Trade's all-time attendance record, held until then by Pierre Trudeau, was broken that day.

Yet almost exactly two years before that standing-room-only performance, demand for Stephen Harper had been so tepid in Montreal that he couldn't find a downtown business audience for his maiden speech in Quebec as leader of the new Conservative Party. So on April 16, 2004, Harper test-ran the tenets that would underpin his 2006 Quebec campaign in front of a modest business audience in the suburban city of Laval. The speech was barely reported on. Falling on the day the NDP's Svend Robinson stunned Canadians with his admission that he had committed a theft, Harper's Laval visit got lost in the ensuing media shuffle.

His speech may have been buried quickly, but it turned out that it was not forgotten. A month later, when Paul Martin used the same venue for what his entourage billed as a "vision speech," it was widely noted that while the new prime minister had used a lot more words than Stephen Harper, and had consequently made his much larger audience wait a lot longer to dig into their lunch, he had given them a lot less substance to chew on.

Only one section of Paul Martin's speech really stood out as newsworthy: an unqualified promise to give Quebec a place at UNESCO, the UN forum that deals with issues of culture. "Quebec should not only be seated with us at the table at UNESCO, but it must be able to speak when we discuss things like cultural diversity," the prime minister said, adding, "Quebec is the cradle of the French language and culture in North America. It is one of the pillars of the French fact in Canada and in the world. It should be able to express itself on the major subjects that affect it directly. The door should be wide open to it, without ambiguity. And it will be."

That was one Martin undertaking that the Liberals would fail to deliver. On the campaign trail in 2006, Stephen Harper claimed it for himself, and the Liberals who rushed to attack the promise were in fact taking shots at one of their own unfulfilled commitments.

—

## CHAPTER SIX

## THE EMPEROR'S NEW CLOTHES

I n Quebec, the incessant and often acrimonious federal-provincial chatter about power and money is the white noise of daily political life, a permanent background sound that many Quebecers have come to tune out. But when the conversation switches to the more symbolic side of politics, Quebec is all ears. It is on this shaky ground, rather than on cerebral matters of policy, that politicians here are more often made or broken. As Sheila Copps found out with the flag episode, one slip can undo years of careful nurturing of a credible image. In the summer of 2005, just months prior to the election campaign, such a test awaited Stephen Harper.

In August, Paul Martin put an end to months of hesitation and appointed Quebec broadcaster Michaëlle Jean to serve as the next Governor General. At first it seemed that the prime minister had scored a home run. The Haitian-born Jean was a picture-perfect representative of a face of Quebec that is often ignored in the rest of Canada—its increasingly diverse and inclusive francophone society. From the Liberals' partisan angle, it also did not hurt that she hailed from one of the cultural communities that the Bloc Québécois was courting most assiduously in the lead-up to the election.

Then, in what will stand for a long time as one of the more

bizarre episodes of the Quebec–Canada saga, some sovereignists resolved to "out" Jean and her husband, Jean-Daniel Lafond, as two of their own. In a singular twist, they joined with the minority of Canadians who consider a vote for a legal sovereignist party a seditious act, and accused CSIS, the country's security service, of having been delinquent in its background checks of the future vice-regal couple. In particular, they claimed that, for the sake of national security, the prime minister should have been warned that Lafond, if not necessarily Jean herself, was known to be actively sympathetic to sovereignty.

Some of the loudest English-speaking commentators in the country, and some of the pundits closest to the Conservative Party, called on Paul Martin to rescind the appointment. Alberta premier Ralph Klein, New Brunswick's Bernard Lord and British Columbia's Gordon Campbell all put their doubts as to the couple's credentials on the record.

Noticeably absent from the largely Conservative chorus that wanted Martin to review her appointment, was the leader of Her Majesty's Loyal Opposition, Stephen Harper. Against the counsel of some of his advisers, the Conservative leader resisted calls to take a lead role in the debate.

Instead, he started by accepting the prime minister's assurances that all was aboveboard. When that turned out not to be enough to end the controversy, and when Jean—at the request of Harper and many others—issued a statement affirming her devotion to Canada, the Conservative leader immediately took her word for the fact that she and her husband had never had anything but love for Canada, and put the issue behind him.

It may well be that Paul Martin's PMO did not exercise due diligence prior to the appointment. It certainly seemed at the time that the prime minister's entourage was blindsided by the assertions of Jean's critics, and at a loss to mount an effective defence. In that case, principal secretary Hélène Scherrer, who shepherded the operation, and Martin himself, who spent hours chatting with Jean prior to making the appointment official, were at fault—not the security service, which had no business looking into her and her husband's political views. But in another sign that Harper had no interest in keeping the issue alive, his party did not raise it when the Commons resumed sitting a few weeks later.

In hindsight, it was a providential call on his part. Upon her installation, Jean conquered her critics outside Quebec. In the manic-depressive style that often characterizes Canada's national debate, calls for Jean's political execution gave way to cries of adulation as some of the same people who had denounced her appointment fell head over heels for the new Governor General. If Stephen Harper had joined the chorus, Michaëlle Jean's days as a Governor General nominee might have been numbered. The divisive witch hunt that the sovereignist activists who set the affair in motion had openly hoped for would probably have materialized. The Conservative leader would have made the day for some of his core supporters at a time when many doubted his capacity to lead the party to bigger and greater things.

But this would also have been the kiss of death for Harper's chances of securing a hearing in francophone Quebec in the coming election. There, the entire affair would have been seen as Canadian-style McCarthyism, with Harper cast in the unflattering leading role. The new Conservative Party would have turned back the clock and retreated—in the minds of many people both inside and outside Quebec—to some of the anti-Quebec, anti-bilingualism roots of the early Reform Party. Its nascent bid to become the federalist alternative in Quebec would have been dead on arrival.

If Gilles Duceppe and Paul Martin had wanted a sign that Stephen Harper was playing a longer game, and that he seriously had his eye on the Quebec ball, the Jean episode would have provided it. But in the summer of 2005, neither the Bloc leader nor the prime minister had any sense that the Conservatives would be at play in Quebec any time soon, and indeed assumed that they probably wouldn't be for the rest of their respective political lifetimes. Not until past the halfway mark of the campaign did they notice that there was an unexpected third contender on the ice. By then the Liberals had grown so weak in Quebec, and the Bloc had been flying on automatic pilot for so long, that it took a single push to knock them off their game.

Stephen Harper delivered that push less than a week before Christmas. On day twenty-one of the election campaign, the Conservative leader travelled to Quebec City and put his remodelled party back on the Quebec map. The speech he delivered on December 19, 2005, was pivotal, yet it contained just one generic promise and made only two specific commitments, neither of which was totally new or particularly bold. Harper said that a Conservative government would practise federalism in a way that was more respectful of the provinces, one of the articles of faith the Canadian Alliance and the Progressive Conservative parties had readily agreed to in the lead-up to their merger. As the federal government raked in ever-increasing budget surpluses after 1997, the premiers complained that while revenues kept growing in Ottawa, the burden of social expenses kept getting heavier on the provinces. Harper undertook to fix that fiscal imbalance between the federal government and the provinces, by clarifying the roles of both orders of government, and divvying up the fiscal pie accordingly. Finally, he promised to give Quebec a distinct place at UNESCO.

Those who had followed Harper attentively over recent months and years had heard most of this before. The main part—the section dealing with federalism—was a variation on his speech in Laval in 2004. The UNESCO commitment was lifted straight out of Martin's voluble address to the same audience a month later. The biggest difference was that by this time, many Quebecers, on the lookout for an option outside the white and black boxes of the federal Liberals and the Bloc Québécois, were paying attention.

Conservative senator Hugh Segal—a long-time Tory insider who has had occasion to watch his current leader at close range—told me shortly after the 2006 election that if one asked Stephen Harper to name just one reason why he wanted to become prime minister, his ready answer would be: to usher in an era of disciplined federalism. That has been the recurring theme of Harper's successive political incarnations.

If Segal is right, if bringing rigour back to the practice of federalism is to Stephen Harper what patriation of the Constitution was to Pierre Trudeau, then his supporters were right to jump for joy every time a Conservative was declared victorious in Quebec that election night. For without some clear signal that Quebecers were willing to buy into his vision of federalism, it would have been impossible to move that vision forward.

Without Quebec, Stephen Harper might still have woken up as Canada's next prime minister on January 24, 2006. But he would have been a leader without a decent mandate—an emperor with no clothes.

# PART II

# KILLING FEDERALISM, ONE DOLLAR AT A TIME

—

## CHAPTER SEVEN

# HELTER-SKELTER FEDERALISM

By the time Paul Martin left office, his government had its fingers in a lot of half-baked pies. To put it mildly, Stephen Harper inherited a messy kitchen in the winter of 2006. The fiscal discipline brought about by the mid-nineties war on the deficit had quickly given way to an era of Liberal profligacy, as recurring annual surpluses filled government coffers to the top.

Canada was enjoying one of its longest postwar growth cycles ever. There was relative quiet on the unity front for the first time in nearly forty years. It had been almost as long since a federal government had had such extensive resources at its disposal. Paul Martin, whose father, Paul Sr., had been one of the architects of Canada's twentieth-century social infrastructure, was eager to put his own mark on it.

It should have been an exciting time to work on Parliament Hill, an occasion to finally leave behind the shrinking expectations of the past two decades and think forward to the realities of a new century. Instead, it was a time of helter-skelter federalism, replete with conflicting signals, unpredictable reversals, declining morale within the top ranks of the civil service and all-around loss of respect for the competence of the federal government.

As finance minister, Paul Martin had brought order to the chaos of the nation's finances; as prime minister, he brought chaos to the order of federalism. To the dismay of the many who had expected him to raise Canada's governance standards, confusion presided over his running of federal affairs. While the Liberal government looked for new activist ways to spend its riches, most of the federal core missions had already gone to the dogs.

By all independent accounts, Canada's international influence was waning, the result of an overdose of lofty rhetoric combined with a paucity of consistent action. A case in point was foreign aid, a file on which successive governments had long talked the talk of more generous performance without walking the walk. In 2005, thirty-six years after Lester B. Pearson had urged First World countries to devote 0.7 percent of their national income to foreign aid, Canada did not have even a self-imposed deadline to reach that target.

Rock singer and anti-poverty activist Bono had been the keynote speaker at the 2003 Liberal leadership convention that had crowned Martin. The megastar's presence at the side of the incoming prime minister had suggested that the foreign-aid file would sit on top of his desk. Any such assumption was wrong. In the spring of 2005, Italy, Germany, Austria, Portugal and Greece signed onto the United Nations' ten-year plan to halve world poverty. They committed their governments to reaching the Pearson foreign-aid target by 2015. Paul Martin declined to follow suit.

Canada was a fading presence in other landmark UN activities. Over the Liberal years, its participation in international peacekeeping efforts had been reduced to a trickle. By the summer of 2006, only about sixty Canadian soldiers, sprinkled across half a dozen missions around the world, would still be under the UN flag.

Those numbers would have come as a surprise to many Canadians. In the post–Cold War era, Canada had increasingly traded peacekeeping duties for the more muscular business of peacemaking. At the time of the Iraq war, it had harnessed much of its flagging military resources to the rebuilding of Afghanistan. There were valid arguments to be made for the redefined terms of engagement under which these troops operated abroad, but successive Liberal governments had largely avoided making those arguments, preferring to keep the debate beneath the radar of public opinion. Meanwhile, Canadian soldiers were fighting with obsolete equipment, and with resources, human or otherwise, stretched to the limit. When a tsunami hit large sections of coast in Southeast Asia in December 2004, Canada did not have the logistical capacity to send help quickly.

One of Jean Chrétien's last acts in office had been to sign the Kyoto Protocol in 2003. Canada had taken an active role in negotiating the international agreement in 1997, and there was never any serious question that its Liberal government planned to ratify the treaty. But in the six-year interval between the conclusion of the negotiations and formal ratification by Canada, the Chrétien government had made few efforts to prepare the country for the obligations involved. Upon taking office back in 1993, the Liberals had promised to reduce greenhouse emissions to 20 percent below their 1990 levels by 2005. By the time the Conservatives took over, carbon dioxide emissions were 20 percent *above* 1990 levels.

So unimpressed was the environmental movement with the general performance of the Chrétien-Martin team on the emerging issue of the new century that many environmental activists had come to remember the Brian Mulroney era with nostalgia. In the winter of 2006, some of them passed over both Chrétien and Martin, to reach back and designate Mulroney as the country's greenest prime minister.

All was not in hand on the Canada–U.S. front, either. NAFTA—the North American free-trade agreement, which was meant to ensure that Canada's central trade relationship ran smoothly—was not living up to the expectations of its authors. A lingering dispute over softwood lumber was casting serious doubts on the value of the dispute-settlement mechanism at the heart of the agreement.

Overall, mixed signals seemed to have become the trademark of Ottawa's relationship with Washington. Jean Chrétien and his government had kept the Bush administration guessing on Canada's participation in the Iraq war almost until the first missiles landed on Baghdad, before declining to join the coalition. Paul Martin followed the same pattern over partaking in the American project for a continental anti-ballistic missile shield, blowing hot and then cold on the idea and ultimately turning it down on the eve of a national Liberal convention. Chrétien had been accused by some of his critics of making his decision on the basis of an upcoming provincial election in Quebec, where opposition to the war ran by far the highest. Now it appeared that even smaller considerations—in this case Martin's wish to avoid a battle on the convention floor—were driving Canadian policy towards the United States.

Other signs also hinted that the Martin team was ambivalent about the way to go with the Canada–U.S. relationship. Upon taking office late in 2003, the prime minister had turned Canada's envoy to Washington, Michael Kergin, into a lame duck by offering the post to his former Cabinet colleague and rival John Manley. When Manley turned him down, Martin left the post in limbo for almost a full year before he finally appointed former New Brunswick premier Frank McKenna.

McKenna himself was to fall prey to the mixed signals coming from Ottawa on missile defence. On the eve of taking up his appointment in Washington, he was clearly under the impression that Martin would sign onto the plan, for he hinted as much to a parliamentary committee, telling MPs that Canada—as part of NORAD—was in any event a de facto participant in missile defence. As it turned out, Ambassador McKenna had been kept out of the ever-twisting PMO loop. Only days later, Martin announced his decision to reject the American invitation. Choosing McKenna from the ranks of former politicians rather than anointing someone from the diplomatic corps had been a precedent-setting move, meant to signal that the new occupant of Canada's embassy in Washington would have a direct political line to the top in Ottawa. Yet one of McKenna's first tasks in Washington turned out to be wiping PMO egg off his face.

Past Liberal governments had often had prickly relationships with the White House, and never more so than when a Republican president was in office. Even when the more popular Bill Clinton was presiding, Jean Chrétien had felt it was good politics to keep his distance, at least in public. But there were other glaring discrepancies between the Liberal government's talk and its actions, in matters even closer to the party's soul.

The 1982 Charter of Rights and Freedoms is the jewel of the federal Liberal crown, an accomplishment of iconic proportions. An overwhelming number of Canadians in every region of the country have come to revere this parting accomplishment of Pierre Trudeau.

As part of his efforts to position his party as the champion of progressive values, Paul Martin spent the tail end of the 2006 election campaign hammering home the message that Charter rights would be immensely safer under the continued protection of a Liberal government than under a Conservative one. Yet the government of Jean Chrétien had had to be dragged to the altar of gay marriage by the courts, and Martin himself had dragged his feet on the way to the ceremony, leading many Liberal opponents of the measure to hope he would be a no-show. In June 2003, the Chrétien government had already put three questions

to the Supreme Court pertaining to the place of same-sex marriage within the larger framework of the Charter of Rights and
Freedoms of the Constitution. One of Martin's first acts in office
had been to expand the federal reference by adding a fourth question to the list. The additional question Martin put to the court
was described by legal experts as a mere delaying tactic, designed
to get the Liberals over the hurdle of the 2004 election before
they had to act on gay marriage. Those suspicions were not without foundation. As it turned out, a year later the nine justices
found that the extra question was redundant. They declined to
answer it.

By the time Parliament belatedly adjusted its laws to accommodate the courts' interpretation of the Charter, the vast majority of provinces were routinely performing same-sex marriage
ceremonies. On Charter rights—as on many other issues that the
Liberal Party likes to claim as its own—federal leadership too
often gave way to political convenience.

Ask most Liberals which federal party is the champion of
Canadian cultural institutions, and chances are they will point
proudly at their own chests. The notion that strong cultural
institutions are the trademark of a vibrant country is a tenet of
Liberal faith, as is a belief in the need to support a public
broadcaster such as the CBC/Radio-Canada. That, at least, is
the theory.

While they were in opposition in the eighties, the Liberals
had promised to provide the CBC with stable multi-year funding
that was in line with its unique mandate. The 1995 war on the
deficit had pre-empted that promise. But in the era of federal
surpluses, the government continued to keep the CBC guessing.
By the time the Liberals left office in 2006, the situation of the
CBC was as schizophrenic as ever, its mandate to offer distinct
Canadian programming still not reconciled with its need to

compete with commercial outlets for audiences and revenues in a fragmented television universe.

The federal government is solely responsible for the equalization system, through which it redistributes funds to level the fiscal playing field between have and have-not provinces. Early in his tenure, Martin made side deals with some provinces, throwing a wrench into the workings of the system.

The first equalization program began in the 1950s. Since then, the system has become so convoluted that few people can figure out what makes it tick. At a Liberal leadership debate in Winnipeg in the spring of 2006, Michael Ignatieff, a scholar of international standing, admitted that the intricacies of the system were well beyond his understanding. With one exception—Stéphane Dion, who had been federal minister for intergovernmental affairs for seven years (over the course of which equalization had been a recurring topic of discussion with the provinces)—none of Ignatieff's opponents disputed his point. Most of them had held senior government positions in Ottawa or at Queen's Park, but they remained at a loss when it came to the fine print of the equalization program. Not surprisingly, it didn't take much Liberal tinkering to make this Byzantine system even worse. By the time Paul Martin left office, it was programmed to produce aberrant outcomes—not the least of which was to raise the fiscal capacity of Newfoundland, a have-not province, over that of Ontario, a net contributor to the system through its taxpayers. As a result, taxes raised from the earnings of Ontarians were ensuring that the government of Newfoundland had more per capita money to spend on programs than Ontario itself.

When Stephen Harper became prime minister, he asked his officials to provide him with figures on the upcoming round of equalization payments. To his amazement, they did not seem able to agree on a set of numbers.

In 1989, the House of Commons unanimously voted to eradicate child poverty in Canada by the year 2000. Instead, child poverty has gone up, peaking in 1996, the high point of Martin's war on the federal deficit.

During Martin's brief tenure, Liberal ministers travelled from province to province to sign accords on child care, to great fanfare. But with the exception of Quebecers, whose provincial government had not waited for Ottawa to act, few working parents saw tangible signs of an emerging, affordable universal child-care system.

The Liberals had promised a national child-care program in the lead-up to their first victory in 1993. Once the deficit was eliminated, they seemed to lose interest in their commitment, until Martin resuscitated it for the 2004 campaign.

In the spring of 2000, Canadians watched with dismay as the Ontario town of Walkerton struggled with the country's worst outbreak of E. coli contamination of a community's drinking water. At a time when the Ontario Conservative government was unloading many of its responsibilities onto the municipalities and the private sector, the town's water treatment system had fallen prey to reckless negligence. Seizing on the fact that Ontario's Conservative regime was philosophically inclined to reduce the size and scope of government, many federal Liberals saw the Walkerton tragedy as vindication of their own brand of government activism. But their activism was selective. In 2005, scores of aboriginal reserves under the sole jurisdiction of the federal government were revealed to have no reliable access to safe drinking water.

Upon taking office, Martin had vouched to put in place mechanisms to measure the performance of the province's health-care systems. But the Liberal government might have proved unable to meet the most minimal standards. To this day, the federal government presides over the worst health outcomes in the country. The aboriginal people to whom the federal government provides services endure longer waits for care and are generally in poorer health.

Over the decade between 1995 and 2005, the country's bigger cities emerged as the strategic forces of a more global Canada. Their socio-economic health, and that of their infrastructures, would largely determine the quality of life in twenty-first-century Canada, and its competitiveness globally. Montreal and Toronto—to name just those two—were more populous and more diverse than most of the provinces. Paul Martin had come into office promising to make this emerging reality an integral part of his government's strategic thinking.

But once he was in power, the initiative lost its focus. The government stopped talking about the big cities and started to use a more generic label, a "communities" agenda. The new label was more politically inclusive for the many MPs who hailed from outside the major cities, but it was a significant distortion of the strategic goals of Martin's original policy.

For years, Canadians had tended to see the federal government as the governance model for other levels of government. Most Canadians, especially outside Alberta and Quebec, had a natural positive bias towards the federal government. In the wake of its success regarding elimination of the deficit, the federal government was widely seen as part of the solution to the country's problems. But after 1997, successive governments found themselves mired in marginal but spectacular cases of mismanagement. A gun registry whose expenses ran wildly off target, a job-grants program employed to help re-elect Liberal MPs—including

Jean Chrétien—in Quebec, and a sponsorship program that plummeted into disgrace, taking the image of federalism down with it in Quebec—this litany of mismanagement made Canadians seriously doubt the competence of their own government.

All this had a corrosive effect not only on the image of the government itself, but on the morale of the civil service. Far from being energized by the arrival of a new prime minister whose buzzword was "activism," the top levels of the civil service were befuddled by conflicting and ever-changing priorities. The Gomery commission on the sponsorship scandal, and the highly publicized police inquiries into the matter, also had a demoralizing effect.

In her landmark 2003 report on the sponsorship program, the Auditor General insisted that she had found no evidence of widespread mismanagement within the civil service. Sheila Fraser took pains to underline the fact that the sponsorship scandal was an exception to a generally commendable regime of public management. If anything, the Gomery commission subsequently brought to light the leading role politics played in the affair. But, understandably, the Martin government seemed deaf to the message that the civil service was not at the root of the sponsorship debacle. The dying months of the Liberal government were spent looking for ways to blunt the impact of the final Gomery report. A dizzying array of new guidelines were drafted, and ever-tighter controls were put in place, often stalling the operations of an already slow government, but often also failing to ensure a more transparent system.

By the time Paul Martin took office in 2004, the years of war on the deficit, the referendum counteroffensive and the Liberal civil war had all left their marks on Canada's premier government address. Many parts of the federal house were in dire need of repair. But the occupants of Parliament Hill saw themselves as builders, not mere renovators. They had grander projects in mind.

—

## CHAPTER EIGHT

# TUG-OF-WAR

Despite its flagging performance in so many of its core missions, the top priorities of the Martin government were all matters that were primarily under the direction of the provinces. Post-secondary education, child care and health care had been the staples of the last two Speeches from the Throne. But while the prime minister had money to spend, the provinces had bad memories about the federal capacity to cut.

They had borne the brunt of the collateral damage of his war on the federal deficit. Having spent years fixing the damage that Paul Martin's cuts to transfer payments had inflicted on their social systems, most premiers were in no mood to take lessons from a nouveau-riche federal government. Martin had not worried about how the provinces could keep their hospitals going when he had tightened the purse strings in the mid-nineties; they were not inclined to let him dictate how they should spend money now that he was willing to untie them.

In the past, prime ministers who had wrested federal-provincial agreements from the premiers had come to the table with a clear set of objectives and the strong wind of public opinion at their backs. Paul Martin had buckets of money and an equal supply of good intentions, but he did not seem to have a road map to lead him to his destination. Moreover, the premiers were determined not to let him seize the high ground.

As the televised portion of Paul Martin's September 2004 federal-provincial summit on health care revealed, the balance of expertise in social policy was decisively tilted towards the provinces. While the prime minister waxed on about saving medicare for a generation—an inflated promise that many Canadians could hardly take seriously—premier after premier shot back with facts and figures. The message to the public was clear: if medicare was to have political custodians, they would be the premiers, who knew the file like the backs of their hands—not the prime minister, whose grasp of the issue came across as well-intentioned but tenuous.

In the end, Paul Martin did get an agreement, but only after the wheeling and dealing stretched late into the night, and only by offering Quebec a separate agreement that basically recognized its constitutional sovereignty over its health-care system. During the following year, Health Canada drafted legislation designed to give federal teeth to the prime minister's agreement with the provinces—but it never saw the light of day. Martin's Quebec ministers made the case that the legislation failed to reflect the asymmetrical terms offered to Quebec in exchange for Premier Jean Charest's signature.

Still, the federal government had achieved its central objective. In the future, the provinces' performances would be measured; waiting times for a select number of medical procedures would be compared to agreed-upon benchmarks. As it turned out, this was a rare instance when Ottawa was marginally ahead of the courts. In the spring of 2005, the Supreme Court would rule that Quebec could not prevent citizens from buying private insurance to pay for essential medical services that the system failed to provide within medically acceptable time frames.

The official opposition supported Martin's health-care accord.

In the 2006 election, reasonable waiting times for medical services surfaced as one of five Conservative priorities. Once in
power, Stephen Harper sought to ensure that the provinces
lived up to their side of the federal-provincial bargain. He too
found that promises were more easily made than kept, as many
provinces responded with a call for yet more federal money for
health care. But at least Harper picked up where Martin had
left off. The other Liberal battle over social policy was destined
for a much less promising fate.

In Quebec, the universal child-care program that began in the
late nineties has become a strong symbol of the input of
women in politics, tangible proof that, given a critical mass at
the top, they can make a significant difference to the direction
of a government. No one who knows him seriously believes
that Premier Lucien Bouchard—a deeply conservative man
from a generation raised on traditional views of the family—
would have taken the initiative on such an ambitious program
if he had been left to his own devices.

After the 1995 referendum, Pauline Marois, Louise Harel and
their female Parti Québécois colleagues fought hard for a regime
of affordable child care. As an aging industrialized society operating in a minority language, Quebec is doubly concerned about
its declining birth rate. It's a threat to its economic future as well
as to the ongoing presence of French as a living language in
North America.

The women in Bouchard's Cabinet argued that the availability
of affordable child care would offer young Quebecers a stronger
incentive to raise families than enhanced baby bonuses, especially
if a generous parental-leave program was put in place to allow
them to stay home for the first years of their children's lives.

According to polls, the conciliation between work and family
was (and remains) the top concern of young Quebec families, a

prime group of voters that had experienced the costs attendant on a financially bereft welfare state more than they had reaped its benefits. Many were increasingly attracted to the tax-cutting policies of the fledgling Action Démocratique Party, at the expense of the social-democrat creed of the PQ.

The progressive wing of the sovereignist party had also grown restless with the fiscally conservative policies of its own government. It was hoped that a new social program would demonstrate to Quebec social activists that the sacrifices involved in getting the province's finances out of the red had not been in vain, or simply the product of a neo-conservative agenda.

Quebec women have traditionally been more wary of sovereignty than their male counterparts. With an eye to the longer referendum game, it was suggested that a bold move on the child-care front might help the Parti Québécois address its gender gap, and connect with the new generation of young urban professionals.

By the time she retired from politics in 2006, Pauline Marois had held all the major portfolios within her government, including health, finance and education. In the late nineties, she and a handful of her female colleagues had key positions within Bouchard's government. As working mothers themselves, they made formidable adversaries for whomever dared tackle them on the merits of a universal child-care program. Very few dared to take them on, or managed to do so effectively, and Quebec became the first North American jurisdiction to set up a comprehensive public child-care system.

Under the subsequent Liberal government of Jean Charest, the program was complemented by a parental-leave system financed by Quebec's share of the federal employment insurance program. In contrast to a parallel federal program, the Quebec version is designed to offer benefits to all working parents, regardless of whether they qualify for employment insurance. Since January 2006, Quebec workers and employers have paid a tax to make up the difference between Quebec's share of the federal parental-leave fund and what the province actually pays out. As a footnote, by the summer of 2006 Quebec was experiencing a modest baby boom.

Inspired by the popularity of Quebec's child-care initiative, Paul Martin decided to make early childhood education the next social frontier of his government. Not surprisingly, he encountered the same provincial skepticism regarding that endeavour as he had regarding medicare. Again, his efforts came to divide the top levels of his government.

Unlike the Parti Québécois government of Lucien Bouchard in the National Assembly, Paul Martin found no support for his child-care plan on the official opposition benches of the House of Commons. In fact, in many crucial ways, the Conservatives seemed to have a better grasp of the optics of the battle Martin was launching than the Liberals did.

Before he became Liberal leader, Paul Martin had repeatedly promised to make room for more women at the top of the government. Once he was in office, though, the power balance of the Cabinet remained largely unchanged. Sheila Copps was replaced by Anne McLellan as the senior woman in the Cabinet, but after the 2004 election the number of women in Martin's Cabinet actually went down, from eleven to eight. Half of those women sat at the junior end of the ministerial table, in posts that Stephen Harper would not even bother to keep when he made up his own first Cabinet a year and a half later.

Compared to their colleagues in the Quebec Cabinet, the women on Paul Martin's team were not equally engaged in the federal child-care bid. On the contrary, some of them found themselves fighting a rearguard battle against their government's sudden activism.

Liza Frulla and Lucienne Robillard—the two ranking female ministers from Quebec—had no incentive to fight a battle in

Ottawa that their sisters had already won in the National Assembly. In Quebec, Paul Martin's child-care efforts elicited little active public support. More often than not, the federal government was seen as once again trying to duplicate existing services to satisfy its endless craving for visibility. So widespread was the sense that the need for child-care services had already been fully addressed by the province that when Premier Charest stated that he would divert whatever federal child-care funds came his way to other priorities, few objected.

In the National Assembly, the Liberals had been generally supportive of the child-care directions of the PQ, if not of their implementation, but in the House of Commons, the Conservative Party had strong reservations. Its vocal social-conservative wing saw state-financed child care as an assault on the traditional family. Moreover, as a general rule, federal incursions into provincial areas of social policy ran counter to the party's view of federalism.

There is a strong case to be made that in a society as ethnically diverse as Canada, early childhood education is a strategic economic investment that can level language and societal inequalities, so that children can start their elementary education on a relatively equal footing. There is no lack of studies demonstrating that the early years play a determining role in successful education outcomes, and that those outcomes impact directly on a modern economy.

By the same token, giving the middle class a stake in a public universal child-care system makes as much sense as doing so in the education system or in medicare. Creating a two-tier system defeats the purpose of such a program; far from levelling the playing field, it can actually make it steeper for less affluent families by forcing the children into low-end daycare ghettos. Under a two-tier system wealthier parents are more likely to spend their money on higher-quality care privately than to push for more quality in the public system. But if anyone on the right was making that case, the point did not get through to the federal Conservatives.

In Quebec, the highest-profile women in the Cabinet had spearheaded the child-care file. They had networked with their opposition sisters to ensure support for the initiative across party lines. Rather than parallel that strategy, Martin handed the child-care mission to Ken Dryden, a political neophyte who spoke no French. Dryden brought much earnestness to the task. His commitment to putting a program in place could not be doubted. But in the public relations battle against the Conservative Party and the provinces, he could not make the grade.

No one would ever accuse Alberta MP Rona Ambrose of being a poster girl for traditional role models. One of the Conservative's up-and-coming young female MPs, she was a natural choice to lead Stephen Harper's battle against the Liberal child-care plan. In February 2005, Ambrose caught flak when she stood up in the House of Commons to accuse Dryden of being an "old white male" trying to impose child-care choices on women—but she had made her point. His well-meaning but wooden responses to his articulate critic reinforced the image of the federal government as a meddling, paternalistic uncle.

A father who, by his own admission, had been relatively helpless on the home front, Paul Martin could hardly make up for the shortcomings of his lead minister on the child-care issue. His record as an advocate for a different work-family balance was non-existent.

Significantly, when Stephen Harper set out to replace Paul Martin's ambitious plan with more traditional family allowances, he made sure that one of his rare female ministers stood at the front line of the debate.

The Conservatives were not the only party giving Martin headaches on the child-care front. Quebec might be the model for the federal plan, but its government's input was often in sharp contrast to the Pollyannaish vision of the plan promoted by the federal government. Quebec officials knew first-hand the recurring costs involved in their program, and they recognized the gap between Ottawa's good intentions and the start-up funding that Martin was willing to put on the table. From its inception, the Quebec child-care program had been immensely popular. In short order it had emerged as a new sacred cow for the middle class, a policy that politicians touched at their peril, and one whose appetite and growth potential put fear in the hearts of government bean-counters.

In his first Quebec election campaign, in 1998, Jean Charest had mused about restructuring the program so that wealthier families took on the burden of financing their share of the system. In the space of twenty-four hours he had had to back off, for fear of hurting his middle-class electoral prospects beyond repair.

Fresh from their experience with keeping medicare afloat, many provinces found the sobering case for caution that Quebec was quietly making to be more persuasive than the enticements the federal government was willing to offer. Like Paul Martin, the premiers believed that the child-care program had the potential to be the medicare of twenty-first-century Canada. Unlike the prime minister, though, many of them found that a daunting prospect rather than an attractive one.

The majority of Canadians liked the concept of a publicly funded child-care system but, like some of the provinces, they found their enthusiasm tempered by hard-earned experience and well-founded skepticism. Successive federal governments had been promising decisive action on the child-care front for twenty years. To date, none had delivered on that promise.

In the 2006 election campaign Paul Martin kept his child-care initiative in the window, but many parents knew better. At best, tangible results of such a program were months and potentially years away; they would materialize too late for most current parents of preschoolers. Most of those parents heartily supported the concept of a program run along the Quebec lines, and would continue to do so in the future—but given a choice between the $1,200 per child per year offered by the Conservatives, and some elusive future system they would never themselves benefit from, many did not hesitate.

In Quebec, meanwhile, the federal child-care initiative was a public relations fiasco. It had taken months for the two governments to agree on the conditions of the transfer of Quebec's share of child-care funds, even though this was the only province that had a full-fledged system in place. The delays were said to be caused by federal calls for more accountability. The notion that Ottawa would try to impose its supervision on a system that existed solely as an initiative of their provincial government boggled the minds of most Quebecers. All of this reinforced the widespread perception that it was an overly intrusive force, bent on duplicating existing policies. Enraged by the daily exposés of sponsorship waste from the Gomery commission, many Quebecers dismissed Martin's child-care crusade as yet another expensive and insulting federal effort to force a flag down their throats with their own tax money.

By the summer of 2005, with only months to go until the prime minister's declared date for the next federal election, Martin's Quebec ministers were at the end of their tether. In January 2004, they had all argued against the setting up of the Gomery commission, predicting that it would paint the entire Quebec federalist camp with the brush of the sponsorship scandal. They had been overruled by Martin's advisers, only to have their direst predictions come true. Now another election was in the offing, and if they were to have any chance to move beyond Justice Gomery and his reports, they needed something more compelling than Martin's obsolete child-care project.

Over the course of a raucous Cabinet discussion on fiscal federalism, matters came to a head between the Quebec and Ontario ministers. Backed by Stéphane Dion and most of his Quebec colleagues, Paul Martin's Quebec lieutenant, Jean Lapierre, complained that the federal government was consistently trampling the provinces' social backyards, while large patches of its own fields were untended. If he had known he would end up running provincial programs, Lapierre said, he would have sought a seat in the National Assembly.

The result was a mega-clash between ministers. Those from Ontario defended their government's hands-on approach to social policy as the very essence of federalism. The Quebecers maintained that it amounted to a perversion of the system. They were not totally without support; some of them left the meeting convinced that David Emerson, senior minister for British Columbia, and Anne McLellan, number two in Martin's government and his sole minister from Alberta, were on the same wavelength.

Be that as it may, the Quebec ministers were on the wrong side of the prime minister. At a subsequent meeting at Paul Martin's farm in Knowlton, Quebec, Lucienne Robillard, Pierre Pettigrew, Stéphane Dion and Jean Lapierre picked up the discussion where it had inconclusively left off at the Cabinet table, and pressed for a more disciplined approach to federal-provincial relations. The Liberal government, they told the prime minister, was turning the logic of federalism on its head. In the process, it was alienating large sections of the population, in particular (but not exclusively) in Quebec. It was also squandering a lot of provincial goodwill by acting as if the Constitution did not spell out the roles and responsibilities of each government. Its energy would be better spent on its core missions than on fighting the provinces, inch by expensive inch, on their own ground.

But Martin had learned his federalism at his father's knee, at the time medicare was created, and he saw himself as a proud descendant of the weavers of Canada's social safety net. He told his Quebec ministers as much.

Forty years had passed since then. The provinces now had mature governments of their own. Strategic thinking was no longer the exclusive purview of the federal government. The creation of the Council of the Federation in 2003 had provided the premiers with a venue to hash out issues among themselves before taking on the federal government. It had also allowed the Quebec government—the provincial administration that had developed the largest federal-provincial expertise over years of Quebec–Ottawa squabbling—to disseminate its knowledge among all the provinces. No longer could a federal government show up at the negotiating table with the advantage of superior expertise. Some of the results of that had been on evidence when the premiers held the line on Paul Martin at the 2004 health-care summit.

The current generation of premiers had an experience of medicare far removed from Martin's romantic memories. Over their time in office, it had turned into their biggest fiscal headache. They were the ones who had had to keep a revered national program going over the lean years, while the federal government shouldered a shrinking part of the expenses. Even now, health care was eating up the bulk of the provinces' social budget. At the September 2004 medicare summit, one premier quipped that at the rate health expenses were increasing in his province, he would soon need only two ministers in his Cabinet, one for finance and the other for health.

The days when the provinces would accept start-up money to open up franchises of a federal program only to find themselves operating them mostly on their own dime farther down the road were gone. If Ottawa insisted on pursuing socially activist purposes with its spending power, it would have to content itself with more modest boutique programs, or else bear the entire burden.

Some of the Liberal leadership aspirants would invite their party to contemplate that reality after the 2006 election defeat. In the spring of that year, Bob Rae—one of only two candidates who had had occasion to sit on the provincial side of the table—suggested that the federal government take responsibility for a national pharmacare program, to alleviate the provinces' social burden. And his leadership rival Michael Ignatieff agreed with the premiers that their share of the revenues of the federation had not kept pace with the rising costs of their social programs.

That night in Knowlton, though, Paul Martin and his Quebec ministers got nowhere. When they parted, they could only agree to disagree.

For the four Quebec ministers, it was a sobering moment. Robillard, Pettigrew and Dion had come to federal politics at a time when the federation had been on the brink. Their loyalty to federalism could not be questioned. They had spent the past decade on the Quebec front line, countering the sovereignist argument that federalism was a straitjacket for Quebec . . . and fully expecting Paul Martin to prove them right. They knew that no Quebecer was willing to turn back the clock after forty years of building a strong social model for the province. The federalism regime practised by Martin's father, as benevolent as it might have been at the time, had no appeal in Quebec.

As for Lapierre, his return to the federal Liberal fold was meant to signal to other Quebec nationalists that the time for sterile confrontations was over. With a federalist in power in Quebec City and a prime minister who purported to admire the Quebec model, surely the two governments would find cause for co-operation.

Some of the Quebec ministers left that night convinced that on the fundamental issue of federalism, they and the prime minister were not on the same page. Paul Martin's view ran counter not only to their well-honed instincts on the unity front, but to the reality of the federation as they thought they knew it.

The fact that Martin and his Quebec ministers had profound differences in their approaches to federalism should have led to an even more troubling question, one that few in Martin's entourage and even fewer on the Ontario side of his Cabinet table seemed to want to pursue. If the most prominent Quebec members of the Liberal government had trouble with Martin's approach to federalism, who in Quebec would not?

The answer—when it came in, January 2006—would reduce Paul Martin to a footnote, and shrink the Liberal Party to its Ontario bones.

In the 2004 federal campaign, no group was less psychologically prepared for battle than the Liberal MPs running for re-election in Ontario. For a decade, the Liberal Party of Canada had virtually owned this most populous province. Over three successive elections, it had had an unprecedented free run. Many of its 2004 incumbents had no personal memories of past battles fought against either a united right or an energized NDP.

A decade earlier, the split within the Conservative movement had turned Ontario into a winning ticket for the federal Liberals. Except in marginal urban pockets, they did not even have to worry about the NDP. The trying days of Bob Rae's one-term NDP government at Queen's Park in the early nineties had not sat well with Ontario voters. Rae's government brought no experience to power at a time when the province was undergoing a deep recession. The result was a stormy mandate, replete with labour strife and deteriorating public finances. In the years between 1993 and 2004, they had turned their backs on the federal New Democrats in record numbers.

That Liberal quasi-monopoly was atypical. With the exception of Alberta, the federal scene had remained competitive in every other province. Outside of Ontario, Liberal candidates usually had to fight for their keep at election time.

The Progressive Conservatives had rebounded from the near-fatal 1993 debacle quickly in Atlantic Canada. Relying on strong provincial infrastructures, the Atlantic PCs had also held their own against the competing Reform/Alliance better than any other group of Tories. As a result, the vote splits that were typical of the right in Ontario were not as much of a factor in Eastern Canada. The NDP under Alexa McDonough, its first leader from Atlantic Canada, had also gained a foothold in the region, for the first time in its history, sapping strength from the Liberals in the process.

For the duration of the Jean Chrétien decade, francophone Quebec had remained the site of vigorous battles between sovereignists and federalists. Over the brief period that Jean Charest led the Progressive Conservatives, some of those battles had been three-way races between the Liberals, the Tories and the Bloc. In all that time, the Liberals came close to winning a majority of Quebec seats only once, in the 2000 election.

In Western Canada, the Liberals had to contend with both the NDP and the Reform/Alliance. The latter was free to take on the Liberals in the absence of any real Progressive Conservative force west of Manitoba. Time and again, Jean Chrétien's party was virtually shut out of Alberta. The Liberals barely held their own in Saskatchewan. In British Columbia, the three-way splits between the NDP, the Liberals and the Reform/Alliance often failed to go their way.

The ten-year discrepancy between the easy ride the Liberals were enjoying in Ontario and the big cohorts that province sent to Ottawa, and the tough battles that Liberal candidates were fighting in every other region, had a profound impact on the personality of their federal party. By 2004, the Liberal Party of Canada had become an Ontario party in all but name.

Like a preview of the replacement of Paul Martin, that of Jean Chrétien was largely an Ontario affair. John Manley and Sheila

Copps, the only two candidates who dared take Martin on, were from the province, as was Allan Rock, who had been expected to run but he determined that he did not have a solid chance of winning. Among the serious pretenders to Chrétien's throne—the handful who had spent months and even years organizing for the succession battle—all but Brian Tobin had strong links to Ontario.

While the federal Liberals from Ontario did not technically replace Jean Chrétien with a leader from their province, they had the next best thing in the shape of Paul Martin. While he was nominally a Quebec MP, and had made Montreal his home base early in his career, his political heart was in his native Ontario. That was particularly evident over the course of his two election campaigns. The Liberal launches in Martin's birth city of Windsor always had more of a party ring to them than the low-key affairs he held in his riding of LaSalle–Émard. In both 2004 and 2006, Martin travelled to Southern Ontario to unveil his party's election platform. As it turned out later, the years he had spent in Quebec had made much less of an impression on his political philosophy than what he had learned in Ontario at his father's ministerial knee.

Martin's board of advisers was also mainly from Ontario. That was where their expertise lay, and where their instincts proved least likely to betray them. When the votes in the 2006 election were counted, that would be credited with allowing the Liberals to salvage a respectable score. But there was a downside. The Martin crew tended to see the world through Ontario lenses, which reinforced their leader's inclinations, rather than open his eyes to larger realities. This put them increasingly out of step with other regions of the country. That tunnel vision was a factor in the rapid shrinkage the Liberal Party underwent over the two short years of Martin's reign.

In fact, there are two ways of looking at the 2006 results. Yes, the Liberals captured fifty-four Ontario seats—a strong showing in absolute terms, as it amounts to slightly more than half the province's 106-seat complement. In comparative terms, though, the number should set off alarm bells in the ears of any thinking Liberal. Since the election of 2000—the last time the right campaigned under two competing party banners—the Liberals have lost half their Ontario seats, and they have proved unable to mitigate that loss with gains in other areas of the country.

In Quebec and Ontario as a whole, the Liberals, in tandem with the Bloc Québécois, have been receding forces, while the NDP and the Conservatives are on the rise. From holding 136 of 181 Quebec and Ontario seats at the time of Jean Chrétien's last campaign, the Liberals were down to 81 after Paul Martin's final campaign, six short years later. Under its fluffy Ontario feathers, the Liberal goose had become a very scrawny bird indeed.

For two decades before Jean Chrétien led his first successful election campaign, the Quebec–Canada battle had defined the federal Liberal Party. But as of 1993, Ontario became the base of the party's power. Shortly after the 1995 Quebec referendum, Ontario dynamics became the primary force that shaped the federal government.

One reason was an ebbing of support for sovereignty, combined with Chrétien's determination to keep the Quebec file within the hands of the tightly knit circle of government insiders. (Significantly, Paul Martin, who was the most popular member of the government in Quebec at the time, was not in the loop.)

More importantly, developments on the Ontario front had a transformative influence on the federal Liberal Party. Just as the election of the first Parti Québécois government in 1976 had a defining impact on the thinking of the government of Pierre Trudeau, the arrival of Mike Harris in 1995 had a profound influence on the outlook of a federal government dominated as never before by Ontario MPs.

—

## CHAPTER NINE

## THE TWENTY-YEAR COLD WAR

B y the time Premier Mike Harris brought his Common Sense Revolution to Queen's Park in 1995, Ontario and the federal regime of the day had already been at cross-purposes for the better part of ten years. Harris's coming to power on a right-wing agenda would raise the cold war between the two to the level of an ice age.

The last time the Conservatives had been in power at Queen's Park at the same time as the Liberals were in office federally had been a golden age of Ontario–Ottawa co-operation. Its memory would quickly fade during the Harris era.

For most of Pierre Trudeau's final mandate, in the early eighties, Premier Bill Davis and the Liberal prime minister had stood shoulder to shoulder on the national scene, and worked hand in hand on the energy front. It was a period of quid pro quos. Ontario reaped providential benefits from the cheaper energy prices that resulted from Trudeau's controversial National Energy Program, designed to give the federal government more control over Alberta's energy output. Trudeau's dream of patriating the Constitution would not have become reality without Bill Davis's unflagging support.

Its supportive role in Pierre Trudeau's most divisive battles would come to cost Ontario dearly in its dealings with the other provinces.

The 1982 patriation debate was the last time in the twentieth century that Ontario found itself on the winning side of a national discussion. The years that followed were a time of volatile political change in the province, and of waning Ontario influence on, and interest in, the rest of the federation. Ontario's leadership on major national issues was repeatedly rejected by the rest of the country.

In 1987–88, Liberal premier David Peterson led a losing battle against Brian Mulroney's free-trade agreement with the United States. Peterson tried and failed to rally other premiers to his side. Even among the Liberal premiers, only Joe Ghiz from Prince Edward Island briefly answered his call. He folded before the battle moved onto the stage of the 1988 federal election. And Quebec—where Peterson's friend and ally Robert Bourassa was in power—tipped the scales decisively in favour of free trade. A few years later, Ontario's NDP premier Bob Rae had no more success in his attempts to mount an effective counteroffensive against the North American Free Trade Agreement (NAFTA), or any major aspect of the federal Conservative economic agenda.

Under both David Peterson and Bob Rae, Queen's Park was at odds with Mulroney's national capital on almost every issue of importance. The exception was the Constitution. Like Bill Davis before them, each played a strong role in a common constitutional front with the prime minister of the day. Unlike Premier Davis, they reaped no benefit at home for their nation-building efforts.

David Peterson was a prime mover of the Meech Lake Accord, supporting it from its hopeful start to its bitter finish. But he could never get the bulk of his Liberal provincial counterparts onside. From Manitoba's Sharon Carstairs to Newfoundland's Clyde Wells, most lined up with Pierre Trudeau in the anti-Meech camp. Their arguments ultimately resonated more loudly with public opinion outside Quebec than those of David Peterson and Brian Mulroney, the highest-ranking politicians in power in their respective political families at the time.

In the same fashion, the Charlottetown Accord that consumed so much of Bob Rae's energy as premier went down in flames, in a national referendum that split the Ontario electorate right down the middle, and galvanized much of the rest of the country against the deal and its authors.

Ontario premier Mike Harris had seen his two immediate predecessors burned in the heat of a losing constitutional fight. He would have no part of one. One of his first behind-the-scenes acts on the unity front was to stop Jean Chrétien from reopening the Constitution. In the aftermath of the 1995 referendum, Chrétien wanted to enshrine Quebec's distinct status in the Constitution quickly. He expected the near-death federalist experience of the referendum to stifle opposition to the move. Ontario nipped the plan in the bud; Harris's answer to Chrétien was a flat no.

The relationship between the Chrétien Liberals and the Harris government went downhill from there. The two had fundamentally different visions of the country and of their core missions, but they drew their power from the same Ontario source, and their rivalry and antagonism permeated every aspect of their relationship. As finance minister, Paul Martin found it immensely easier to get along with Quebec's Bernard Landry than with his Ontario counterpart, Ernie Eves. His experience was far from unique. Over the period when the two parties were simultaneously in power, more co-operation agreements were struck with sovereignist Quebec than with Conservative Ontario.

In the late seventies, the clash between the Quebec federal Liberals and the Parti Québécois over Quebec's political future had defined the government of Pierre Trudeau. In the late nineties, an ideological clash with the Harris Conservatives came to define the Chrétien-Martin Liberals.

Premier Mike Harris believed in a smaller, less activist government. The instincts of a federal Liberal caucus dominated by Ontario leaned decisively the other way. As Queen's Park unloaded responsibilities and shrank the role of government, Ottawa branched out in primarily provincial directions. The cities, post-secondary education, child care, homelessness and the management of medicare all became bigger priorities of the federal Liberal government. Paul Martin, in particular, embraced them even before he was leader.

In the same way that the debate over federalism versus sovereignty had its roots in a Quebec family feud, this power struggle began as a battle over the role of governments between Mike Harris's Queen's Park and Jean Chrétien's Ontario-dominated capital. In time, Paul Martin would try in vain to export that battle to the national scene, to frame his fight against the reunited Conservative Party as a battle for core Canadian values. But there was simply no market for this concept in Quebec, or in many parts of Western Canada at the time.

Taking the battle for the hearts and minds of Ontarians inside the federal government had other unintended consequences.

It led Ottawa to set out to fill non-existent gaps in areas that were already taken care of, in Quebec, by the more activist provincial government. It tested the patience of Alberta, which was at that point putting more per capita into the social envelope than any other province, yet was still treated as a renegade by the federal Liberals in their efforts to paint the Queen's Park Tories as right-wing clones of the Ralph Klein government. It also pushed the federal government in directions that answered no pressing need in many of the smaller provinces.

When Dalton McGuinty came to power in 2003, the federal Liberals were happy to see the last of the Harris-Eves Tories. But the first budget of the new Liberal premier, complete with tax cuts and a deficit, made life more difficult for them on the campaign trail—another first for most of the federal incumbents, who had never had to campaign with a government of the same stripe installed at Queen's Park. No longer could they position themselves as a vanguard against the provincial government of the day.

McGuinty's subsequent vocal battle for a fairer deal for Ontario sent Martin's minority government scrambling to find millions to secure its political base. Over the course of a single afternoon in the spring of 2005, Martin put hundreds of millions of dollars on Ontario's table as a public peace offering. Brian Mulroney could only have dreamed of having the temerity (or the means) to make such a blatant offer, in the days when he was trying to secure unanimous provincial support for his constitutional accords.

Over the decades, Ontario's interests had not favoured benevolence to the rest of the federation. Why should they have? After Ontario's leadership was rebuffed on free trade, NAFTA, Meech and Charlottetown, the province had, quite naturally, set out to look after itself. The realities of the north-south economic axis brought about by freer trade with the United States had made the workings of the federation less vital to Ontario's economy. No longer could anyone assume that Ontario's interests automatically coincided with those of the rest of Canada—or that it cared all that much if they didn't.

David Peterson, Bob Rae and Mike Harris had all kept their distance from a federal government that they felt was adversarial to their agendas and to their province's interests, but they had all cultivated an alliance with Quebec. The first two were seen by Robert Bourassa as his closest provincial allies at the constitutional table, and Mike Harris always had a better working relationship with Lucien Bouchard than with Jean Chrétien.

By comparison, the relationship between Dalton McGuinty and his Quebec counterpart, Jean Charest, was defined almost from the start by their differences rather than by their common interests. Charest's Council of the Federation—whose founding had preceded McGuinty's election as premier—was more likely to constrain Ontario's influence on the federal government than to enhance it. And Ontario was bound to find itself on the wrong side of most of the other provinces in the battle to right the fiscal imbalance through enhanced equalization payments, as its taxpayers were contributors to that fund rather than bene-ficiaries. Moreover, the Harris tax cuts had left Ontario with a lot less room to manoeuvre than its Liberal government would have liked.

With the Liberals out, McGuinty was basically a free agent. With Quebec re-engaging itself in federalist politics at the national level, Ontario could no longer bank on its status as the political base of the federal ruling party in its dealings with Ottawa.

That was not necessarily bad for Dalton McGuinty. More often than not, Ontario premiers have benefited at election time from an adversarial relationship with the federal government. Ontario voters have been even more inclined than Quebecers to put their eggs in different federal and provincial baskets. But there was no silver lining for the Liberal Party of Canada. Over its decade in power, it had come to speak for Ontario more than for Canada, and what was left of it after the 2006 election reflected that reality.

The line between the federal Liberals and their Ontario cousins had become so thin that Gerard Kennedy, the Ontario minister of education, thought nothing of jumping from the Cabinet at Queen's Park straight into the leadership campaign of the federal party. That would normally be a huge stretch for someone with little or no profile in most regions of Canada, and zero federal experience, not to mention a lack of proficiency in French.

Stripped of its thin veneer of support in francophone Quebec, and with not a single seat in Alberta, the Liberal Party of Canada had become a prime manifestation of the regionalism it was always so prompt to denounce in others.

PART III

—

# THE CANADIAN LEFT

—

## CHAPTER TEN

## HEAVEN AND HELL

For the left, Quebec is both heaven and hell: a social democratic paradise where the great icons of the left in this country nevertheless get precious little respect.

Take the NDP. Quebec is its pot of gold at the end of the rainbow, an elusive treasure trove that is always in sight, yet always proves to be out of reach. For as long as the NDP has existed, Quebecers have been impervious to its efforts to seduce them. Even true-blue Alberta is not as indifferent to the NDP as Quebec.

Over the years, the federal NDP has regularly won seats in Toronto, Vancouver, Winnipeg and Halifax, but never in Montreal or Quebec City. In 2006, New Brunswick, Nova Scotia, Saskatchewan, Manitoba, British Columbia and Ontario all sent NDP members to the House of Commons—but Quebec has done that only once, in 1990, and has never come close to repeating the experience.

And yet, to the frustration of many social democrats, Quebec is the province where the party's progressive values are most commonly shared, and most often reflected in public policy. Despite Quebec's insistence on giving the NDP the cold shoulder, without the province life would be harder, not easier, for Canada's left. Without Quebec, some of the great social debates of the past decades might well have gone the other way.

The last time Parliament revisited the death penalty, in 1987, Quebec MPs — most of them members of the Progressive Conservative Party — voted against its return in overwhelming numbers, and the measure died.

Quebec is the province where Henry Morgentaler launched his battle for free access to abortion in Canada in the late sixties. Long before the Supreme Court waded into the debate to strike down the section of the Criminal Code pertaining to abortion, in 1988, Quebec juries had skirted the legal restrictions by repeatedly refusing to convict Morgentaler. As a result, abortion on demand was available in Quebec decades before federal efforts to restrict it were dropped as a result of a parliamentary stalemate in 1990.

In 2002, the three parties in the Quebec National Assembly unanimously supported the introduction of civil unions for gay couples. The Quebec parties stopped short of full-fledged marriage only because that was a federal responsibility. All three parties welcomed the court decisions that ultimately forced Parliament's hand and opened the door to the legalization of same-sex marriage. In the House of Commons, the issue bitterly divided Ontario's 106 MPs, often along rural-urban or religious lines, but only a handful of Quebec's 75 MPs voted against the 2005 bill permitting same-sex marriage. In the fall of that year, the Parti Québécois elected André Boisclair, becoming the first mainstream party in Canada to elect an openly gay leader.

If the participation of women in electoral politics is a benchmark of sexual equality, Quebec is once again ahead of the national curve. With 38 women out of 125 National Assembly members, the province currently has the highest proportion of female legislators: 30 percent, versus 22 percent in Ontario and British Columbia, the runner-up provinces. Since entering the provincial arena, Quebec premier Jean Charest has spared no effort to bolster the number of women running for his Liberal

Party, going out of his way to run female candidates whenever he can find them. The results speak for themselves.

At the time of the debate over Iraq, the anti-war movement elsewhere looked on in envy while as many as 250,000 demonstrators (versus fewer than 10,000 in Toronto) braved sub-zero February weather to take to the streets of Montreal to plead for peace. Quebecers mobilized against the war in greater numbers than any other provincial group of opponents. A Quebec election was called the week that the U.S.-led coalition moved against Iraq, and all three main party leaders sported the white ribbon of the peace movement for the duration of the campaign.

When it comes to being run by activist governments, Quebec takes second place to no other province, regardless of which of its parties is in power. The NDP believes in the benevolent power of the state; Quebec has lived by that creed for more than four decades, with the state a presence in virtually every aspect of life.

In his days as NDP premier of Ontario, Bob Rae used to muse wistfully about Quebec's powerful economic tools — especially the Caisse de Dépôt et Placement, through which the retirement savings of Quebecers are put to work in the economic development of the province. To no great regret in the office towers of Bay Street, Rae never managed to get a similar institution off the ground in Ontario. Nor did he deliver on a public no-fault car insurance system, a feature of Quebec's makeup for more than twenty-five years.

Most Canadian social democrats can only envy Quebec's seven-dollar-a-day child-care system. No other province has come anywhere close to matching it. During his 2003 election campaign, Dalton McGuinty promised to create a comprehensive provincial child-care system for Ontario; despite that undertaking, Canada's largest province still lags far behind Quebec on the child-care front.

In the summer of 2006, Quebec became the bright spot in a depressed Canadian environmental movement when the Charest government set out to unilaterally bring the province's greenhouse gas emissions into line with the Kyoto Protocol, regardless of the federal decision to walk away from the targets of the international agreement. In a move that created much angst in the backrooms of Stephen Harper's government, Premier Charest introduced plans for a carbon tax, a measure that is anathema to the federal Conservative regime and to its base in oil-rich Alberta.

Quebecers pay more tax than anyone else in North America. In exchange for that, their universities (including McGill and Concordia) are more accessible than average, their children take on less debt to acquire a post-secondary education, affordable child care is immensely more available, and the growing number of workers who do not enjoy the side benefits of permanent employment can get paid parental leave from the province and partake in a public pharmacare regime.

Whether this is a trade-off that Canadians in other provinces would accept is very much an open question. The average tax bill of a middle-class Quebecer is not to be taken lightly, and those taxes are a source of vociferous irritation, but the evidence is that the tax burden is widely accepted. Over his first term in office, Charest forsook a promise to bring down taxes but left the fiscal structure of the child-care system intact, raising fees from five to a still-modest seven dollars a day. He also became a champion of the environment, a crusade that stands to cost Quebec taxpayers yet more money in the future, as the carbon tax, for instance, is passed down to them, in whole or in part, by the industry. In contrast with the federal Liberals, who have found a winning recipe in campaigning on the left and governing on the right, the Charest Liberals campaigned on the right but came to feel that their electoral salvation required them to govern from the progressive centre.

Yet Quebec is not all roses and rainbows for the left. Some of the biggest storm clouds on its horizon have had their origins in Quebec.

In 1988, it was Quebec that tilted the balance in favour of Brian Mulroney's original free-trade deal with the United States. The NDP and the Liberals split the anti-free-trade vote outside Quebec by both campaigning against the deal, but it was Quebec's role that was most bitterly resented by some sections of the Canadian left. The feeling in many progressive quarters was that the left's longstanding sympathy for Quebec's aspirations had not been reciprocated. That created a chill between the Quebec progressive movement and its counterparts elsewhere that endures to this day.

Many progressive activists from the rest of Canada felt doubly betrayed, because not only had Quebec voters supported Brian Mulroney in relatively large numbers, but the influential Quebec chattering class had also lined up behind the Conservative prime minister. In 1988, the Parti Québécois, the Quebec Liberal Party, including its progressive wing, and many of the progressive Quebec groups associated with the sovereignty movement all signed onto free trade. It was the first time it had been so apparent that the aspirations of Quebec nationalists could trump those of the Canadian left.

The chill brought about by the free-trade debate ricocheted off the ensuing constitutional debate over the Meech Lake Accord, and later, after the 1995 referendum, off the parliamentary alignment on the Clarity Act on Quebec secession.

Manitoba's NDP government, under Howard Pawley, was one of the first to encounter rough sailing over the Meech Lake Accord. It did so both at the hands of the opposition parties in the provincial legislature and at those of some of its own party members. In 1990, Elijah Harper, an aboriginal NDP member of the Manitoba legislative assembly, dealt the Meech accord the death blow.

Eight years later, in the House of Commons, the federal NDP supported the Liberal Clarity Act, a gesture that many progressive Quebecers saw as a betrayal of the party's longstanding support for Quebec's right to self-determination.

For years, social democrats in Canada have kept an eye on Conservative Alberta, on the watch for any deviation towards a two-tier health-care system. When it came to challenging the tenets of medicare, Premier Ralph Klein was always on top of their list of usual suspects. Yet in the end it was progressive Quebec that broke away from the status quo. In June 2006, Quebec's Liberal health minister, Philippe Couillard, introduced a bill to allow Quebecers to buy and use private insurance for a handful of surgical procedures. While initially limited, the number of these procedures could be expanded at the will of the Quebec government, paving the way for a full-fledged private stream operating in parallel with the public system.

Couillard stated that his objective was to bring the province in line with a landmark Supreme Court ruling on the issue of private access to essential medical procedures. But in fact his law goes beyond that, building on the ruling to try out a different health-care mix. Many medicare defenders feel that Quebec has opened the first real breach in the system. Some of them wonder why progressive Quebecers did not put up more of a fight.

The reality is that Quebec is a political ecosystem operating under rules that are largely foreign to the rest of Canada. Its climate has been shaped by the different forces of the debate over the province's political future. Because that is a battle that neither side can win with the support of just the left or the right, both sides have had to reach out and find areas of consensus that straddle the left-right ideological divide, to try to build a winning coalition.

Sovereignists tried to stake out the social justice agenda for themselves early, consistently arguing that as a sovereign state

Quebec would have more leverage to build an egalitarian society than it ever would have within the more limited scope of provincial status. But federalists had no interest in letting their rivals claim a monopoly on the social conscience of future Quebec governments. Back in the days of the Quiet Revolution, in 1960, the Quebec Liberal Party was responsible for putting in place much of the province's modern social infrastructure, and it has never allowed itself or its leaders to forget that for very long.

When federalists argued that sovereignty was a pipe dream that would leave Quebec in economic ruins, sovereignists set out to prove that they were the more fiscally competent of the two camps, developing strong economic expertise, recruiting fiscally conservative politicians to bolster their ranks and, in time, leading and winning the battle against the Quebec deficit.

Until recently, at least, there has not been space in Quebec for a left-right or progressive-conservative ideological divide of the type the NDP is more familiar with. In sharp contrast with British Columbia, or with Ontario at the time of the Common Sense Revolution of Mike Harris, Quebec has not so far polarized along left and right lines. Day in and day out, it operates in the centre.

So foreign has the black-and-white view of right versus left been to Quebec's approach to politics that in 2002 it was not until commentators from outside the province started to describe Mario Dumont as Quebec's version of Ralph Klein that Quebecers really focused on the right-leaning flavour of his policies. They didn't like what they saw, and Dumont promptly went from first place in the polls to a distant last place on election night.

In the late eighties, the Quebec political establishment saw Brian Mulroney's free-trade plan as a way to expand the province's economic horizons. Largely sheltered by the French language from the cultural swamping that so many anglophone nationalists feared, most Quebecers found little wrong with a project that stood to put their province on a more solid economic footing while diminishing its dependency on the rest of Canada.

The fear that the U.S.–Canada deal would in time force a shrinking of the Canadian social safety net also did not cut deep in Quebec. The province maintains a social safety net that is wider than that of its immediate neighbours, including wealthier ones such as Ontario. The proposition that Canada, with the powers of a country, would not be able to preserve a distinct social model in a more integrated North American economic environment, while Quebec managed to do so within Canada, had no legs with most Quebecers.

In the same spirit, the medicare debate in Quebec does not play out along left versus right or progressive versus conservative lines, and it certainly does not involve issues of national identity. Outside Quebec, nationalists often see medicare as a program that distinguishes Canada positively from the United States. But when Quebecers think of other models for their health system, they are just as likely to think of France, whose public system involves a greater private component than Canada's, as of the American pay-as-you-go system.

Quebecers are increasingly conscious of the toll that health care is taking on the province's budget. Over the past decade, politicians as diverse as Stéphane Dion, Jean Charest and Lucien Bouchard have made the point that the health-care budget has become an elephant, crowding out other needs. For many progressive Quebecers, trying a different medicare mix makes sense, inasmuch as it frees up public resources for other social priorities — as long as the new mix isn't a two-tier American-style system.

To this day, the will to preserve their provincial government's capacity to lead in the social-policy area trumps most debates in Quebec. In the 2006 election, it pushed a significant number of voters into the arms of Stephen Harper. Those voters hailed from a variety of milieus, including the union town of Jonquière, the civil-service city of Quebec and the entrepreneurial Beauce. The Conservatives also made promising inroads in the middle-class francophone suburbs around Montreal, by far the richest vote market in the province.

In the months that followed, Jean Charest emerged as Stephen Harper's closest provincial ally. He was the premier whom the new prime minister visited most often over his first hundred days in office, and the one with whom he struck his first federal-provincial deal, an accord to formalize Quebec's participation at UNESCO. It became apparent that Quebec's support for Harper could be more than a passing fancy. Quebecers were at least willing to look at the federal Conservatives as a longer-term option, cutting Harper a good deal of slack as he settled into office.

While the NDP and the Liberals were up in arms over the defection of British Columbia's David Emerson to the Conservatives, Quebecers took in stride the appointment, through the Senate, of Michael Fortier as public works minister and political minister for Montreal.

By the end of the first sitting of the new Parliament, Quebecers were second only to Albertans in expressing approval of the new government, despite the fact that many of its policies—on the environment and the Afghan mission, for instance—rubbed the province against the grain.

If an election had been held in the summer of 2006, Harper could have doubled his score in Quebec. But for all that, there was no sense that Quebecers were in any hurry to get the Conservatives out of their minority situation. Despite an initially favourable impression, the Quebec jury was still out on the wisdom of granting Harper a majority.

—

## CHAPTER ELEVEN

## LEFT OUT IN THE COLD

There was a big climate change in Quebec in January 2006, as many voters warmed to the Conservative Party but the NDP was once again left out in the cold. The Liberal Party fell to a historic low, but only an insignificant fraction of its votes went to the New Democrats. When the ballots were counted, the only consolation for the NDP was that the Liberals were now its companions in misery. They too had been banished to single-digit territory in francophone Quebec. This was a heartbreaker for the NDP in more ways than one. The party had put its best foot forward in Quebec, after a long period of disengagement. In the decade and a half that had followed the advent of free trade, the party had treated Quebec virtually as if it were no longer on its map.

The 1988 free-trade campaign had earned the NDP its first double-digit Quebec score ever. At 14 percent, Ed Broadbent's relentless efforts had brought the party to the threshold of establishing a foothold in the province. Two years later, Phil Edmunston had been elected for the NDP in Chambly.

But under the surface all was far from well within the NDP after the free-trade vote. The party's mood was swinging away from Quebec, not towards it. The 1988 election had been a particularly bittersweet moment for the New Democrats. They had collected their best results ever, nationally, as Canadians sent a record number of NDP MPs to Parliament, but the numbers had fallen far short of the hopes kindled by pre-election polls that had actually given Broadbent a shot at becoming prime minister.

Worse, the party had improved its standing by sharing the anti-free-trade vote with the Liberals, a split that had allowed Brian Mulroney to secure a second majority and execute his controversial plans. For many NDP supporters, the party had won a battle at the cost of losing the war. It was Quebec's role in ensuring that Brian Mulroney won that war, rather than the NDP bounty in the province, that stuck with many New Democrats.

Some of them trained their sights on the Meech Lake Accord, a deal they felt would endanger the federal government's capacity to act on matters of social policy. If Canada was to embark on free trade with the United States and emerge with its national character intact, its central government should not have its arms tied any more than they already were by the provinces.

Had they specifically sought a leader who would annihilate Ed Broadbent's work in Quebec, the New Democrats could hardly have found a better-qualified successor than Audrey McLaughlin. The MP for Yukon had come into federal politics in a 1987 by-election on an anti-Meech ticket. She felt that the accord offered a raw deal to both women and aboriginal Canadians. Upon her arrival in the House of Commons, she had secured a rare dispensation from Broadbent to vote against the party's pro-Meech stance.

McLaughlin's French was painfully hesitant. Among the federal leaders who competed in the 1993 campaign, only Preston Manning was more helpless in Canada's other official language. But then, unlike the NDP, the Reform Party was not running candidates in Quebec at the time.

Audrey McLaughlin's knowledge of Quebec was on a par with her French. No NDP leader before or since brought to the job as little understanding of the forces at play in the province. Under her leadership, the NDP vanished from the Quebec radar.

Alexa McDonough succeeded Audrey McLaughlin as NDP leader in the middle of the Quebec referendum campaign. No one in Quebec took much notice. Those who did remembered mostly that she beat out Svend Robinson for the job. Robinson was to the NDP what Sheila Copps was to the Liberals, a rare MP from outside the province who had actually made it onto the Quebec radar.

While her French was superior to McLaughlin's, McDonough had more pressing business to attend to than giving Quebec the full-court press. Her absolute priority was to breathe new life into a parliamentary wing that had been put on life-support in the previous election. The NDP had not managed to elect even the twelve MPs required for official party status in the House of Commons, and had been effectively silenced for the duration of that Parliament as a result.

Alexa McDonough was from Atlantic Canada, and under her leadership the federal party put down roots in the region for the first time. In 1997, it got enough MPs elected to win back its official party status. But in Quebec the well-meaning McDonough was simply no match for the competition. She had campaigned against three federal leaders from Quebec, Jean Chrétien, Gilles Duceppe and Jean Charest. The election of two French-speaking NDP MPs from New Brunswick, Angela Vautour and Yvon Godin, gave the party a chance to raise its profile in Quebec, but that did not translate into support. Besides, by the time the 2000 election came around, the NDP had landed itself on the wrong side of the national debate in Quebec.

Under pressure from part of her caucus and from the NDP premiers, McDonough lined her party up behind the Clarity Act. In the sixties, the NDP had been the first federal party to formally recognize Quebec's right to self-determination. For backing the

Clarity Act, a law that subjected Quebec's eventual secession to conditions set by a majority of MPs from the rest of Canada, the party was widely seen—in Quebec as well as in some NDP quarters elsewhere—as walking away from its historical stance. The move generated a chill between the Quebec left and the NDP, on a par with the feelings of many New Democrats towards the province after the 1988 free-trade election.

Even if the NDP had joined the anti–Clarity Act camp, it probably would not have fared any better in Quebec in the 2000 campaign. The act polarized Quebec between the Bloc Québécois and the Liberals. As a result, Tory leader Joe Clark, the only federalist leader to oppose the Liberal law, lost support in Quebec, where his divided party was not seen as an effective vehicle to protest the move, and in the rest of the country, where his opposition to Jean Chrétien's tough post-referendum stance was unpopular.

As for Chrétien, he rode back to power in 2000 with his best Quebec score ever, winning more votes than the Bloc Québécois. A few months later, Lucien Bouchard stunned everyone by abruptly resigning as premier; at the time, he cited the Quebec results of the recent federal election and the Liberal success in the aftermath of the adoption of the Clarity Act as major factors in his decision to retire rather than work towards another referendum.

The NDP stance on the Clarity Act confirmed the psychological break between the party and Quebec. Most Quebecers came to the conclusion that the New Democrats had lost interest in them—and they weren't much interested in the NDP, either.

By the time the NDP set out to replace Alexa McDonough, in 2002, it had had little or no presence in Central Canada for a full decade. Only one of its MPs had been elected in Ontario in the 2000 election, and none in the two federal votes before that. Despite regaining official party status in 1997, it was an anemic presence in a five-party House of Commons. In the seventies the NDP had been a major influence on the Liberal governments of Pierre Trudeau, but in the nineties that role had been taken over by the Reform Party. It was from the right that Jean Chrétien had been stealing ideas for the better part of a decade.

Up to a point, Jack Layton was the answer to many New Democrat prayers. A bilingual municipal politician from Toronto, he also had strong roots in Quebec, where his father had served as a Tory MP under Brian Mulroney. As a result, Layton was more comfortable in Ontario than Audrey McLaughlin and Alexa McDonough had ever been, and brought to the job inside knowledge of Quebec that Ed Broadbent had taken years to acquire after he became leader.

Many New Democrats had expected Broadbent to throw his support in the leadership contest to his friend Manitoba MP Bill Blaikie, who was also bidding for the job. Instead, he gave Layton the nod, a decision influenced in no small part by the latter's comparative advantage in Central Canada.

The 2004 election was Layton's baptism of fire, a time consumed by learning the ropes of federal politics in the heat of battle, securing a seat for himself in downtown Toronto and trying to prevent the Liberals from spooking NDP sympathizers into switching to them to fend off the right. The new NDP leader barely broke the Quebec surface. But once he was ensconced in an influential position in Paul Martin's minority Parliament, Layton started to turn his mind to Quebec matters.

Like Stephen Harper, the leader of the NDP became more present in the province, making frequent and successful appearances in the French-language media and paying regular visits to Montreal. The NDP was back in town, after a fifteen-year absence.

In 2006, the NDP sent its most Quebec-savvy leader ever into the fray. For months prior to the election, Layton championed the social causes closest to the heart of Quebec's progressive movement. While the Bloc focused on the sponsorship scandal, the NDP wielded its influence to force a rewrite of the federal budget that accommodated many of the demands of the Quebec social movement. Layton never let an occasion pass to remind Quebecers that the Bloc had voted against this budget that he himself had forced Martin to rewrite with his left hand.

To no avail. When the ballots were counted on January 23, 2006, the NDP had failed to get one in ten votes in Quebec. Its best score in any riding was under 20 percent. On the morning after the election, Layton seemed destined to go the way of Joe Clark, a federal leader whom everyone in Quebec liked but few wanted to vote for.

The NDP had lacked a strong team of Quebec candidates. It had not had an organization to deliver its vote to the ballot box. But then, neither had the Harper Conservatives. They too had supported the Clarity Act and, compared to the NDP, had done so enthusiastically. And, as opposed to the NDP, their general ideology went against the grain of the province. Yet the Conservatives had emerged as the new default federalist alternative in Quebec, while the New Democrats, for all their progressive talk, had gone nowhere.

On the morning after the 2006 election, the NDP had run out of excuses for its repeated failures in Quebec. Its leader was clearly not the problem; Jack Layton was more comfortable in French, and more at ease in Quebec, than Stephen Harper. If Quebecers had been asked which of the two federal leaders they would rather take home to dinner, most would readily have picked the more personable Layton. As Stephen Harper self-deprecatingly pointed out on his first visit to Montreal as prime minister, in the spring of 2006, the Quebecers who had supported him in the election certainly hadn't done so for his looks or his diffident charm. Given Jack Layton's roots in the province, he, not Stephen Harper, was the next-best thing to a Quebec leader on the 2006 ballot.

For years, the NDP had rationalized that it was being shut out of Quebec by the sovereignty debate. The progressive vote, they lamented, was spoken for by the Bloc Québécois, and the federalist vote—most of it progressive too, by the way—by the Liberals. But in 2006, the Conservatives had successfully raided both the Liberal and Bloc pools of votes. Furthermore, on some of the issues that Quebecers felt strongly about—like globalization, same-sex marriage, the war on Iraq, the American anti-missile shield and the environment—the NDP was on the side of angels, while the Conservatives clearly were not. And if having been on the wrong side of the Clarity Act was a major liability, it should have come back to haunt Stephen Harper, who had pushed for something very similar during his first spell in federal politics, in the mid-nineties, and had urged Preston Manning to vote for the Liberal bill— not Jack Layton, who personally opposed the law, and the federal NDP, which had only reluctantly supported it.

When all the rationalizations are stripped away, what is left is stark evidence that, for many Quebecers, the NDP poses more of a threat—or at least a hindrance—to the province's progressive social model than does the federal Conservative Party. They have recognized a point that the federal NDP is missing, at its peril.

On the campaign trail, New Democrat politicians often boast that while the Liberals talk the talk of progressive policies, it is the NDP who walk the walk. When it comes to Quebec and the interventionist form of federalism at the heart of the federal NDP's creed, that only makes their party sound worse than the federal Liberals. Based on Quebec's social-activist experience, and also on recent Canadian political history, a reasonably progressive person can arrive at the conclusion that, in matters of social policy, it is better to live by the separation of powers decreed by the Constitution than to spend one's life alternately pushing on and fending off an inconsistent federal government.

The federal NDP, of course, begs to differ. It brings every battle to Parliament, as if every fight for social justice in Canada could be won or lost there. In so doing, the party is ignoring both the political structure of the federation and its own history. Even as it kneels at the altar of medicare, it conveniently brushes off the fact that, in this country, the mountain down which iconic social programs are brought is a provincial one, not Parliament Hill.

In the latter half of the twentieth century, the provinces have of necessity shown themselves to be the true keepers of social programs. As Paul Martin's 1995 war on the deficit demonstrated, the federal government has little concern for the fate of such programs when they stand in the way of its own objectives.

Over the years, that relative lack of concern has gone largely unpunished by voters. Even as a majority of Canadians profess to want the federal government to play a strong role in social policy, most are not inclined to hold it responsible for its actions or lack of action in that arena.

In the nineties, Canadians gave the federal Liberals credit for balancing the books, and gave the provinces flak for the glaring deterioration of medicare. Despite the federal NDP's strenuous efforts to draw the obvious link between the two, the connection did not echo strongly with voters at the national level.

At the peak of the medicare crisis, between 1997 and 2000, Alexa McDonough campaigned single-mindedly on the issue of health care. She certainly didn't lack for examples of a system in disrepair. Still, she never managed to make the issue a central theme of the two federal campaigns she participated in, and instead emerged as a marginal player in the election debates.

Over that same period, though, opposition parties in a number of provinces took the incumbent governments to task for waiting times and overflowing emergency rooms, and regularly succeeded in galvanizing voters into protest.

As for the Canada Health Act—the legislation that had pride of place in the trophy gallery of the federal NDP because it validated the federal role in overseeing medicare—the benefits brought to this country's most cherished social program by virtue of the 1984 act are infinitesimal versus the damage wreaked on the system by the federal cuts of the nineties, cuts that went politically unpunished.

It's not only medicare. When Jean Charest mused about tinkering with the Quebec child-care program in the 1998 provincial campaign, he had to back off over the course of a single day in the face of a full-fledged middle-class backlash. But when Brian Mulroney cancelled plans for a national child-care program after the 1988 election, his decision barely caused a ripple in public opinion. And in 2006, Paul Martin's dire warnings that the advent of a Conservative government would once again send child care to the federal back burner fell on a lot of deaf ears, even if a majority of voters maintained that they would like to see a better system. In federal politics, the penalty for non-delivery of social promises ranges from light to non-existent.

The story is completely different when it comes to income-support programs. Successive federal governments have learned the hard way that they tinker at their own peril with employment insurance, old-age pensions or farm-income supplements. Because the political price for cutting subsidies to individual Canadians is much higher than that for reducing transfer payments to the provinces, the latter has often been the preferred route of federal finance ministers in search of dark corners to cut at budget time.

When it comes to social programs, Ottawa is afflicted with a long-standing case of attention deficit disorder that no amount of NDP pressure has managed to cure. Over time, it has disengaged from medicare, transferring more and more of that burden to the provinces, to move on to new areas of political interest. For instance, the past few federal governments have been mostly content to pay lip service to the cause of modernizing the system through home care and pharmacare.

If a national child-care program ever saw the light of day, there is no doubt that the federal role in its funding would gradually fade. Judging by the experience of medicare, provinces who go down the road of a universal child-care system based on the Quebec model can expect to end up paying for its long-term maintenance out of their own treasuries. That doesn't mean they shouldn't or couldn't set up such a system. In a diverse society that will be increasingly dependent on learning for its living, a comprehensive public early childhood education system brings undeniable strategic, economic and social advantages. But the provinces should enter into the bargain with their eyes wide open.

Voters insist—as they should—on holding provincial governments primarily accountable for the health of their social programs. Those are, in any event, an exclusive provincial constitutional responsibility. Logic and the track record of each level of government, if not the orthodoxy of the left in Canada, would suggest that the provinces should have control over and access to the funds to direct social programs, rather than depend on the not always good graces of the federal regime of the day.

In the real world, the federal government is not a disinterested, benevolent player in matters of social programs. While it writes standards for the provinces to respect with its right hand, it has its left hand on a fiscal tap that it turns on at will—usually according to its own needs, not those of the provinces' social programs.

Like the Bloc Québécois, the NDP purports to be an element in a larger movement, rather than just a partisan vehicle for federal power. One of its main goals is to exert progressive influence on Canada's central government. But, in sharp contrast to the

Bloc, it often acts as a solo show, and it does not pick its battles. If the Bloc went about its relationship with the Parti Québécois the way the federal NDP approaches New Democrat provincial governments, it would be a breakaway sect within a religious movement, rather than the federal section of a disciplined political coalition devoted to a greater cause.

Despite its status as a permanent opposition party, the Bloc Québécois is often more pragmatic in its positions than the federal NDP. That's at least in part because it doesn't treat the experience of power, and its trade-offs, as regrettable deviations from a dogma, but as tokens of pragmatism.

In the nineties, the Bloc used Lucien Bouchard's success in eliminating the Quebec deficit to enhance the credibility of its own critics of the federal fiscal performance. The NDP, for its part, looked the other way when some of its provincial governments engaged in their own wars on the deficit. Only when it became obvious that the public would not easily tolerate a return to deficit financing did the federal NDP grudgingly get in step with the fiscal discipline that had become part of the life of every government in Canada, regardless of ideology.

In the end, it's no wonder that the federal NDP paid for the shortcomings of Bob Rae's rookie NDP government in Ontario without sharing credit for the efforts of its more successful but often more conservative governments in the Prairies.

The relative contempt of the federal NDP for the exercise of power too often permeates its daily life. Its decision in the mid-nineties to campaign for a strong voice in Parliament rather than for power has become an evasion of the difficult choices that governance involves. It has also liberated the NDP from the obligation to strive to be a truly national party, rather than one that routinely runs sacrificial lambs in more than half of the country's 308 ridings, including all of Quebec's 75.

It is significant that some of the politicians who had been in power under the NDP banner provincially chose the Liberal Party as their vehicle federally. Ujjal Dosanjh, a former premier of British Columbia, and Bob Rae, the only New Democrat to have brought the party to power in Ontario, both resurfaced as federal Liberals.

New Democrats generally scoffed at the news, arguing that the shortcomings of both ex-premiers had turned them into albatrosses for their party. But the Liberals were happy enough to put Dosanjh in charge of the federal Health Department, and to entertain Rae's bid to become their leader. The ex-premiers that the federal NDP described as rejects were seen as catches by the Liberals, a group not predisposed to offer refuge to all-around losers.

For Canada's progressive movement in general, and the NDP in particular, Stephen Harper's determination to bring about an era of more disciplined federalism may be an opportunity, rather than another battle waiting to be lost. The future of Canada's social union will play itself out in the provinces, and voters, rather than the federal government, will be the disciplining force in this debate — as they have been in the struggle to maintain medicare, or to uphold child-care gains in Quebec.

The days when the provinces could be bought into signing onto a comprehensive program such as medicare by a wealthy, more knowledgeable federal government are over. The scars of the provincial battles against the deficit, the end of public tolerance for deficit financing, the demands that medicare has put on provincial resources as successive federal governments have disengaged from its funding, have all robbed the provinces of their innocence.

Even at the peak of their belated daycare crusade in 2005, the best the Martin Liberals could hope to put in place was a set of checkerboard arrangements. They implicitly admitted as much when they set out to negotiate separate agreements with each province. The physical and demographic disparities between the provinces make anything else unrealistic. These days, the metropolitan region of Montreal alone offers affordable child-care services to a population greater than the combined total of New Brunswick, Nova Scotia, PEI, Newfoundland, Saskatchewan and the territory of Nunavut.

The big debates of the twenty-first century are going to involve Canada's relationship with the outside world, rather than domestic arrangements. Already, Canada's role in the war on international terrorism, the trade-offs between immigration and security in the post–9/11 era, Canada–U.S. relations and the environment are capturing increasing attention from Canadians—including Quebecers, younger voters and new Canadians.

These debates are all within the uncontested purview of the federal government.

Stephen Harper connected with Quebec in 2006 because he found a thread between his essentially right-wing agenda and the aspirations of Canada's least conservative province. That thread is the tenuous one of respect for the areas of responsibility devolved to the provinces by the Constitution. The NDP and the Liberals share a lot more common ground with mainstream Quebec than the Conservatives do. If the federal NDP and Liberals practised the same discipline in their approach to these respective turfs, they might stand a chance of turning their chase after social rainbows into a richer take of Quebec's pot of progressive gold.

But that is unlikely to happen if the parties to the left of the Conservatives spend the next decade killing each other off on the electoral battlefield.

CHAPTER TWELVE

—

## BACK TO THE FUTURE—CIRCA 1988

After the 2006 election, political strategists of every federalist persuasion turned their minds to a radical reconfig-
uration of Canada's federal landscape.

The Conservatives and the NDP jointly set their guns on the
wounded Liberals, looking to deal them an electoral *coup de
grâce*. Throughout the latter half of the twentieth century, the
Liberals had acted as Canada's natural governing party. Now that
he had control over the levers of power, Stephen Harper was
determined to install the Conservatives in their place. The NDP
too could imagine a Canada without the Liberals in a pivotal
position. Its boldest strategists dreamed of a future when the NDP
would be the main progressive alternative on the federal ballot.

Some of the Liberals who had benefited immensely from the
disunion of the right during the Chrétien era started to ponder a
union of the left. And the Bloc Québécois, paradoxically, had
cause to fear being squeezed out of existence by both the right
and the left.

The 1993 campaign had set the stage for an election earthquake
that almost claimed the lives of two of the country's three traditional parties. A decade later, the NDP was barely starting to come
back in Central Canada. The Canadian right, for its part, had taken
ten years to patch the cracks that had split it down the middle.

The end result was not an exact replica of the party that Brian Mulroney had successfully led in the eighties. The new Conservative Party was more right-wing than its previous Progressive Conservative incarnation, and its leader was conceivably the most conservative Canadian prime minister to hold office since the Second World War. On the way to the altar with the Tories, the Canadian Alliance had insisted on having the word "progressive" removed from the name of the new party.

At first, that name change turned out to be less significant than expected. To the dismay of his political foes and some of his friends, Stephen Harper originally proved to be less ideologically driven than they had hoped.

In Ontario, the Harris Tories had polarized their way to power in 1995, and again four years later. Many had expected Stephen Harper to follow the same route. But by 2006, Ontario had fallen out of love with the more radical policies of the right provincially, and Quebec had never had any appetite for them federally. And so, while Harper had borrowed part of the Harris recipe and focused on appealing to the small-c conservative middle class, he also campaigned close to the consensual centre. If an influx of Quebec and urban voters was to materialize in the next federal election, that process would have to accelerate.

Once the party was in government, it promptly discovered it would have to try to smooth more hard-right corners if it was going to have a hope of a majority. By the summer of 2006, for instance, the Conservative government had to turn its mind to the environment.

In the immediate aftermath of the election, this issue had not loomed large on its agenda. The appointment of Rona Ambrose to the file had been an afterthought; Harper had originally considered starting off his mandate on that front with an absentee minister from the House of Commons. In an early Cabinet plan, Michael Fortier, the prime minister's Senate appointee, would have taken the portfolio with him to the upper house—where he would have been largely sheltered from daily opposition attacks over the Kyoto Protocol.

In hindsight, it was providential for the Conservatives that the scheme fell through. By that first summer, the last thing Harper needed was another sign that his government dismissed the environment as a minor distraction. In opposition, the Conservatives had railed at the Liberals for not having a realistic plan to meet the targets of the Kyoto Protocol. They had had a point, but they too had failed to do their homework, showing up in office without a better plan. They would have to fix that if the party was to move forward in the next election—in particular in Quebec, but also in much of urban Canada. But that turned out to be easier said than done.

During his first months in office, the issue revealed itself as an Achilles' heel. The green plan Harper eventually put forward was dismissed as a delaying tactic, mostly because it seemed to ignore climate change to focus on air quality. The only saving grace for the government was that the Liberals' own record on the same issue gave them little to brag about. But in spite of its obvious flaws, the Conservative Clean Air Act still amounted to a major effort on the part of the government to fix an overlooked omission in its ongoing makeover.

The Bloc Québécois had taken francophone Quebec by storm in 1993 and never let go of it since then. In 2006, it had taken a much bigger hit to its expectations than in the ballot box. In the lead-up to the election, a string of polls had led the Bloc to expect that it was headed for a historic victory.

That record score did not materialize, but nor was the final result of fifty-one seats and 42 percent of the popular vote the worst score the Bloc had ever had. The first time the party had campaigned without its charismatic founder, Lucien Bouchard, in 1997, it had been pushed under the 40 percent mark and had kept only forty-four seats. And in 2000, it had again failed again to rise over 40 percent, salvaging only thirty-eight MPs, or thirteen fewer than those it brought into Harper's 2006 minority Parliament.

For the Bloc, the post-election polls told a more sobering story than the actual results. At first, they showed the Conservatives poised to make new strides in the next federal election, and to do so at the Bloc's expense. Then, when some of the less attractive features of the Conservative agenda started to sink in, it was the Liberals that showed new signs of life while Bloc support remained stable. It was not the first time that polls played yo-yo with the Bloc in between elections. But the last time that had happened, the Bloc had been saved by the once-in-a-lifetime thunderbolt of the sponsorship scandal.

Quebec voters have been window-shopping for an alternative to the federal sovereignist party for almost a decade, setting their sights first on Paul Martin in his pre-leadership days and then, when he and his party were found wanting, turning to Stephen Harper. If not in the next election, then in the one after that, the many Quebecers who are not diehard sovereignists and who still vote for the Bloc will take their marbles to the dominant federalist option. Only an improbable quick advent of sovereignty is likely to pre-empt this shift. If one connects the federal dots of the past decade, they outline a slow but likely return to Canada's pre-1993 three-party system.

That pattern may pose an acute problem for the left in particular, and the Canadian progressive movement in general. It means that the difficult questions left unresolved in the wake of the divided votes of the 1988 free-trade election, and then buried in the debris of the 1993 electoral earthquake, are about to resurface with a vengeance. If Canada reverts to pre-1993 patterns federally, it is as likely to be entering a Conservative era as just going through a phase between Liberal governments.

After the patriation of the Constitution in 1982, the Conservatives secured a winning coalition that kept power out of reach of the Liberals for a decade. It was because that coalition imploded that Jean Chrétien led back-to-back majority governments throughout the next ten years. As soon as the right reunited, the Liberals lost first their majority and then, in short order, their place in the sun.

For a decade, that divided right allowed the Liberals to overcome their structural weaknesses in francophone Quebec and Western Canada, and to go on to build solid governments. It also allowed the NDP to sweep under the rug the unintended consequences of the divided 1988 anti-free-trade vote and ponder whether progressive causes might not be better served under a single banner. Now that question and those Liberal weaknesses were back to haunt both parties.

In similar circumstances in the mid-eighties, the NDP had overtaken the Liberals in the polls. By the summer of 1987, Ed Broadbent had had cause to believe that he might be the next occupant of the prime-ministerial residence at 24 Sussex Drive. On the day after the 2006 election, New Democrat strategists were keen to pick up where they had left off back then, hoping that this time they would go all the way. In the spring session of the new Parliament, the NDP caucus divided its attention between taking shots at the Liberals and attacking Harper and the ruling Conservatives — but keeping the Liberals down took precedence.

The Liberals were staging the weakest official opposition performance in recent history; it did not take a huge leap of imagination for the NDP to think they were easily replaceable in that role. But outside the rarefied atmosphere of Parliament Hill, their hopes seemed wildly optimistic. In theory, one could add the seven consecutive defeats of the federal Liberals in francophone Quebec to their ongoing lack of representation in significant sections of Western Canada, and to their limited growth potential in

Atlantic Canada, and arrive at the sum of a party reduced, in essence, to a large Ontario base.

But while the Liberals emerging from the 2006 election were certainly less than a healthy national party, they had nothing to envy the NDP. On the path to bringing a progressive government back to power, the New Democratic Party is the blind trying to lead the one-eyed.

On January 23, 2006, twice as many Canadians voted for the Liberals as supported the NDP. The two parties were tied in the popular vote in British Columbia, Manitoba and Saskatchewan. The Liberals actually did better than the New Democrats in Alberta. In Atlantic Canada, they outscored the NDP by a wide margin in every province. And, as bad as things had become for the Liberals in Quebec, they were still in infinitely better shape than the NDP with thirteen MPs and 20 percent of the vote versus 7 percent of the vote and no seats at all.

And while, in a two-way contest in many parts of Western Canada, the NDP would be more likely to beat the Conservatives than the Liberals would be, the reverse is true in most of the 213 federal seats east of Manitoba.

Even the Progressive Conservative Party—when it tried to play David to the Reform Goliath—had a stronger base from which to take on the Reform/Alliance in the 1997 and 2000 elections. The Tories had a number of national governments under their belt, and had recently had MPs in every province. In 2006, the federal NDP could hardly say as much. Their decade-long battle against the Reform/Alliance party eventually sapped the energy of the weaker Progressive Conservatives, leaving them with no option but to engage in a merger. Less than a year after the 2006 election, there were ominous signs that the NDP was headed down the same path.

On November 27, 2006, the voters of the Ontario riding of London North Centre went to the polls in a federal by-election.

The result was a stinging disavowal of the NDP idea that it could overtake the Liberals. While the Liberals kept the seat, the New Democrat vote plunged nine points from 23 percent in the general election to 14 percent. The spoiler was the Green Party under its new leader Elizabeth May. She vaulted to second place capturing 26 percent of the vote. Far from crowding the Liberals out of the picture, the NDP was in danger of being squeezed out of existence.

—

## CHAPTER THIRTEEN

## TO MERGE OR NOT TO MERGE

I f the mathematics of the 2006 election add up to any new equation, it is not the zero-sum game of the NDP winning a war of attrition against the Liberals any time soon, but the potential multiplication of progressive momentum if the two merge into a single, reconfigured party. The very idea is anathema to many New Democrats. Much as the Tories used to decry any rapprochement with the Reform/Alliance, New Democrats proclaim that coming together with the Liberals would narrow rather than expand voters' choices. The NDP brand of idealism, they say, would be diluted by crass Liberal pragmatism. And yet. . . .

The successful New Democrat governments of Western Canada—where the base of the federal NDP is currently located—are much closer in their approach to the federal Liberals than to their federal cousins. The differences between a New Democrat premier like Gary Doer in Manitoba, a Liberal like Jean Charest in Quebec and a Progressive Conservative like Bernard Lord in New Brunswick have more to do with style than substance. That is probably why the three emerged as close allies over the last federal Liberal mandate. And in Quebec, the cohabitation of pragmatism and idealism within the Parti Québécois and the Quebec Liberal Party since 1960 has produced more progressive policy than any other mix on the Canadian landscape.

For more than a decade, New Democrats have been trying to convince the antiglobalization activists that they should not bypass the conventional political arena on their way to a larger battlefield. But the examples they use to drive home the importance of electoral politics in the advancement of global causes actually highlight the importance of being in power rather than the benefits of the actions of permanent opposition parties such as the NDP.

New Democrat politicians have been boasting for years that they are Liberals in a hurry. In fact, the Liberals may be likelier to be hurried from the inside than to be hurried off the electoral map.

The end of the division on the right is a serious loss to the federal Liberal Party, one it cannot but try to recoup on the left. While the reunited Conservative Party will have low cycles, there is unlikely to be a return to the Liberal free ride of the nineties.

After the departure of Jean Charest for the Quebec arena in 1998, the split in the right allowed Jean Chrétien to pick up the federalist pieces of the Progressive Conservative Party in Quebec win more seats and bring his Liberals up to a competitive score. That advantage vanished in the 2006 election; the handful of former Tories running under the Liberal banner were all defeated. Had they stuck to their original party, chances are they would all be in the House of Commons today.

In Ontario and Atlantic Canada, the reluctance of many former Progressive Conservatives to support the new party was instrumental in helping the Liberals hold on to power in 2004, and retain a respectable amount of ground in 2006. But that could change, if the Conservative government becomes more centrist.

When the Progressive Conservative Party and the Reform/Alliance finally merged, they had many differences, but they did agree on their vision of federalism; that agreement was what bound them, and it turned out to be central to their success in becoming a national party again.

The Liberals and the NDP are united in their sense that the federal government is the primary force in the federation. But that core belief finds no traction in key areas of the country. In the aftermath of the 2006 election, these parties face a stark choice.

They can take a cue from Stephen Harper, make peace with the conservative approach to federalism, mend fences with francophone Quebec, temper their centralist approach and mass their cannons on more consensual fronts, where there is common ground among progressive forces right across the country. In a matter of only a few months, the Conservatives have offered plenty of targets, on the environment, foreign policy, the future of the military, Canada–U.S. relations and the Middle East. Those targets will multiply as the Harper regime focuses on its core missions.

But if the NDP and the Liberals stay apart, they can only fight each other for the territory to the left of the Conservatives. It may be a large band of terrain, but—as the free-trade election demonstrated—it can't be divided, productively, to infinity. In the best-case scenario for the NDP, that kind of fight would produce a replay of the 1988 free-trade election, and another Conservative government. In a worst-case scenario, the NDP could continue to be stuck on the periphery, as more voters in Central Canada rally to the Liberals to keep the Conservatives at bay.

A merger of the NDP and the Liberal Party would restore the patina of integrity that the latter lost over the course of the sponsorship saga. A new federalist left-of-centre coalition that was not centralist to the core would be more attractive to a large pool of voters in Quebec and elsewhere who are both socially progressive and interested in having their ideas put into practice in government.

It would give many Quebecers a reason to vote, finally, for a party that not only includes Jack Layton, Alexa McDonough, Bill Blaikie and others, but also offers a policy mix much closer to the successful, pragmatic one of the Parti Québécois or the Quebec Liberal Party. No longer would Quebecers have to look to the right for a federalist party that respects the autonomy of the provinces in their areas of constitutional jurisdiction, or to a permanent sovereignist opposition party for one that reflects their progressive values. Such a merged NDP-Liberal party could stack the decks of future federal elections in favour of progressives rather than conservatives.

But if the NDP and the Liberals want to both stick to their guns on federalism, and go to the wall to defend their notion of a strong central government against the Harper approach of a looser, more collegial federation, it's even more imperative for them to unite rather than spend the next few elections at each other's throats. For if that is their choice, they will have to win power without Quebec or Alberta, two regions that these so-called progressive national parties ignore at their own peril.

But it's also possible to make a compelling case against such a merger for the very reason that the result could have a divisive influence on Canada. Even if the NDP and the Liberal Party of Canada married tomorrow, their union would be missing some of the key attributes of a full-fledged national party. Initially it would be a formidable Ontario vehicle. Under the right circumstances, it could probably sweep the Conservatives out of Canada's biggest province, and also do them serious damage in Atlantic Canada. But because of this massive Ontario presence, the new party might be more beholden to that province than the NDP and the Liberals are currently, as separate entities.

The tendency of the Liberal Party to be a voice for Ontario could be exacerbated by a merger with the NDP. The Western Canada voices of the NDP might be all too easily drowned out by the chorus of an overbearing Ontario caucus. Such a political creature might drive away rather than attract new constituencies. When the Canadian Alliance and the Progressive Conservative parties merged a few years ago, their congruent view of federalism, rather than their common affection for right-wing policies, was the glue that initially bound them together. If the NDP and the Liberals came together around their shared current vision of federalism, they would likely veer away once and for all from Alberta and francophone Quebec, the two regions where the vision of a strong central government holds the least attraction. That vision would stand to be reinforced by the partnership of the staunchest keepers of the Trudeau legacy and the more rigid elements of the NDP.

In time, such a single party could turn out to be a more divisive force, and certainly one more likely to polarize the federation into two irreconcilable camps, than the various regional forces that emerged in the post-Meech era.

In the end, for Canada's progressive voters, a more promising route to a productive exercise of power lies in the common-law relationship of a coalition government, rather than a formal marriage. But this is also a longer route, and the path leading to it is strewn with at least as many obstacles as the road to an NDP-Liberal merger. In particular, it is littered with the debris of two successive minority parliaments. If there is one cause that the experience of the Martin and Harper governments has hurt, it is that of electoral reform along the lines of proportional representation.

Most Canadians remember the Martin minority era for the partisan brinksmanship that presided over its governance of the House of Commons, rather than for the brief co-operative venture that produced a popular NDP-Liberal budget.

Paul Martin spent the last half of his short mandate running away from defeat in the Commons, until he ran out of hiding places and had to face the inevitable. Stephen Harper had not been in power six months when he started to dare the Opposition to take him and his party to an election.

The result on the policy front has been a bust.

Martin tried to run the country with an agenda that was so cluttered that it became impossible to put one's finger on exactly what his government was about. There were times when the government itself was unsure. Martin's Liberal regime could never have died on the battlefield of a policy, since it was ready to change its policies as need be. Witness the dance of the spring of 2005, which saw two consecutive budgets brought to the fore and defended with equal passion — often with contradictory arguments — by the same government, over a matter of weeks.

Conversely, Stephen Harper has gone the minimalist route, limiting his initial agenda to a handful of items. In theory, what one saw on the 2006 Conservative platform was what one got; in practice, that was precious little of anything. Only in the rarefied air of partisan politics or in a country mercifully devoid of intractable problems could a cut in the GST or a tougher regime for some criminal offenders be described as important national priorities. The implicit bargain between Stephen Harper and Canadian voters in 2006 was that if they elected him, they could trust him not to do anything overly ambitious.

Having been treated first to the spectacle of a minority government that could change course at the snap of the Opposition's fingers, and then to the sight of one that would sooner break over a tempest in a teapot than bend an opposition inch, many Canadians have no appetite for a reform that would virtually guarantee minority governments as the rule rather than the exception.

That's too bad. While there are reasons to be wary of a more proportional system of election, they should not include the mediocre policy performance of the two recent minority governments.

If minority outcomes were the rule, the kind of co-operation that prevailed between the NDP and the Liberals around the time of the 2005 budget would also no longer be the exception, nor would an act of deathbed brinksmanship be required to bring it about. Coalition governments would be common rather than non-existent. Third parties such as the NDP would regularly have to subject their demands to the test of the realities of power, rather than doing so once in a blue moon. They would actually have representatives in the Cabinet. One of the more interesting by-products of the 2005 NDP-Liberal budget was that it forced New Democrats to defend some of the trade-offs they had accepted along the way to a successful outcome, rather than just offer criticism of the government's choices.

With majorities few and far between, the test of any government would include demonstrating a capacity to make Parliament work for Canadians, rather than using it to show that the government absolutely needs a majority to get any work done.

Contrary to the rhetoric of many of its proponents, though, a more proportionally representative electoral system would not solve many of the problems that currently plague the federal political arena.

There is no compelling evidence, for instance, that it would significantly raise participation in federal elections. While every individual vote would have more impact on the outcome, the complexities of the new system might drive away as many voters as the first-past-the-post system does, if for different reasons.

That, at least, has been the experience of countries that have a long experience of more proportional systems. While none of them would want to go to a Canadian-style system, voter participation is not the main reason for their preference. They simply think that their system is better adapted to a sophisticated and diverse society.

As for the fundamental problem of the participation of Canadian women in politics, it has its roots elsewhere than in an unresponsive electoral system. There is not one party that would not like to run more women candidates, and no party has found it harder to get women elected than men.

On the contrary. The Conservatives, who have done the poorest job of all federal parties in recruiting women as candidates, have found that they face a significant gender gap in people's voting intentions. Unless they convince more women to vote for them in future elections, the majority government they seek may continue to elude them. In their case, the relative paucity of women within the ranks of their candidates cost them votes.

For the Conservatives, as for every party, convincing women to run for office is the main problem, and the reasons for it go far beyond the specifics of party programs. The contortions involved in juggling a family and a political life are a prime reason for the reluctance of many women to enter politics. It is no accident that there are proportionally more women involved in local politics and advocacy groups, where living away from home and travelling long distances are not routinely required, and where the impact of one's work is often more quickly visible.

Over the past decade, the toll that a political life takes on families has also become an issue for male politicians. As they have played more active roles at home, fathers have become less willing to sacrifice time with their children for the sake of time in a legislature. It has become more common for men declining a run at politics, or even at leadership, to explain that they want to devote more time to their families. Brian Tobin, Frank McKenna, and François Legault in Quebec all gave this reason for refusing to enter a leadership campaign. And while the argument has sometimes sounded like a convenient excuse to avoid certain defeat, there is no doubt that the era when it was a given that a man could, like Paul Martin, presume to pursue his personal ambitions, while his wife handled the home front on his behalf, is largely behind us. These days, even stay-at-home mothers require an increasing amount of paternal participation in the daily lives of their children. Thus, while it has not become easier for women to juggle politics and family, it has become harder for men with families to do so.

But something else is also at play and it has nothing to do with parental responsibilities. At the very time when women have come into their own in the upper levels of the professional job market, the image of the career politician has plummeted. It is a sad fact that these days, many Canadians think less of a man or woman in politics than they do of one in almost any other sector of professional activity . . . including journalism. As a result, top-tier entries in the political arena have become fewer and farther between. A sharp reduction in parliamentary pension benefits, coupled with further restrictions on the jobs one would be allowed to embark on after politics, stand to accentuate that trend.

As men have come to find life in politics less attractive, women have not stepped forward to take their places. That, in a backhanded way, is a positive outcome. Plenty of other professions have become more female-oriented as they became less glamorous. From that perspective, it's a small blessing that politics is not one of them.

And then, politics is a business defined by winners and losers. The history of women in Canadian politics has been punctuated by small victories and bigger defeats, with happy endings all too rare. With one exception—Catherine Callbeck in PEI—no woman in Canada has ever led her party to electoral victory. Kim Campbell and Audrey McLaughlin, the first women to lead federal parties in Canada, led them to stinging defeats on the occasion of their first and only election campaigns. Under Alexa McDonough, the federal NDP stayed resolutely in fourth place. Ontario's Lynn McLeod saw promising Liberal fortunes deflate over the course of her single campaign as leader in 1995.

In their time, Sheila Copps and the Reform Party's Deborah Grey were the best-known women in their respective parties, and those who came closest to the top. Both were iconic figures in their own right. Copps was the country's first female deputy prime minister, under Jean Chrétien. Grey was the first female Reform MP, and the first woman to lead the official opposition (albeit in an interim capacity, over the course of the Canadian Alliance's 2000 leadership campaign). But both ended up being pushed to the sidelines of their parties. Copps's life in politics was terminated by other Liberals over the course of a local nomination campaign. Grey made enemies when she split from her party over the leadership of Stockwell Day; after her return, she never regained her influential position. It would have been interesting to see what role she could have had in Stephen Harper's government, had she chosen to run again after the tumultuous term that resulted in the Conservative merger.

Anne McLellan, who served as Martin's deputy prime minister, lost her precarious seat as part of the 2006 Liberal debacle. Her role as number two in his government was not enough to save her from a local defeat.

Finally, Pauline Marois—probably the woman who brought the most government experience to a leadership bid—did not even come close to robbing André Boisclair of an easy victory in the autumn of the 2005 Parti Québécois campaign. Over the next few years, the short shrift given by the PQ rank and file to a leadership candidate of Marois's stature is likely to further alienate women from politics in Quebec.

For all of these reasons, it will take more than a change in the electoral system to redeem the good name of politics, and to reverse the trend set by the difficult history of women in politics, so that greater numbers of them agree to enter the arena.

As for the divisions on the left, a different electoral system might actually multiply rather than decrease them, as splinter groups seize the chance to get some of their own into office, and possibly into government, rather than water down their wine by signing onto larger coalitions.

But in twenty-first-century Canada, there would be one significant advantage to a more proportional system: it would likely yield a better inter-regional mix within each of the federalist parties. Under a more proportional system, there could have been more Liberals from Alberta, more Conservatives from urban Canada, and possibly even a New Democrat from Quebec in the 2006 Parliament.

That would certainly be less conducive to alienation and polarization than the current system, which renders voiceless, in government and in various parties, large sections of the population of key provinces.

It would also be the beginning of a cure for the regionalism that has seen the once proud Liberal Party of Canada shrink into Ontario's federal party, rendered progressive Albertans invisible at the federal level, and forced progressive francophone Quebecers under the permanent opposition banner of the Bloc Québécois.

—

# PART IV

# THE LAW OF UNINTENDED CONSEQUENCES

—

## CHAPTER FOURTEEN

# THE END OF THE LANGUAGE WARS

Over the past two decades, the law of unintended consequences has made changes in the dynamics of the Canadian national debate that no act of Parliament could have achieved. The Internet and the new global village have had more impact on the evolution of the Canadian language debate than forty years of official bilingualism. The Quebec sovereignty movement, at least as we had known it since its inception in the sixties, died on the bloody fields of the country once known as Yugoslavia. And the downing of the twin towers in New York City has accelerated the coming of age of a second distinct society in the federation, one based on the riches of oil and gas rather than on those of language and culture.

On the surface, Canada continues to operate according to a text drafted by a group of relatively wealthy white males working under the colonial auspices of the nineteenth century. Modernization has so far passed its political institutions by. But in spite of the passivity of the political class, it has been anything but business as usual within the federation since 1990, with one of the biggest changes taking place on both sides of the French-English divide.

Canada is not now the country that tore itself apart over language in the seventies and eighties. It is infinitely more complex, and slightly more mature. While there will always be rearguard skirmishes, this country will likely never fight over language again. In fact, the Canada that went to bed with language aches at the end of the twentieth century may have woken up in the twenty-first with a cure for some of the world's migraines.

It is no accident that the political debate over the federal official-languages policy died with a whimper in the nineties. Was it only a bit more than ten years ago that the Reform Party was scoring points in large sections of Western Canada by promising to take the battle against official bilingualism to Parliament Hill? These days, no mainstream politician would see turning back the clock to an English-only era as a positive signal to the rest of the world. Too much of Canada's international profile has been vested in its duality, and too much of its economic future rests on its diversity.

In a 2004 survey titled "Official Bilingualisms: Part of our Past or Part of our Future," the Centre for Research and Information on Canada—an adjunct of the now defunct Council for National Unity—found that 77 percent of anglophones who live outside Quebec feel it is important for their children to learn a second language. Seventy-four percent said French was the most important second language for their children to acquire. That same survey found that 75 percent of all immigrants agreed that "having two official languages has made Canada a more welcoming place for immigrants from different cultures and ethnic backgrounds." Overall, new Canadians were even more supportive of official bilingualism than those born here.

While francophone Canadians still prize official bilingualism, precious few of them believe that this will be the hill on which the battle for the survival of French in North America will be won or lost. Indeed, many have come to realize that the decisive hill in that fight is located neither in Quebec nor in Canada.

In the rest of the country, the notion that learning French is a gratuitous gesture towards national unity, a good deed performed to keep Quebec happy, has largely been replaced by the less romantic but ultimately sounder realization that acquiring languages—including French—is a sound investment in one's own future. It is a rare bilingual or multilingual young Canadian who does not feel lucky to command more than one language—so it's hardly surprising that new Canadians, who already tend to speak more than one language, are so supportive of official bilingualism.

From Haiti to Darfur to the courts of the new international justice system, Canada's capacity to operate in French adds value to its contribution to the world scene. Its hard-earned expertise as a binational country is an asset to conflict-resolution missions, and there is sadly no lack of need for those. And French opens doors that English—the language of the last remaining superpower—does not, precisely because it is not the language of the superpower.

At the same time, the multilingual face of Canada has became one of its prized assets. In an interview with the Quebec magazine *L'Actualité* in June 2006, three leading aspirants to the Liberal leadership were asked to spontaneously finish a sentence that started with the words "Immigration is . . ." Michael Ignatieff and Stéphane Dion answered that immigration was the future of Canada, and Bob Rae added that it was the core reason why he was a Canadian.

It is impossible to know how Jean Chrétien, Sheila Copps and Paul Martin would have answered the same question when they ran for the Liberal leadership in 1990, or what Brian Mulroney, Joe Clark and John Crosbie would have said on the topic in 1983, because it would simply not have crossed anyone's mind to put the question to them.

Since then, immigration has become more than just a policy feature of federal politics. At a time when some industrialized nations have come to see immigration as at best a necessary evil, and at worst something to be feared, fought against or severely controlled, Canadians have grown resolutely convinced not only that it is a positive economic force, but that it contributes significantly to the national fabric. Most Canadians—be they of French or English descent—cannot imagine returning to the days of a less diverse Canada.

They may not always realize it but, as their society has been reshaped by immigration, Canadians outside Quebec have increasingly come to see English as a common language rather than a native one, and their society as one that *operates* in that language, rather than be defined by it.

Helped along by the province's language laws, that same pattern has surfaced vis-à-vis French in Quebec. It is ironic, given all the negative ink expended on lamenting the isolationism of Bill 101 over the years, that that particular law has been instrumental in making francophone Quebec more open and diverse, rather than less so. If steps had not been taken to channel the bulk of new Quebecers into the francophone mainstream in the seventies, that mainstream would now be a backwater, rather than a vibrant, multi-ethnic, French-language society in its own right.

The historical background of Canada, and its demographic reality, commanded that its default second language be French. The decision to nurture its diverse roots rather than bury them has emerged as one of the country's most effective weapons in the battle to be a distinct voice in the chorus of nations, rather than just melting in with other mid-sized Anglo-Saxon tones.

Paradoxically, Canada's face to the world is often more reflective of its founding languages and peoples than its own capital is. *Atanarjuat* (*The Fast Runner*), the first feature film ever made in Inuktitut (the Inuit language), won the prestigious Palme d'Or at Cannes in 2001. Denys Arcand brought home the Oscar for best foreign film for *Les Invasions Barbares* (*The Barbarian Invasions*) in 2004. Céline Dion and Cirque du Soleil are top marquee acts (in English) in Las Vegas.

In the same way that Dion and Cirque have carved significant niches for themselves and for Canada on a more global scene by exporting their talent to the other side of the language barrier, these days, francophone and anglophone journalists increasingly report on the international scene to both French and English audiences in Canada. The message, at least to the outside world, is that Canada moves fluidly from one language to the other, an achievement that is still a work-in-progress at home.

When Stephen Harper gave Quebec a larger role at UNESCO, as one of his first moves as prime minister, he might as well have formally appointed Quebec one of the prime keepers of Canada's diversity abroad. (He may not have seen it that way.) Some critics feared that he was hampering the country's capacity to speak with one voice on the global scene. In fact, he was handing an insurance policy to the nationalists who worry that a rapprochement with the United States, under a more American-friendly government, will come at the expense of Canada's independence on the world stage.

If Canada loses its nerve and stops standing up to the commercial imperatives of the United States in matters of cultural diversity; if it proceeds to a realignment on the culture front along the lines of the one the Harper government presided over on the Kyoto Protocol, and agrees to treat Canada's cultural output as just another industrial product governed by the same non-protectionist rules as any other, Quebec can be fully expected to make its voice heard at UNESCO, crying foul.

The past two decades have seen an explosion of Quebec talent onto the international stage, as a growing number of French-speaking artists have made names for themselves in both their native language and English. Their success is a source of pride in Quebec. That too is a change; not long ago, becoming successful in English almost automatically meant abandoning French, or at least being perceived as doing so. Language is no longer an either/or proposition.

As English has become the dominant language of the world market, living in French in English-language North America has acquired a silver lining. It still involves swimming against the current, but there is a bonus: a head start on much of the non-anglophone world.

If Canada's official languages had been Flemish and French, like Belgium's, or if the two languages had been Spanish and Catalan, as in Spain, the creation of the Internet would not have been an insignificant event, but it would not have had the profound consequences that it has had on the tenor of our national politics.

The emergence of English as the lingua franca of the wired world has changed the thinking on the necessity to learn it. In the past, the addition of English to French was too often an obligation forced on francophone Canadians. Without it, they might not be able to attain as full a professional life as their English-only counterparts, even in Quebec. But even if France had prevailed on the Plains of Abraham back in 1759, Quebecers today would be striving to master English, if only to own one of the best pass-keys to the rest of world. For many talented Quebecers, English has actually become a means to bypass Canada on the way to a broader stage.

When the Parti Québécois government of Lucien Bouchard set up the Larose commission, to probe Quebecers' opinions on the future of the province's language policy in 2000, the group found massive support for the status quo. Few witnesses came forward to urge a change to the rules that make French the language of instruction for everyone in Quebec except those whose parents were schooled in English in Canada. But there was clearly a lot of pent-up demand from francophone parents for more effective English-as-a-second-language (ESL) instruction for their children. In the end, one of the key recommendations of the Larose commission was that better ESL instruction be offered in Quebec's French-language schools.

Many English-speaking Canadians bemoan the fact that it's hard to master French in the many places across the country where the language is not commonly spoken. But a francophone Quebecer living in Jonquière or Rimouski has to struggle equally to acquire English. In the not so distant past, regions like the Saguenay were considered linguistically pristine because they were so homogeneously French. Now, many French-speaking parents no longer see that as an advantage.

Finally, the language debate has become less passionate on the federal scene because the survival of the French language in North America has less and less to do with Canada's domestic arrangements. Yes, the failings of the official-languages law will remain irritants that grate on francophone Canadians whenever they encounter them. And Quebecers are not about to revert to the days when federal leaders who addressed them through a translator could hope for their support; on the contrary, as more and more of them become bilingual or trilingual, fewer and fewer will have patience with the notion that they should give an anglophone politician credit just for uttering a few disjointed sentences in Canada's other national language.

But the real challenges to the continued existence of a strong francophone presence on the North American continent are on a more global stage. And that means, paradoxically, that Quebec's battle to preserve its French identity has become a less lonely one, as non-English-speaking countries—including France—strive to preserve a place for their culture in the face of the mounting influence of all things English.

In the summer of 2006, I sat on the Berlin U-Bahn alongside two annoyed women who spent the entire ride riffling through a

German-language magazine and pointing out to each other the many English words that had found their way into its titles. For a francophone Montrealer, there was something eerily familiar about the exercise. By virtue of geography, Quebecers may be more isolated from languages other than English than the international average, but they are clearly less and less alone in worrying about preserving their linguistic heritage.

In the aftermath of the last referendum, sovereignist strategists found that language—once the primary engine of the sovereignty drive—had become a relatively neutral factor in the debate. Most Quebecers no longer believed that it was essential to support sovereignty to ensure the future of the French language in North America.

Over that same period, the general perception of identity-driven struggles changed even more dramatically as ethnic-based nationalism lost its shine forever. And that too had profound unforeseen consequences for the Quebec sovereignty movement.

—

## CHAPTER FIFTEEN

# THE DEATH OF IDENTITY POLITICS

A s they watched the Berlin Wall tumble in 1989, most Canadians did not suspect that part of their country's carefully constructed defence against Quebec sovereignty was coming down with it.

Two years later, on December 1, 1991, the Ukrainians voted massively to secede from the Soviet Union, in a referendum. The very next day, Canada announced that it would officially recognize the new country of Ukraine. Later that same month, the federal government opened formal diplomatic relations with eleven more former Soviet republics.

Over the course of less than thirty days, Canada had abandoned a long-standing cornerstone of its foreign policy, opening what initially appeared to be a gaping breach in its domestic defence of federalism.

Up until then, Ottawa had held the line on recognizing the independence of regions of countries seeking secession, convinced that recognizing them would set a dangerous precedent for Quebec. Accordingly, the Biafrans at the time of the civil war in Nigeria in the sixties, and the Palestinians, until the year of the fall of the Berlin Wall, had failed to secure Canadian support for their right to self-determination.

By 1991, with the Soviet empire crumbling fast in the wake of the fall of the Berlin Wall, the Canadian approach to breakaway states had become untenable. In August of that year, Canada recognized the independence of the Baltic States: Estonia, Latvia and Lithuania. Given that Ottawa had never accepted their annexation to the Soviet Union in the first place, that in itself did not amount to a complete break—but everyone who knew anything about the file also knew that there would be no turning back.

Four months later, in January 1992, Canada, along with its European and American allies, accepted the breakup of Yugoslavia, and welcomed Croatia and Slovenia into the club of independent states.

The emergence of new states in the heart of old Europe could not have come at a better time for Quebec's sovereignist leadership, or at a worse time for the federal government. Canada was in the midst of a crisis of its own. Support for sovereignty had skyrocketed in Quebec in the wake of the failure of the Meech Lake constitutional accord the year before. Another referendum was in the offing, and momentum was on the side of sovereignty.

The events in Europe meant that if and when Quebec attained sovereignty, it would hardly be an anomaly. Many of the emerging European countries had economies smaller than a sovereign Quebec's would be. And if the two parts of a country like Czechoslovakia were able to negotiate a divorce peacefully—as the Czech Republic and Slovakia were doing at that point— Quebec and the rest of Canada certainly could too.

"Twenty years ago, when we said we wanted to develop a project to create a country, we were told we were going against the tide of history. But considering what is happening now in several places in the world we should be declared prophets," crowed Parti Québécois leader Jacques Parizeau in August 1991. It was difficult not to agree with him on that or on his attendant conclusion: "The decision of Western countries to officially recognize the tiny countries also holds promise for Quebec. For all those in Quebec who doubt whether we will be recognized if we become sovereign, there is a lesson to be learned here."

In fact, what looked to Parizeau like a dream come true was really the beginning of a sovereignist nightmare. In very short order, the world's attention would be diverted from the certain prospects of Slovakia and Lithuania easing smoothly into NATO and the European Union. And Parizeau would use the changing map of Europe as an argument in his referendum campaign at his peril—for all eyes would be on the former Yugoslavia, where ethnic strife and "cleansing" on a scale that Europe had not seen since the Second World War had become a daily occurrence.

Before it broke into several pieces, Yugoslavia had not been a backward country, nor one deprived of public institutions. Until the fall of the Berlin Wall sent it tumbling into civil war, it was one of the more open economies operating behind the Iron Curtain, a prime vacation destination of Western Europeans. Prior to taking arms against each other, many of its people had lived mundane middle-class lives, not all that different from those of the citizens of Toronto and Montreal. Serbs and Croats, Muslims and Christians, had been working side by side for generations, often living as neighbours, sometimes marrying each other.

Canadian soldiers were among the first peacekeepers to set foot in the former Yugoslavia. By the time the Bloc Québécois arrived in strength in the House of Commons in 1993, Canada's mission in the Balkans was a top political issue. Jean Chrétien's first overseas trip as prime minister, in January 1994, was dominated by the fratricidal war taking place in the former Yugoslavia. One of the first debates of the new parliament had to do with whether the peacekeeping troops should be maintained in a region that was proving intractable to traditional blue-helmet efforts. Peace*keeping*, as Lester B. Pearson had imagined it in the sixties, was being redesigned into peace*making*, and the dynamics of the Quebec sovereignty debate were about to be redefined along with it.

The images from the war theatre of the Balkans cast a dark cloud on sentiments that had until then been accepted as normal and reasonable—such as national pride based on language and race. A few years later, the genocide in Rwanda would finish the job. Set in francophone Africa, in a region familiar to Quebec missionaries, and with Roméo Dallaire, a francophone Canadian general, at centre stage in the drama, that conflict was to leave a deep impression on Quebec. Rwanda would eventually inspire the first Quebec movie to be filmed entirely abroad, and a rare one in that it did not deal with a story directly germane to the province.

The early generations of Quebecers who had founded the sovereignty movement had done so in the heady atmosphere of decolonization, and the attendant struggles of previously stateless people to affirm their right to self-determination. It was in the context of the liberation struggles of the post-colonial era that the NDP had been the first federal party to recognize Quebec's right to self-determination, in 1961.

The new generations that would determine whether Quebec progressed to independence were bringing a different mindset to nationalism. In contrast with their parents, many of them had been in close contact with children from all horizons as they grew up—a by-product of the language law that prescribed that French be the main language of education for all but children of parents educated in English in Canada. They were more likely to see French as a common language than as one necessarily spoken in every "authentic" Quebec home. By and large, English had never been a domineering force in their lives, just a dominating one. Like their contemporaries in the rest of Canada, the younger generations of Quebecers were children of Pierre Trudeau's Charter of Rights and Freedoms. They spoke the language of civil liberties over that of historical grievances, and they were profoundly North

American. Even without Yugoslavia or Rwanda on their minds, their model of citizenship would have been that of the civic nationalism that is the norm on this continent, where everyone belongs equally to the American or Canadian nation regardless of race or origin, rather than the ethnic-based one that was setting parts of Europe aflame.

For a short while, Quebec federalists were a rare step ahead of their sovereignist competition in catching the spirit of the era. The concept of Quebec as a distinct society that Premier Robert Bourassa convinced the other provinces and the Mulroney government to enshrine in the Constitution in 1987 was more inclusive than exclusive. It was one that the vast majority of Quebecers could easily embrace, then and in the future. Fortunately for the sovereignty movement, Canada dropped the Meech ball before the federalist camp managed to kick it into the net and score a decisive goal.

The practice of inclusiveness was hardly foreign to Quebec sovereignists, in particular those who hailed from the more diverse Montreal area. Prominent sovereignists such as Bernard Landry, Pauline Marois, Louise Harel and Gilles Duceppe, to name just a few, were trailblazers in reaching outside the native francophone circle to bring new Quebecers on board. They brought relentless determination to the task, and their version of nationalism was at least as civic as the one being preached by Canadian federalists, if not more so.

But in other sovereignist quarters, the culture of inclusion often came across as skin deep. Just prior to the referendum, a Bloc MP had suggested that only Quebecers who were native to the province should have the right to vote. At the tail end of the referendum, Lucien Bouchard himself got in trouble when he suggested that Quebecers should have more children. At the time, he seemed to have a specific kind of Quebecer in mind. "We are one of the white races that has the fewest children. That doesn't make sense!" Bouchard pronounced at a referendum rally. (He quickly recanted the statement as poorly phrased.) And Jacques Parizeau set his movement back years when he suggested on referendum night that "big money" and the "ethnic vote" were responsible for his camp's defeat.

In October 1995, the razor-thin federalist victory had allowed sovereignists to hope for an imminent rematch, one that would, this time, be in their favour. But the very closeness of the vote was giving many Quebecers, including some prominent sovereignists, second thoughts about the wisdom of rushing into another winner-take-all contest. And with storm clouds over the Balkans, the international community took a darker view of the prospect of Quebec sovereignty.

When Jean Chrétien travelled outside Canada shortly after the referendum, many of his world-leader colleagues gave him an earful about the close referendum call. United Nations secretary-general Boutros Boutros-Ghali, in particular, is said to have told Chrétien point-blank that he was mystified that Canada would allow itself to be broken up on the basis of a one-vote majority. "How can you let something like that happen? If you accept secession so easily, there will soon be five hundred new states and the world will become impossible to govern," he told Chrétien, according to L'Actualité.

In a report published by the magazine on the occasion of Chrétien's 2003 retirement, Marcel Massé, who served as minister for intergovernmental affairs at the time of the referendum, told journalist Michel Vastel that the prime minister had come back from that trip a changed man. According to Massé, before he left, Jean Chrétien's priority had been to arrive at some form of quick constitutional accommodation with Quebec, but when he returned, he was more like a man on a mission to make Canada's breakup as legally arduous as possible. With "ethnic cleansing" rearing its ugly head on European soil (and soon in francophone Africa), the rest of the world had a greater need for a successful example of nations cohabiting under the same state roof than for a model of peaceful, orderly secession.

A few years later, Boutros-Ghali became secretary-general of La Francophonie, the international organization of French-speaking states and the prime international venue where Quebec has a voice independent of Canada, and in 1999 he staged a summit in Moncton, New Brunswick. The event showcased the staunchly federalist Acadians as a people on a par with Quebecers, and gave France's president Jacques Chirac, Quebec's staunchest ally on the international scene, an occasion to temper his support for the cause of sovereignty.

—

## CHAPTER SIXTEEN

## THE FRENCH CONNECTION

From one referendum to the next, France had been the sovereignists' preferred remedy for the global hangover that would undoubtedly materialize on the morning after a Yes vote. As the leading francophone world power, a veto-holding member of the Security Council and a prime mover within the G8, France was counted on to be the first to recognize the referendum results and plead Quebec's case in international circles. It was expected to act as a counterbalance to Great Britain within the European Union, and to the United States in a variety of other forums.

In the lead-up to the referendum, Jacques Chirac had given the sovereignists no reason to believe that he would let them down. When Jacques Parizeau had travelled to Paris on an official visit in January 1995, the mayor of Paris had rolled out the red carpet for the Quebec premier. On that occasion, Chirac — who was in the middle of his first presidential campaign — had publicly assured Parizeau that France and the other francophone nations would answer his call for recognition, should his side prevail in the upcoming referendum.

From South America, where he was leading an economic mission, Jean Chrétien had angrily retorted that Chirac's overtures didn't matter because he had as much chance of becoming president of France as Parizeau had of winning the referendum. Nine months later, Chirac watched from the presidential Élysée Palace as Chrétien came perilously close to being wrong on the other half of his prediction.

In his days as mayor of Quebec City, Chrétien's chief of staff Jean Pelletier had developed a rapport with his Paris counterpart. A bit more than a decade before, they had co-founded the Association Internationale des Maires de la Francophonie. In the years after the referendum, with his ardour for secessionist causes cooled by the bloodbath taking place in his European backyard and the casualties France was enduring trying to maintain peace in the Balkans, Chirac effected a rapprochement with Pelletier's former schoolmate Jean Chrétien. The two leaders became so close that when the Liberal prime minister retired, he and a handful of his francophone Cabinet loyalists travelled to Paris for a farewell dinner hosted by the French president.

A few years before that, Jacques Chirac had sealed his friendship with Jean Chrétien by tempering his support for Quebec sovereignty. In 1999, when Chirac attended the Moncton summit of La Francophonie, the event was relatively uneventful. For sovereignty-watchers, however, Chirac's two side trips were not. The French president first travelled to Memramcook, New Brunswick, to speak about France's privileged relationship with the Acadian people. Then, for good measure, he trekked up to Nunavut, where he praised the Inuit nation (and placed a few orders to supplement his collection of Inuit art). The underlying message was crystal clear. On the proposition that nations could coexist within a single state, Canada and France were on the same page.

The 1995 referendum had come within about fifteen thousand votes of going the other way. Jacques Parizeau—who had resigned as premier the next day—had clearly been heartbroken by the near miss. Others, like his successor, Lucien Bouchard,

were more ambivalent, fearing that it would have been exces-
sively difficult to negotiate a decent separation agreement with
such a slim basis of support.

The narrow result also drew attention to a Pandora's box of
possible consequences, each uglier than the one before, and
many reminiscent of the drama unfolding in the Balkans. The
doomsday scenario of the flight of large sections of the population across the Quebec borders, the possibility that the Canadian
armed forces would take up positions in the aboriginal territories
of Northern Quebec, the suggested partition of some regions of
the province—all these were routinely dismissed by sovereignists
as fear tactics. And there was an unmistakable dose of such
strategy in some of the hare-brained schemes being put forward.
But in the context of events taking place around the world, these
predictions were more alarming than they would have been in
other circumstances.

At one time, a group that included Marc Lalonde, formerly
one of Pierre Trudeau's top Quebec ministers, suggested that if
Quebec separated, Montreal could become a Canadian enclave.
Some prominent federal politicians, such as Stephen Harper
(then intergovernmental affairs critic of the Reform Party), associated themselves publicly with the Quebec partition movement
and promoted the concept that the federalist regions of Quebec
could vote to continue to be part of Canada even after separation. Others, like Jean Chrétien and his new referendum point
man, Stéphane Dion, simply refused to dismiss any scenario out
of hand, thus allowing imaginations to run riot.

There were also questions as to what would really have happened if the referendum results had been reversed and the Yes
votes had been marginally ahead of the No votes at the end of the
evening. The prime minister hinted broadly that he would not
have recognized a close result, arguing in the House of Commons
that Canada was not about to be broken up on a recount. What

was certain was that the main proponents of the federalist camp would have been deeply divided. In the days before the referendum, the question of whether or not a positive result should be accepted had caused furious discussions within the ranks of the No committee, and those had remained unresolved.

On Parliament Hill, Stéphane Dion and Jean Chrétien began to make the case that a simple majority should not be enough to set Quebec's secession in motion. It was an argument that most Quebecers—sovereignists and federalists—resisted strenuously, as did the other federalist parties in Parliament. If a simple majority was not enough, sovereignist leaders asked, then what was, and who would decide? They suspected (not entirely without cause) that the introduction of a floating floor to launch sovereignty negotiations was first and foremost a trick to rob them of an eventual victory.

In a 1996 federal reference on the issue, the Supreme Court was not asked to pronounce on what would be an acceptable level of support to bring the parties to the table to negotiate the terms of Quebec secession, nor did it offer a number or even a range. The court said that the secession of a province from the federation was legally possible, ruling that if Quebec was given a clear mandate to enter into such talks, the government of Canada would have to at least come to the table. But the court did not define what such a clear mandate entailed, in mathematical terms.

The Clarity Act that was subsequently introduced in the House of Commons was likewise silent on the issue of what threshold should trigger secession talks. But the debate did not go away, and polls subsequently showed that, in their own minds, many Quebecers had come to the conclusion that a sound victory for sovereignty should be more consensual than the mere act of achieving a simple majority. In particular, the notion that the old Quebec would drag the new, more diverse Quebec, kicking and screaming, into nationhood, was not sitting well with a growing number of voters.

Those who argued for the 50 percent-plus-one rule also increasingly found themselves on the wrong side of the international trend. In May of 2006, the citizens of Montenegro were asked in a referendum whether they wanted their Balkan province to become independent. Europe, with France and Jacques Chirac leading the way, set 55 percent as the minimum threshold the Yes side would have to reach for the vote to carry.

In Quebec, both the sovereignist opposition and the federalist government of Jean Charest reiterated that, notwithstanding Montenegro, the threshold in a future Quebec referendum would remain 50 percent plus one. But that condition, a basic tenet of Quebec faith only a decade before, had become eminently debatable even within sovereignist ranks.

Over a very short time on the vast scale of history, the law of unintended consequences had changed the dynamics of the sovereignty debate. Language had been neutralized as the defining issue in the debate, in part by the relentless growth of English as a lingua franca. The genocidal strife in the Balkans and in Rwanda had taken any romanticism out of ethnic nationalism, and removed much of the fervour from flag-waving (except for soccer's World Cup). At least in the minds of many Quebecers, the bar for a successful referendum had been raised.

In the future, it would be almost impossible for Quebec sovereignists to walk the walk of civic nationalism without significantly enlarging the support for their project, beyond its traditional francophone base. And that meant that a new paradigm for the sovereignty debate would likely have to be found if the cause of Quebec secession was going to move forward. What had looked like a quasi-formality on the morning after the 1995 referendum— i.e., the moving of fewer than twenty thousand votes from the No column to the Yes column—no longer seemed realistic, even from inside the sovereignty movement.

———

Quebec was hardly the only province undergoing profound changes over that period. Canada's failure to enshrine Quebec's distinctiveness in the Constitution in 1990 had not stopped the province from continuing to build a distinct society. Now out of the ashes of 9/11, a second Canadian distinct society was emerging—one that stood to change the rules of the federation game in ways that were different, but just as fundamental.

—

## CHAPTER SEVENTEEN

## ALBERTA: THE GIANT AND THE DWARF

In 1989, most Canadians could not imagine that fragments of the crumbling Berlin Wall would ricochet into the Quebec–Canada debate, or what impact they would have. Nor did sovereignist strategists foresee in 1991 that the dramatic transformations taking place in Western Europe would make their own project of a separate Quebec a different and potentially harder sell, at home and abroad. By the same token, in September 2001, Canadians had little cause to suspect that the events unfolding on their television screens would exacerbate some of the structural tensions within their own federation.

Once the immediate shock over 9/11 started to wear off, attention turned to the collateral damage that would inevitably result from the attacks. In Canada, the first thoughts were for the fate of the world's longest undefended border. That it would come under intense scrutiny was a given. That the free flow of goods and services, the backbone of both countries' most important trade relationship, could become a headache was also in the cards.

Business leaders worried about their bottom line, and that of the national economy. Nationalists anguished about getting drawn farther into the net of an integrated North America. The United States, they correctly assumed, was bound to be tempted to turn the northern half of the continent into part of "Fortress

America." After 9/11, the American message was that one was either with the United States or against it. For Canada, that sounded like an in-or-out proposition.

Everyone suspected that passenger air traffic would never be the same. At a minimum, flying anywhere, but especially to the United States, was bound to become more tedious and time-consuming. Those who worried about Canada's struggling air industry, whether in the business of transporting people or of building planes, feared that Bombardier, Air Canada and others might have to fly on a wing and a prayer.

The fate of civil liberties, the future of Canada's immigration policies, the potential institution of racial profiling, the possibility that police-state powers would squeeze their way into the country's security apparatus, all came to mind as Canadians took stock of the immense damage wreaked by 9/11.

In those first months, though, few thought of connecting the debris of the towers to an unprecedented surge in energy prices, and then on to one of the most significant changes in the balance of the Canadian federation since Quebec's Quiet Revolution in the 1960s.

At first, Iraq did not have a central spot on the post–9/11 radar, except (as it turned out) within the inner circle of American president George W. Bush. To most of the outside world, the leap from the twin towers to Iraq and a second Gulf war was not immediately obvious. In short order, though, international events set in motion by 9/11 raised concerns over the world's dwindling supply of energy; that in turn sent energy prices skyrocketing, which dramatically improved the economic prospects of oil-rich Canadian provinces while those of Central Canada declined. Throw the dollars of an energy powerhouse such as Alberta into the mix, and one had the ingredient of a major challenge to the workings of the federation. Canada's failure to reform its institutions in the aftermath of the patriation of the Constitution in 1982 was now coming back to haunt it.

Prior to 9/11, Alberta was already a "have" province on the move. Even without a war in Iraq and rumblings of one in Iran, the surging economies of China and India were bound to push global energy prices to new highs. Even in the unlikely event that the Middle East situation stabilizes tomorrow, the Canadian energy equation is not about to change fundamentally.

Today, Alberta stands head and shoulders above the other provinces in fiscal might. If Canada were a forest, the province would be a Douglas fir towering over a patch of mulberry bushes. In 2005–06, Alberta's gas royalties alone exceeded its revenues from personal income taxes. At $8.7 billion, its surplus for that fiscal year is beyond the wildest hopes of the other provinces; indeed, that surplus is more than the total expenses of a number of them. Alone of all of the provinces, Alberta is also debt-free.

Because they are collectively richer than their counterparts anywhere else in Canada, Albertans contribute more per capita to the federal treasury than people in any other province, including Ontario. In the spring of 2006, an expert federal panel explored various models for updating the formula through which the federal government redistributes funds to even out the fiscal capacities of the provinces. But no equalization mechanism can come close to levelling the current playing field. Under the model advanced by the group—chaired by Al O'Brien, a former deputy treasurer of Alberta—the post-equalization fiscal capacity of the other nine provinces would have ranged from a low of $6,500 per capita to a high of $7,000. But Alberta would have been left with the princely amount of $11,000 per capita, a sum that knocked it way out of the ballpark, and into an entirely different field.

Variations on the formula all produced the same striking gap. The issue is not that Alberta is not paying its share of the financing of the federation—it is doing that and more—but that its current revenues have placed it in a unique position vis-à-vis the rest of the country. And the gap has profound consequences for the shape of Canada's social union. Conservative Alberta already spends more on government programs for its citizens than state-enamoured Quebec or social-democrat Saskatchewan, the two runners-up.

The dying days of the Ralph Klein reign were a time of relative government nonchalance, as a lackadaisical attitude to running the province and figuring out what to do with its riches set in. But the options within the reach of Alberta, if not yet on its planning board, remain extraordinary. Alberta could eliminate provincial income taxes, which would put a significant strain on the capacity of its neighbouring provinces to remain competitive, and might turn Calgary and Edmonton into magnets for the head offices of Central Canada. Or Alberta could offer tuition-free post-secondary education—or, alternatively, endow its institutions to give them academic and physical resources unparalleled anywhere else in Canada. Or it could purchase the best academic talent on offer and, in doing so, attract the best and brightest of Canadian students. It could turn itself into a North American centre of knowledge and learning.

Alberta already pours more money per capita into its health-care system than its provincial partners. If its government so chose, it could completely overhaul its medicare system to tilt the mix towards more private-sector solutions, and thumb its nose at the federal government in the process.

All that really stands in the way of greater privatization of Alberta's health-care system is the province's public opinion. The Canada Health Act is a paper tiger for such an affluent province; its financial penalties would likely be more of an irritant than a deterrent. And the act is a double-edged sword for Ottawa; the more Alberta disengages from federal funding for health care, the less motivated it will be to contribute to the maintenance and expansion of the federation's social safety net.

Alberta could set up a universal child-care program tomorrow, and make it as attractive as Quebec's, or even more so. It could afford to pay its early education workers the best such wages in Canada. The same applies to medical specialists, nurses and public service professionals. All or any of these measures have the potential to suck oxygen from many of the other provinces. Most are already facing a shortage of labour to staff their social services at a competitive cost—as well as, in the manufacturing heart of Central Canada, a slowdown in their economies as a result of the rising Canadian dollar and mounting energy costs. In recent years, even Quebec has found that the language barrier is no longer so effective in preventing French-language professionals from being lured by higher salaries in Alberta.

In theory, one of the strengths of a federative system such as Canada's is that it allows the provinces to innovate in matters of social policy, and Alberta certainly has the means to do so. But whatever it eventually chooses to do with its wealth, most of the other provinces will find it hard, if not outright impossible, to keep up with its standards.

Alberta is both the richest partner per capita in the federation, and one of its poorest political cousins, a combination that can only corrode the ties binding the different parts of the country. It is by far the most politically alienated province. Even British Columbia—its sister in federal institutional misery— has at least been getting a bit more respect from politicians from Central Canada. And as for Quebec, by all common measures it doesn't come even close to Alberta's degree of estrangement from Canada's central institutions. Quebecers—for all their talk of jealously guarding their autonomy from the federal government—are on average a lot less suspicious of the federal government than Western Canadians in general and Albertans in particular. In 2003, a Statistics Canada study found that Quebecers were "consistently more likely than those in other provinces to have high levels of confidence in public institutions," while confidence in the federal parliament and the justice system ran lowest in the Western provinces.

And how could that not be? If Quebec were as underrepresented in the power centres of the federal capital as Alberta is, the federation would have broken up a long time ago. And if Ontario, the other province (with Alberta) that routinely contributes more than it gets back, had so little relative input into the affairs of Canada, it would be clamouring for reform, rather than acting as the staunchest pillar of the status quo.

The system is set up in a way that condemns Alberta and British Columbia to a lack of power in both houses of Parliament. By virtue of a constitutionally entrenched formula that stipulates that no province shall see its representation in the House of Commons fall below a certain floor, the less wealthy provinces have been sheltered from the consequences of their dwindling populations.

The four provinces of Atlantic Canada hold a combined total of thirty-two seats in the current Parliament, while their population warrants twenty-one. Alberta, with a larger population, has four fewer seats than the provinces of Atlantic Canada. The even more populous British Columbia has thirty-six seats, only four more than the sum of PEI, New Brunswick, Nova Scotia and Newfoundland—a group whose total population barely equals that of metropolitan Vancouver.

The discrepancy is even more acute in the Senate, where the four Atlantic provinces have thirty seats among them. Ontario and Quebec came into Confederation with twenty-four each, but Alberta, like every province west of Ontario, has only six.

To compound this systemic injustice, two of the country's socalled national parties, the NDP and the Liberals, have little or no traction in Alberta—and have paid only lip service to fixing the situation in the recent past.

Neither under Jean Chrétien nor under Paul Martin did the Liberals expend on Alberta the amount of attention Stephen Harper devoted to Quebec. In the last election, the loss of the one remaining Liberal seat in Alberta barely elicited a shrug, at least in public, from the top ranks of that party. And no major candidate from Western Canada emerged to contend the Liberal leadership. Over the years, the Liberal Party consumed itself in winning back francophone Quebec. But in Western Canada it bypassed Alberta to focus on gaining ground in British Columbia. Ironically, the route of a more collegial practice of federalism might have led the Liberals to a more promising destination in both Quebec and the West.

Jean Chrétien once spent an entire campaign without setting foot in Calgary. In the 2000 election, he brushed the federal leaders from Alberta with the same kind of divisive tar the Reform Party once tried to apply to leaders from Quebec. "I like to do politics with people from the East," he said, on a campaign stop in Atlantic Canada, adding, "Joe Clark and Stockwell Day are from Alberta. They are a different type."

In 2006, NDP leader Jack Layton visited Alberta only twice over the course of a two-month campaign. Both times, he went to use the Alberta government as a foil for his message that his party was the champion of medicare. "Back off," Layton warned Premier Ralph Klein (*in absentia*) on a visit to Edmonton a few days before the federal vote, adding, "You are not going to destroy public health care." As in Quebec, the federal NDP had only ever won one seat in Alberta.

Even the Bloc Québécois got into the Alberta-bashing in the last phase of the 2006 election campaign, running ads that featured a cowboy hat to warn Quebecers that under a Harper government, federal decisions would be made in Calgary. Bloc strategists credit the ads and Gilles Duceppe's verbal warnings on the same topic for bringing party support back from 38 per-cent in the last week of the campaign to its 42 percent election score. The same strategy is unlikely to help the party repeat this marginal gain in future campaigns.

The recurrent absence of Alberta from the corridors of federal power and from the ruling sides of the Senate and the House of Commons fosters a culture of envy among those whose provinces do not enjoy such riches. That feeling is matched by paranoia among Albertans, who are prompt, since the years of the National Energy Program, to look for a hidden agenda behind every federal policy decision.

For both systemic and political reasons, Alberta endures a boom-and-bust cycle in federal politics that is even more pro-nounced than the cycles it goes through on the resources front. Even Quebec, with a permanent opposition party of its own, has been more of a presence in power than Alberta has, in between Conservative governments. Today, Quebecers are in the caucus of three of the four parties in the House of Commons—the Liberals, the Conservatives and the Bloc Québécois—while Alberta has voices in only one, the governing party led by Stephen Harper. As a result, the Alberta political scene is as one-sided federally as it has been provincially under its current Tory dynasty.

In one of the greater ironies of the past two decades, the Bloc's presence on Parliament Hill has actually helped reduce the alienation of Quebec from the federal system, while the Reform Party's presence did little to alleviate Alberta's resentment.

—

## CHAPTER EIGHTEEN

## LUCIEN BOUCHARD'S GIFT TO CANADA

The end of the 2006 federal election campaign did not come a day too soon for the Bloc Québécois. By the time Canadians went to the polls, the sovereignist party was perilously close to choking on the pretzel of its own twisted logic.

For two years, the Bloc had relentlessly made the case that under successive leaders from Quebec, the Liberals had abused the sponsorship program and thus disqualified themselves from office. But in the dying days of the election campaign, Gilles Duceppe switched gears to argue that a vote for the Conservatives was a vote to put Alberta in control of federal affairs.

It was a strange argument coming from a party that was not itself in contention for government. At first glance it was hard to see why it would matter to the Bloc whether Ontario or Alberta had the most influence on the federal government. The Bloc's paradoxical assertion was that while the Liberals did not merit re-election, Quebecers should take no part in bringing a different government to power.

The partisan rationale behind Bloc thinking was easier to grasp than its logic. A Liberal victory—achieved without francophone Quebec and on the heels of the sponsorship fiasco—would come across to many Quebecers as an affront to their sense of government ethics. But a Conservative victory achieved without them could be construed as an assault on their progressive values. Under either scenario, the Bloc thesis about Quebec's ideological isolation from the rest of the federation would be validated. Although Bloc strategists would later credit their last-ditch assault on the Conservatives with having saved as many as ten of their seats, one in four Quebecers still voted for Stephen Harper.

Since 1990, the Bloc has unwittingly done more to legitimize federal political institutions in Quebec than all of Jean Chrétien's flag campaigns. Instead of reinforcing the belief that there is an unbridgeable gap between the values of Quebec and those of the rest of Canada, it has undermined it.

Over the years, the NDP has made common cause with the Bloc on most international, environmental and social-justice issues. In the matter of same-sex marriage, the two prodded the Liberals into putting their money where their mouths were, Charter-wise. The Liberals, the NDP and the Bloc agreed that Canada had no place in the Iraq fray. And the Conservative Party was more than just the Bloc's ally in the bid to bring down the Martin Liberals over the sponsorship scandal; Stephen Harper actually took the lead in the operation, at considerable risk to himself and his party outside Quebec.

In hindsight, it was always a given that a federal sovereignist party would find common ground with one or more of the federalist parties on a fairly comprehensive range of issues. Those outside Quebec who expected the Bloc Québécois to come to Parliament Hill to wreak havoc on the system, and those in Quebec who predicted that the sovereignist MPs would be shunned because of their secessionist goals, were equally guilty of underestimating each other's respect for democratic institutions.

From day one, the Bloc worked to play a constructive role in the House of Commons. Its founder, Lucien Bouchard, would not have had it any other way, nor would the many Quebec voters who had supported the party. By definition, the Bloc was destined to become the main window into the sovereignty movement for the rest of Canada, and for the diplomatic community; it was in the Bloc's interest to put its best foot forward in the House of Commons. Sabotaging federal institutions or paralyzing them from the inside may have been on the minds of some sovereignists, but that was never on the Bloc's radar. Long before Stephen Harper handed duct tape to the loose-lips in his Cabinet and caucus in 2006, Lucien Bouchard had his rookie MPs on a short leash. Few federal parties have ever exhibited as much discipline in public as the Bloc has. The fact that over the years, a large part of the Press Gallery has operated as if the Bloc barely existed has helped the party patch up the cracks in its façade quickly and discreetly.

After the 1993 election, the Chrétien Liberals soon discovered that they had a vested interest in having a functional sovereignist opposition across from them in the House of Commons. The Bloc's presence kept the rest of Canada focused on the threat to the country's unity. Canadian voters are never more faithful to the Liberals than in the face of an enemy on the unity front.

The Bloc also made it conveniently difficult for another federalist party to grow roots in Quebec and challenge the Liberals for power. Even if the Conservatives reunited, it was assumed by Liberal strategists (wrongly, as it turned out) that the sovereignist party could be counted on to keep them out of Quebec.

But perhaps even more important, the Bloc, a party that everyone expected to act like salt on the Quebec–Canada wound, often managed to take some of the sting out of the debate. When historians look back on the Bloc Québécois, they may find that the party's most striking and unexpected contribution to Canada's public life was to reduce the alienation of Quebecers from federal politics. Its record on that counterintuitive front is at least on a par with that of the four prime ministers from Quebec who led Canada between 1968 and 2006.

That was obviously not the plan. When Lucien Bouchard founded the Bloc Québécois at the time of the Meech Lake constitutional crisis, the legitimacy of Canada's Parliament in Quebec was certainly not on his mind. On the contrary. In 1982, 74 Liberal MPs from Quebec had stood behind the patriation of the Constitution while their 122 colleagues in the National Assembly had unanimously denounced it. With the Meech Lake Accord dying the death of a thousand provincial cuts, Bouchard had vouched that Quebec's federalist representatives in Parliament would never again acquire legitimacy by default—in the absence of a non-federalist alternative at the federal level—and then use that legitimacy to undermine the National Assembly.

Lucien Bouchard would contradict his own logic at the first opportunity. Less than two years after its founding, the Bloc campaigned against the Charlottetown constitutional accord. In doing so, Bouchard was not taking his cue from the National Assembly—any more than the Trudeau Liberals had done at the time of patriation. Quebec premier Robert Bourassa had already signed the Charlottetown Accord. The majority of the members of the National Assembly were Liberals in 1992, and they had campaigned for ratification of the deal.

In fact, Bouchard had cobbled the Bloc together, out of the debris of the Meech Lake Accord, as a vehicle to carry him to one main destination—another referendum on sovereignty. At least in the early years, it was clear in his mind that the Bloc should not branch out in the direction of a permanent presence on Parliament Hill after the conclusion of the referendum operation. Win or lose, he repeatedly promised, he would be gone soon afterwards. But while he personally kept that promise, bowing out of federal politics to become premier three months after the referendum, his party stayed on—and in so doing, changed the texture of federal politics for the better.

In pre–Bloc Québécois days, Parliament was a surrealist place, divorced from the reality of the Quebec–Canada debate. That was never more obvious than in the two years that immediately followed the failure of the Meech Lake Accord. Under Joe Clark's leadership, the nine non-Quebec premiers and the federal government tried to find enough common ground to rally the country to a new Quebec–Canada constitutional deal. They might as well have donned a blindfold to pin a tail on a paper donkey.

The entire process was happening without direct input from the Quebec government, since Robert Bourassa's government had walked away from the federal-provincial table after the Meech failure. Like doctors examining a patient on the opposite side of a curtain, the other premiers were trying to grope their way to a compromise that their Quebec colleague could live with.

The three main parties in the House of Commons were also once or twice removed from the reality of post-Meech Quebec. Instead of worrying about the surging support for sovereignty, the NDP, the Liberals and the Conservatives were preoccupied with haggling among themselves to make sure that whatever deal emerged would satisfy their respective factions outside Quebec.

Meanwhile, those whose contrary views would ultimately prevail in the 1992 Charlottetown referendum were watching from the outside, reduced to silence by parliamentary tradition and by the common agreement of the gentlemen's club of Canada's traditional parties. The handful of Bloc Québécois members who sat around Lucien Bouchard, next to the green curtains of the House—as well as Deborah Grey, the lone Reform MP elected to Parliament in 1989—did not have official speaking rights in the Commons. For most of the Meech-to-Charlottetown period, they operated in the margin of the Commons, outside the organized routine of Parliament Hill.

While the three traditional parties talked to each other, the Bloc and the Reform Party were talking to their constituencies, and those were growing exponentially. The stunning rejection of the Charlottetown Accord demonstrated that its high-profile promoters had been out of touch not only with post-Meech Quebec, but also with the mood of the rest of Canada.

At the end of the spring that followed the Charlottetown rout, the federal Tories chose a successor to Brian Mulroney in the same surrealistic atmosphere. If the polls showing that Lucien Bouchard was poised to wipe their party out in Quebec while Preston Manning was about to do the same thing in Western Canada were on the minds of the Tories who selected Kim Campbell as their leader, it seemed to be only as an afterthought.

The arrival of fifty-plus Bloc MPs in 1993 put Parliament Hill squarely on the Quebec map. In the past, the federal scene in Quebec had revolved mostly around the narrow cast of characters who were both from the province and in the government. With the Bloc in the House, Quebecers were treated to a much wider stage, and a much more interactive drama.

For the first time, the main operating language of Canada's official opposition was French, and the two leading characters in the House—the prime minister and the leader of the official opposition—were Quebecers. In deference to its status as official opposition, the Bloc would occasionally throw a question in English into its question-period lineup, following an approach fairly similar to the way previous official oppositions had handled French. For the most part, though, the Bloc Québécois conducted its parliamentary business in French.

More than a decade after the fact, many of the journalists who cover Parliament Hill have no personal recollection of how predominantly English-speaking the House of Commons was, prior to the Bloc's arrival. French was a token presence in question period, its place in the exchanges largely left to the changing whims of the official opposition of the day and its rotation of speakers. The Quebec media would keep score and occasionally report on the French-English ratio, and their reports tended to bring about a surge in French-language exchanges, but only for a while.

After the Bloc Québécois arrived in force, the House of Commons became a venue where French and English Canada seemed to finally converge. To this day, the more bilingual image that has resulted from the Bloc's presence on Parliament Hill remains an improvement on the reality of the federal capital as a whole.

The Bloc brought a host of federal issues closer to home in Quebec, as its MPs developed expertise on the files that are the domain of the Canadian government. One of Lucien Bouchard's first and most eloquent speeches as leader of the opposition dealt with Canada's peacekeeping tradition. Topics that had seemed, if not out of bounds, at least restricted to the purview of a psycho-logically remote Parliament—where business was more often than not conducted in a language other than French—became routine items on the *Téléjournal*.

If the Bloc Québécois had not existed, it is quite possible that the Clarity Act would never have seen the light of day. In the unlikely event that it had, it is almost certain that it would have driven support for sovereignty to new heights.

It was no accident that Jean Chrétien recruited Stéphane Dion, an articulate intellectual from Quebec, to lead the debate. Both at home and abroad, Dion's presence on the front line was designed to dispel the impression that the rest of Canada was attempting to put Quebec's aspirations in a legal straitjacket. Allan Rock, justice minister when a reference to the Supreme Court on the issue of Quebec secession was drafted, and Anne McLellan, Attorney General by the time the judges heard the reference, both took back seats to their intergovernmental affairs colleague, in Parliament and in the media.

Chrétien was playing to a dual audience, showing the rest of Canada that he was taking steps to prevent a replay of the 1995 campaign while lobbing questions as to the sovereignist approach to secession in Quebec. But to all intents and purposes, he framed the clarity debate in Parliament as a family discussion, with Stéphane Dion on one side of the table and Gilles Duceppe and his MPs on the other—or at least, that was how it came across in the Quebec media.

It takes two to tango. The Clarity Act could never have been packaged as a dance between Quebecers if the Bloc had not been in the ballroom. Without the sovereignist party, showing federalist politicians outbidding each other to put limits on Quebec's capacity to determine its future would likely have been akin to striking a match next to a nationalist bonfire. Tensions within the federalist caucuses would have risen dramatically as Quebec MPs questioned their role in the affair. More non-Quebec politicians might have been willing to enter the fray against Dion's act, if it had not meant fighting side by side with sovereignists on a daily basis. Canada would likely have come across as deeply divided on its approach to a possible Yes vote—a perception that would have been closer to the truth but would have hindered Jean Chrétien's message to Quebecers. Instead, under a daily barrage of attacks from the Bloc Québécois, federalist politicians of all stripes and from every region basically closed ranks behind the Clarity Act.

While the Liberals were using Stéphane Dion as a damp rag to extinguish the incendiary perception that Quebec was being shackled by the rest of Canada, the Bloc was using its parliamentary stage to reignite the recent passions of the post-Meech period.

The Bloc never expected to win the parliamentary debate on the Clarity Act in the House of Commons, a forum where its MPs were greatly outnumbered. But it was confident that it would win the battle for Quebec public opinion. After all, outside Parliament Hill, not a single prominent Quebec politician—including federalist opposition leader Jean Charest and his caucus—supported the act.

Yet that was not how things turned out. In the 2000 federal election, on the heels of adoption of the Clarity Act, Quebecers voted for Jean Chrétien's Liberal Party in greater numbers than they had since the early eighties, prompting Lucien Bouchard's resignation less than two months later. While they might not have supported the gist of the Clarity Act—and very few within the province's federalist ranks did, at least openly—francophone Quebecers had not felt alienated by the clarity debate in the way they had at the time of the patriation of the Constitution and the Meech Lake Accord.

For strategic reasons, the Bloc and the PQ had settled early on fighting their battle against the Clarity Act on the field of indignation, dismissing the entire federalist case as a trampling of the basic democratic rights of the Quebec people, rather than addressing the specific issues raised in the bill. In time, Liberal and Conservative senators would poke more holes in the Clarity Act than the Bloc had, pointing out how its shortcomings made it an unlikely road map for Canada to fall back on if it ever needed to extricate itself from the jungle of a Yes vote. Some in the Senate were also alarmed by the fact that Canada had just put a legal recipe for its own dismantling on its books. But by then, few Quebecers were paying attention.

An immediate result of the sovereignist strategy of fighting form over substance was that Quebecers, who only five years before had walked to the threshold of sovereignty, heard a lot of solemn, indignant affirmations from the sovereignist leadership as to the illegitimacy of the Clarity Act, but very few substantive answers as to where Quebec should go from there. And while many Quebecers could easily agree with the argument that the Clarity Act was not a constructive undertaking, they were still left with unanswered questions about the sovereignists' own work plan.

To this day, the decision to steer clear of the actual issues raised by the clarity debate continues to haunt the sovereignty movement. In an open letter to *Le Devoir* in the spring of 2006, a group of academics and PQ insiders publicly challenged the notion that Quebec sovereignty could be achieved on the basis of a simple majority; a bit less than ten years after the fact, the seeds planted by Stéphane Dion had bloomed in unexpectedly fertile sovereignist soil. His and Jean Chrétien's argument that the threshold of 50 percent plus one was not a realistic political turning point had found a sovereignist audience, and one that was willing to pick up the discussion where they had left off.

Over the years that the Bloc has been on the federal scene, Quebecers have become more rather than less engaged in the debates of Canada's Parliament. That is particularly true of foreign affairs—one of those rare files that successive Liberal governments handled to the relative satisfaction of Quebec, and one that Stephen Harper soon discovered that he could manage differently only at his peril in that province.

As well, the House of Commons has come to be seen in Quebec as a legitimate forum for launching discussions, and even legislating, on some of the issues closest to the hearts of Quebecers—issues that used to be considered the exclusive and quasi-sacred purview of the National Assembly, in pre-Bloc days.

The definition of the national identity of Quebec is one of those. Catching itself at its own game, the Bloc brought the issue of the recognition of Quebec's national character to the House of Commons in the fall of 2006. Throughout the fall, Liberal leadership candidate Michael Ignatieff had been enduring a barrage of flak in the rest of Canada for supporting a call by the Quebec wing of the federal Liberals to move to recognize Quebec as a nation.

Sovereignist strategists never expected the prime minister to seize on the opportunity presented by their motion to make his own overture to Quebec by asking the House to recognize that the "Quebecois form a nation within a united Canada." Nor did they imagine that the NDP and the Liberals—even in the midst of their own cat fight on the issue—would massively support the Conservative motion.

On November 27, 2006, 266 MPs endorsed the recognition of Quebec's national character and only 16 opposed it. The move was controversial in much of the rest of Canada. It particularly divided the Liberal party. But none of Harper's diehard Conservative MPs stood up to oppose it. They accepted the rationale that the alternative was to forego their hopes for a lasting reconciliation with Quebec.

But a larger agenda than the Conservative future in Quebec than was also at play. In Quebec, the motion stands to make the advent of another referendum more unlikely, for nothing fuels the sovereignist momentum like the sense that Canada would rather risk a break-up than recognize the uniqueness of Quebecers.

Without the failure of the Meech Lake accord and the rejection of Quebec's status as a distinct society, it is unlikely that a second referendum would have taken place in 1995 and just about certain that the results would not have been so close. In the event of another vote on Quebec's political future, the motion would stand all federalist politicians—including Harper if he were still the prime minister—in good stead, for it would allow them to campaign on an overture to Quebecers rather than on a glaring failure to accommodate their aspirations.

At cost to the Bloc's bigger game of sovereignty, Gilles Duceppe had once again underestimated Harper's determination to rebuild a Quebec–Alberta Conservative coalition.

—

## CHAPTER NINETEEN

## THE END OF PORK?

The 1984 election revealed that the federal Liberals did not own Quebec. Never at a loss for a new theory, political pundits promptly replaced that piece of conventional wisdom with the proposition that Quebecers held their finger to the federal wind and went with the flow.

That had not been true in 1979, when Joe Clark had won in the rest of Canada but failed to sway Quebec. With their customary reverse logic, proponents of the bandwagon theory ascribed that to Pierre Trudeau's exceptional ascendancy in his home province. It took almost another decade after 1984 for Quebecers to demonstrate that following the money was not one of their prime voting considerations after all. Until the sponsorship scandal brought the darker side of patronage to the surface in an unprecedented way, that message consistently fell on deaf ears.

In the summer of 1990, fresh on the heels of the Meech debacle, a federal by-election was called in the Montreal working-class riding of Laurier–Sainte-Marie. Located in one of the poorest urban areas in Canada, the seat had been held by Jean-Claude Malépart, a popular Liberal social activist, for a decade, until his untimely death from cancer in 1989.

Malépart's passing paved the way for the first test of both Jean Chrétien's recently acquired Liberal leadership, and the nascent

Bloc Québécois. Throughout his leadership campaign, Chrétien had insisted that the Quebec constitutional debate was elite-driven. In the world of real people, he maintained, bread-and-butter issues were what mattered. In the riding of Laurier–Sainte-Marie, he had a perfect socio-economic testing ground for his theory, and it was found wanting; Gilles Duceppe romped to victory for the Bloc Québécois.

The misguided notion that Quebecers would put proximity to the honeypot of the federal government above their strongly held views on a defining issue such as their political relationship with the rest of Canada should have died that night. Instead, the by-election unleashed a decade of federal patronage spending, as successive federalist governments set out to show Quebecers the merits of voting for the "right side."

With the federalists on the run in Quebec after the Meech Lake failure, the Mulroney government scrambled to put together an alternative set of proposals to relaunch the constitutional debate. Those proposals were presented to the Quebec Tory caucus in the early fall of 1991. The discussion did not go well. In many ways, the package fell short of the previous accord—but that, as it turned out, was not the biggest hitch.

Like the passengers who insisted on not leaving the *Titanic* without taking all their valuables, many Tory MPs were up in arms over the suggestion of devolving some relatively minor powers, such as forestry and tourism, to Quebec. Their government, they complained, was trying to make them obsolete by putting them out of the business of handing out grants.

In the years between the Meech crisis and his retirement, Brian Mulroney found himself constantly looking for glue to keep his fragile Quebec caucus together. On at least one occasion, a Tory MP gave the prime minister (via one of the Quebec ministers) the forty-five minutes of question period to either make good on a grant for his riding, or watch him cross to the Bloc Québécois.

The personable Benoît Bouchard was appointed Mulroney's Quebec lieutenant, and a separate department was carved out of the government structure to deal exclusively with Quebec regional development. It would be Bouchard's task to give a new twist to the role of political father-confessor. Rather than impose penance on those who confessed that they were sensitive to the sovereignist temptation, Bouchard would deal out rewards for the ridings of suitably repentant MPs.

Brian Mulroney survived the post-Meech era with his Quebec caucus almost intact. By doing that, he probably avoided the fall of his government. But the money his MPs dispensed on pet projects for their ridings did little to save them. In the 1993 election, Mulroney's entire Quebec caucus, with the sole exception of Jean Charest, was sent packing. Almost all were replaced by Bloc Québécois rookies, MPs who would, by definition of their permanent place in opposition, never have their hands anywhere near the government till.

Canada changed governments in 1993 but the federalist approach to francophone Quebec remained the same, as Jean Chrétien picked up where Mulroney had left off. The federal Liberals brought in a national infrastructure program, and opened its taps wide in time to help the provincial Liberals in the 1994 Quebec election. Their efforts were once again in vain. In the fall of that year, the Parti Québécois came back to power with a solid majority.

After the patriation of the Constitution, Jean Chrétien's riding of Saint-Maurice could no longer be considered a Liberal fief. After he lost the leadership to John Turner in 1984, Chrétien was re-elected then on the basis of his personal popularity; but as soon as he packed his bags to await his second shot at the crown in the private sector, Saint-Maurice switched to the Conservatives.

When Jean Chrétien came back to lead the Liberals some years later, he had to re-enter the House of Commons through the door of a New Brunswick riding. In the 1993 election, the Liberal Party invested massive amounts of resources to get him re-elected in his former Quebec seat. Liberal senators and those MPs who enjoyed the luxury of holding safe seats pounded the pavement of Saint-Maurice on Chrétien's behalf throughout the campaign. Pundits and pollsters predicted his defeat, but he proved them wrong. He was naturally jubilant at the outcome, and he thought it would be easier to campaign for re-election next time, as incumbent prime minister. This time, he was wrong.

Notwithstanding its prime-ministerial MP, Saint-Maurice followed the francophone trend in the 1995 referendum. A solid majority of its voters came down for sovereignty. If they stuck to their referendum guns in the following federal election, Jean Chrétien's seat would be at risk. If he lost his seat, his moral authority, already sapped by the close results of the referendum, would suffer a potentially fatal blow.

After the referendum, Martin Cauchon, a Chrétien loyalist, was put in charge of regional development in Quebec, in place of Paul Martin. Following that, francophone Quebec was showered with job-creation grants, courtesy of the Human Resources Development Council. The riding of Saint-Maurice received particular attention. Over that same period, Chrétien came precariously close to facing an election fight he could not win.

With Lucien Bouchard gone to Quebec City, the Bloc Québécois went in search of a new leader. Michel Gauthier, Bouchard's immediate successor, soon decided that he did not have the stomach for the job. He quit within a year. Yves Duhaime, a former Parti Québécois minister who had served under René Lévesque, decided to throw his hat in the ring. Whether he won or lost the leadership race, he was set to run against Chrétien in Saint-Maurice in the following election.

The prime minister and his Quebec entourage spent the Bloc leadership campaign privately cheering on Gilles Duceppe.

They were immensely relieved by his victory. In the larger scheme of things, the Bloc Québécois had made the right choice. Duceppe had more federal experience. He was a bigger asset in the urban markets of the province, where the Bloc would have to remain popular if it was going to avoid being reduced to a rural rump. In time, Gilles Duceppe would grow to be the most popular sovereignist figure in Quebec.

But in 1997, his victory over Duhaime was a blessing for Jean Chrétien. The latter's efforts to show the merits of having the prime minister as MP might well have fallen short in Saint-Maurice if his opponent had been the leader of the Bloc Québécois rather than just a has-been who happened to be an also-ran. In the end, Chrétien beat Duhaime by 1,600 votes.

Jean Chrétien kept his seat until his retirement. As soon as he left, it fell to the Bloc. By then, the fact that Saint-Maurice had never ever been represented by the Bloc made it almost unique among francophone Quebec ridings. In 1997, sowing job-creation seeds throughout francophone Quebec with job-creation grants had not produced much of a crop of federalist MPs. In fact, in their efforts to swing Quebec back to them, the federal Liberals were more often than not going after the wrong targets.

Between the time when Jean Chrétien first went into politics in the sixties and the end of his reign as prime minister in 2003, Quebec had become a heavily urbanized province. The demographics of the sovereignty movement had changed along with it. In the 1995 referendum, support for the Yes side in the suburban middle-class belt around Montreal was as high as in the more traditional francophone strongholds of the Saguenay or the Lower St. Lawrence area, or even higher.

Like their counterparts in Mississauga and Calgary, urban Quebecers are impervious to the politics of pork. Their ballot-box issues, especially at the federal level, are more likely to have to do with macropolicies such as taxes, child care, clean air and urban transport. In many such areas, the Liberals were shooting blanks as they spent money to make themselves more visible at the expense of the Bloc.

There is a chance that the sponsorship program was the last full-fledged eruption of federal pork politics in Quebec. Even if it had not given rise to dubious, fraudulent practices, the program would have been a failure.

There is a case to be made for government support for events that have significant spinoff effects on tourism or cultural industries. But the underlying aim of the sponsorship program, with its heavy emphasis on Quebec, was unity. There is no evidence that the recurring sight of a federal logo (courtesy of the taxpayer) has ever turned a sovereignist into a federalist, any more than a plethora of crucifixes will turn an atheist into a believer.

For fifteen years the Bloc defied conventional wisdom, settling permanently on the wrong side of the House of Commons, and winning more seats in rural and urban francophone Quebec than the governing parties that competed against it with taxpayer money. The Bloc's resilience should have convinced its Liberal opponents of the futility of their ways. It did not, and in the end they paid a hefty price for trying to buy their way to the votes of Quebecers with constant reminders of the federal capacity for largesse. While the Bloc did not bring the sponsorship scandal to light, it was much more persistent in demanding and exacting a penalty for it than a party with power expectations might have been.

From beyond the political grave, Jean Chrétien has pointed to the rising Liberal numbers in Quebec immediately preceding his retirement to argue for the worthiness of his approach. But Chrétien does himself a disservice when he credits his government's simplistic quest for visibility with his improving status in the province.

Quebecers liked Paul Martin when he handled the federal deficit with determination, and they particularly appreciated Jean

Chrétien's last year in office because he made them proud with his decisions on issues such as Iraq and Kyoto—files, as a bonus, that were clearly within the purview of the federal government.

In the 2006 campaign, the Quebec wind did not turn for Stephen Harper until he promised to practise a more open federalism, one more respectful of the provinces. Without that commitment, no amount of selective local Conservative cajoling would have delivered one in four Quebec votes to his party on election day. For Harper's Conservatives in the future, as for the Chrétien/Martin Liberals and the Mulroney Tories in the past, the real test of success in Quebec will not be determined by local patronage. There, as elsewhere in Canada, the way the Harper government handles big-picture items that come its way, rather than its approach to every local file, will determine its fate.

If the more disciplined practice of federalism that Stephen Harper has promoted throughout his career does see the light of day, if the federal governments of tomorrow turn out to be more strategic than political in their choices, it may be Quebec federalists—starting with those who sit in Quebec City, rather than voters in general—who suffer the most acute withdrawal symptoms. While the Parti Québécois has a strong culture of state intervention, it is Quebec federalists who have grown addicted to punctual transfusions of federal cash in the name of the greater cause of Canadian unity. Time and time again, they have come calling on Parliament Hill for special help in their hours of electoral need.

In this fashion, even as he was publicly calling for exclusive Quebec control over a host of federal jurisdictions after Meech, Liberal premier Robert Bourassa was privately wary of cutting the umbilical cord between his government and the federal treasury in many of the policy areas involved.

In the past, federalist governments have basically picked up where their predecessors had left off in matters of patronage.

There was ultimately not much difference between the Trudeau Liberals' patronage approach to Quebec, and that of Brian Mulroney and, after him, Jean Chrétien. But the current Conservative government is of a different mettle. There is little in its Reform/Alliance baggage to predispose it to pork-barrelling. The new Conservative Party's anti-establishment bias has already backfired a few times, notably when Stephen Harper clumsily painted the civil service, the courts and later the parliamentary media with a Liberal brush. But where patronage is concerned, that bias may turn out to be more of a virtue than a fault.

For five consecutive elections, the Bloc has demonstrated that the way to the votes of Quebecers does not necessarily pass through the back pocket of federal patronage. In so doing, it may have helped change one of the less appealing sides of federal politics. If so, that change has not come a moment too soon for the good name of federal governance.

PART V

—

# THE WAY AHEAD

—

## CHAPTER TWENTY

## SPINNING WHEELS

Over the past decade, a major crisis of relevance has plagued the electoral politics of Canada. Between the 1988 and 2006 elections, participation in federal elections has dropped an average of more than ten points.

Only 64 percent of eligible Canadians voted in 2006, down from 75 percent in 1988. Despite the presence of the Bloc Québécois—which should have given sovereignists a stronger incentive to stand up and be counted—Quebec registered one of the sharpest drops in provincial voter turnout over that period. By the time of the 2006 federal election, it had become as hard to sign up promising recruits for the main federal parties as to bolster the dwindling ranks of the Canadian military reserves. Morale among MPs was running low, in particular (and paradoxically) among those on the government side of the House.

Pierre Trudeau once dismissed MPs as nobodies outside the immediate sphere of Parliament Hill. In the Chrétien era, many of the MPs who toiled in the House of Commons came to feel that they were nobodies even within the parliamentary precinct. By the end of Jean Chrétien's third successful campaign, in the fall of 2000, the majority of the Liberal incumbents had been in Parliament for at least seven years. Many had lost hope of being appointed to Cabinet as long as Chrétien remained in office. By will, in the case of the Bloc and the NDP (at least at that particular juncture), or by the design of their own internal divisions, in the case of the Canadian Alliance and the Progressive Conservatives, the four opposition parties were made up of MPs who had little expectation of sitting on the governing side of the House.

Even during the peak periods of his governments, Chrétien was never much of a legislative activist. As a result, the agenda of the House of Commons was usually underloaded. Most of the matters on the parliamentary menu were the bread-and-butter items that are too often the preferred fare of unchallenged majority governments.

Idle minds are the devil's playground. It was not a good time to be a federal leader. Alexa McDonough resigned and the NDP again went in search of a replacement. The other three federalist parties kept busy by engaging in civil war. In the years between Chrétien's last campaign in 2000 and Paul Martin's first one in 2004, the media were more likely to capture Liberal, Canadian Alliance and Progressive Conservative MPs and insiders squabbling within their parties than arguing a policy issue.

Some of the restlessness manifested itself in the near-implosion of the Canadian Alliance, and the quick toppling of Stockwell Day as its leader barely a year after he had beat out Reform Party founder Preston Manning and Tom Long, one of the architects of the Ontario Conservative Common Sense Revolution, for the job. Restlessness also played a part in the neither-fish-nor-cut-bait debate about a possible merger of the right that consumed the Progressive Conservative Party for the duration of Joe Clark's tenure, and over the course of the leadership campaign that followed his resignation.

The Liberals meanwhile plotted against their aging king. The party was slated to hold an automatic vote on Jean Chrétien's leadership at its first convention after the federal election. Given that he had just secured another majority, it should have been a formality. But within weeks of the Liberal victory, the minds of the Martin clan had turned to whether the occasion might be made into an opportunity to show the prime minister the door.

The malaise did not escape the attention of Parliament's rulers. Jean Chrétien tried to fight it with money, presiding over a major overhaul of parliamentary salaries. He also sought ways to make the life of his backbenchers more meaningful without making the life of his government more eventful. The results were mixed, at best.

The previous Parliament had been rocked by a major controversy over the government's funding of job-creation projects. In what would later become a familiar pattern, the story came to light after an audit revealed a lack of oversight on thousands of transactions within the job-creation program.

The 2000 Human Resources Development Canada (HRDC) boondoggle, as it was nicknamed by the Opposition, exposed a potentially embarrassing pattern of grants that seemed tailored at least as much to the incumbent government's needs as to those of Canada's economically depressed regions. The initiative dated back to the immediate post-referendum period. In many instances, Liberal Party officials had been involved in the distribution of the public monies while the opposition parties had not been.

Under attack from all sides, the prime minister fended off furious opposition attacks by arguing that it had been essential to give individual MPs—including himself, as the member from Saint-Maurice—more input into the grant process. Doing otherwise, he maintained, amounted to turning MPs into eunuchs, kept at bay from the affairs of their own ridings by civil servants.

But a massive number of transactions had taken place in the months immediately prior to the 1997 election, at a time when the government had an acute interest in making its own MPs and candidates look good. Also, the job funding was often tilted towards Liberal ridings. That was particularly so in Quebec; grants handed to federalist ridings in 1998–99, for instance, exceeded those received by sovereignist ridings by a margin of three to one, even though economically depressed areas of the province tended to be represented by Bloc Québécois MPs rather than Liberals.

Duplicates of grant applications had routinely found their way to Liberal Party officials. In one case, a Quebec organizer was caught luring donors to the party with the prospect of HRDC grants. Opposition MPs were regularly kept out of the loop of job-creation announcements, while their Liberal colleagues were invited by the PMO to make sure they were on hand for the distribution of government largesse.

Investigations into the HRDC affair unearthed no evidence of theft or fraud, at least within the government and the civil service, but it was clear that political discretion had often been allowed to trump administrative oversight in the distribution of the funds.

The HRDC controversy set the stage for the subsequent sponsorship furor. It was at the time of that boondoggle that the perception that the Liberals were willing to bend the rules to suit their political purposes, especially in Quebec, set in. And it was in the context of that crisis that Jean Chrétien first used unity as a justification for politically directed government spending in Quebec, including in his own riding.

Meanwhile, Chrétien's pay hikes led to another blow to the self-esteem of members of Parliament, as the public lashed out at the notion that MPs deserved more money. Given the 24/7 nature of their jobs and the amount of work they do, most MPs are worth every penny they are paid, and possibly more. But they didn't help matters by spending many of their visible hours casting aspersions on each other's integrity, and pursuing the demise of their respective leaders.

As for Paul Martin, once his leadership campaign officially surfaced, his first promise was to empower MPs—a commitment dictated by his self-interest as future leader, as he was supported by far more Liberals than he could ever fit into a single Cabinet. His proposed reforms nibbled at the edges of parliamentary life but left most of its real imbalances unfixed. For instance, it was hard to fathom the purpose of freer government votes on opposition motions if no action resulted from their passage.

Martin's plan to fix the democratic deficit was a bust with the public. It was not that Canadians didn't like his package and the procedural changes it contained, as far as it went; there just wasn't much in it for them to like. It did not address electoral reform, the issue most likely to engage them directly as voters, and it left the Senate—the poster child for institutional sclerosis on Parliament Hill, in the public's mind—intact.

The plan had been conceived in the context of a majority government, and overtaken by the advent of two consecutive minority ones. In theory, the election of a minority government should be a source of empowerment for individual MPs. In practice, the opposite is closer to the truth.

In a minority Parliament, an MP does have more power to put a knife to the throat of his or her leader. (Or to stick one in his back, with devastating results. Belinda Stronach did just that to Stephen Harper when she crossed over to the Liberals on the eve of a crucial vote for the Martin government, in the spring of 2005.) But having that kind of life-and-death power and little else in one's arsenal is like living with one's finger on the red button that triggers a nuclear strike; one can only press the button once. Short of that extreme recourse, a minority setting offers MPs less rather than more options for expressing dissent on various policies.

In the normal course of a minority Parliament, MPs are doubly constrained, by the party line but also by the partisan needs of the moment. And in a bind, in a minority situation, politics almost always trumps policy—on the government side of the House, or on the opposition benches.

Thus, in their efforts to topple the Martin Liberals in the spring of 2005, Bloc Québécois MPs voted against a host of socially progressive measures that they had previously called for over a number of years. And one short year later, many of the same MPs had to support fiscal measures that went against the grain of their social-democrat philosophy to ensure passage of Stephen Harper's first budget, to avoid a painful return trip to the polls by keeping his government afloat.

After the 2004 election, hopes that the first spell of minority federal government in twenty-five years would assuage the relevance crisis in Ottawa quickly evaporated.

As MPs searched their souls, looking for a greater purpose to their existence in the House of Commons in the twenty-first century, part of the answer was just down the hall from them.

Over the very period when the Commons was spinning its wheels in the mud of internal party strife, the Senate was evolving from a chamber of sober second thought into the place on Parliament Hill where complex issues had the best chance of being constructively examined.

In the past decade, the Senate has been a beehive of policy activity. Much of its work has been at the leading edge of the national policy debate. It has waded in where MPs feared to tread; and on some of the key issues it has been well ahead of the Commons. The following is only a sample of its recent work.

In 2000, the Senate became the first (and only) house of Parliament to look into assisted suicide and euthanasia, two sensitive issues that confront a growing number of Canadians as they and their parents live incrementally longer lives.

In 2002, it produced the first comprehensive report on the legal status of marijuana since the Le Dain commission looked into the matter in 1963. The Senate committee, headed by Conservative senator Pierre Claude Nolin, recommended legalization. The House of Commons eventually tried and failed to take modest steps towards decriminalization.

To the collective shame of the House of Commons, the work the Senate has done on medicare has turned out to be embarrassingly more prescient and more salient than anything produced by its own committees. The 2002 Kirby report on the federal role in medicare (named after Michael Kirby, the Liberal president of the Senate committee that produced it) was the first major federal report to focus on wait times as the measure of the system's performance. Paul Martin and Stephen Harper both eventually made that approach their own, as did the provinces. Senator Kirby and his colleagues foresaw the time when the Supreme Court would step in and rule that governments could not deny Canadians both timely medical care, and the right to resort to private options to heal themselves at their own cost. Quebec was handed just such a decision in 2005, and its ongoing reform proceeded from there.

In 2006, the Senate produced a study of the state of the Canadian media in the era of convergence—a strategic topic for a country that thrives on both competition and the free circulation of ideas.

The upper house is also well ahead of the Commons in trying to grasp the policy adjustments that the demographic shock will require. Given the aging of Canada's population and the declining birth rate, it is an issue that is bound to dominate the federal and provincial policy-making environment over the next decade as it will require some fundamental changes to the social safety net.

These days, fans of the Senate point to this impressive body of work to argue for its continued existence in its current shape.

But leaving aside the Rubik's Cube of Senate reform, the compelling question is not whether the current upper house is doing useful work; senators are as likely as the rest of us to want to use their time on earth productively. But the fact that most of them actually work for their money is beside the point. The real question is why the bulk of leading-edge strategic policy-thinking being done by politicians on Parliament Hill is done at the initiative of the non-elected Senate, rather than the House of Commons.

The answer is depressingly simple. Even though MPs would like to be more than legislative short-order cooks, they and their parties, especially when they are in government, often fear the heat of the kitchen so desperately that observers wonder why they went into public life in the first place.

It would have been impossible for an all-party committee of the House of Commons to produce a document as substantial as the Senate report on medicare without thinking outside the box of partisan party lines. And any attempt at that would have led to more of the name-calling that Canadians have been treated to during successive election discussions of health care, rather than any constructive debate.

The issue of euthanasia and assisted suicide divides Canadians along moral and religious lines. Most people are not looking for moral guidance from their elected officials; they want a realistic legislative framework within which to make their own difficult personal decisions. But in the past, when MPs have considered issues on which they themselves had firm beliefs, many have not been prepared to limit their decisions to such a framework.

As topical as planning for the demographic shock of aging may be, it is difficult for the issue to hold the attention of a House whose members think in four-year increments in major-ity times, and within a narrow eighteen-month horizon in minority times.

By ignoring difficult and divisive issues until they fall into the lap of the government of the day—by often failing to tackle even those pressing issues in substance rather than in rhetoric—MPs are rendering themselves and the institution they inhabit more irrelevant.

These days, many members of Parliament lament the leading role that the courts have played in crafting innovative social policy, especially since the advent of the Charter of Rights and Freedoms. There is much talk about judge-made law. That talk used to be most prevalent on the right, which has often been on the losing side of court battles involving Charter rights. Since the 2005 Supreme Court ruling on the Chaoulli case that found that Quebecers should have the option of using private insurance to secure medical care within acceptable waiting times, the lament also echoes in some sections of the left.

But if political parties would rather bury their heads in the sand than stick their necks out to deal with cutting-edge issues, it should not come as a shock to them that Parliament so often finds itself behind the curve of the courts, the provinces and, yes, public opinion.

## CHAPTER TWENTY-ONE

# TOWARDS A MORE STRATEGIC PARLIAMENT

The Cabinet that Stephen Harper put together since the 2006 election was the smallest in decades. At the political level, that was meant as a not very subliminal message that the Conservative prime minister was determined to run a tighter ship than Paul Martin's. The smaller the Cabinet, the easier it is to control, and if Stephen Harper's style of management was shown to be about anything after the election, it was control. But the slimmer lineup also reflected a serious attempt to realign the political command centre of the government along federal core missions.

The Liberal Party was not quick to adjust to this realignment. In reaction to the reduction in the size of the Cabinet, the official opposition appointed two critics for every minister. In most cases, that amounted to splitting a normal load into half-loads or even quarter-loads. It also amounted to a lot less bang for every opposition buck. In hindsight, no one should have been surprised that the result was one of the most anemic official opposition performances in recent Canadian history.

Splitting up the critic loads also meant that every Liberal member had a chance for a turn in question period, the time that has come to matter most to opposition parties. That forty-five minutes is the most adversarial period in the parliamentary day. Not coincidentally, it is usually the time when MPs are at their collective worst, a period when grown men and women regularly debase themselves into intellectual dwarfs, and sink to ever-new lows of demagogic silliness to score a television point.

A successful question-period hit often involves playing dumb, the better to pursue the futile at the expense of the essential. Again not coincidentally, this is the time that gets the most exposure in the media. Thus an MP is more likely to come to national attention for a capacity to reach ever-new heights of fake indignation than for thoughtful contributions to the national debate.

That will not change until MPs resolve to sink their teeth into issues that echo more loudly with the public than the sound and fury of question period. Taking ownership of strategic policy thinking, bringing it from the Senate to the House of Commons, would be a good start.

But that would mean using the House of Commons and its members to shape legislation and policy on a collegial basis, rather than concentrating their energies on their adversarial roles. It would be a radical change in the modern culture of Parliament Hill—but one that could save MPs from sinking farther into the mud of partisan irrelevance. Otherwise, the ongoing waste of talent in the House of Commons will solve itself less desirably. In today's toxic parliamentary environment, talented MPs are already an endangered species. They could become extinct.

The deterioration of the federal parliamentary debate is particularly obvious to those who have spent enough time on the Hill to know first-hand that it was not always so. In 2004, former federal NDP leader Ed Broadbent came back to Parliament after an absence of a decade. His return was short-lived, as he served only one final term before going back to care full-time for his ailing wife, Lucille. But before he left again, Broadbent had ample time to discover that the House of Commons had not matured in his absence. In his farewell speech, on May 5, 2005, he had these parting words for his colleagues:

> Those who will remain after the next election, when-ever it may be, should give some serious thought to the decline in civility in the debate that has occurred in the House of Commons and which occurs daily in question period. If I were a teacher, I would not want to bring high school students into question period any longer. There is a difference between personal remarks based on animosity and vigorous debate reflecting big differences of judgment. They should see what can be done in the future to restore to our politics in this nation a civilized tone of debate. A tone of debate, in the words of the Universal Declaration of Human Rights, acknowledges the human decency and dignity of all other members of the House who recognize this.

In Quebec, over the past decade, a certain pattern has begun to set in: those who can effect change go to the National Assembly, and those who cannot come to Parliament Hill to sit in opposition. Unless that pattern is reversed by ending the crisis of irrelevance that has overtaken Canada's top elected house, it will spread to other regions of the country.

Depending on one's political biorhythm, the end of the Quebec monopoly on the top political job in Canada is either a positive sign of national maturity or—if one is on the depres-sive side of the cycle—yet another disquieting symptom of Quebec's growing disengagement from the federation.

The latter, of course, presumes that Quebecers have been largely responsible for the almost continuous presence of one of their own as prime minister for thirty-eight years. The facts don't

bear that out. Without substantial support in the rest of the country, none of the Quebec prime ministers who have held power
since 1968 would have been in office for any length of time.

Pierre Trudeau and Brian Mulroney beat some perfectly capa-
ble non-Quebec leaders on their own ground. Trudeau took
Quebec as part of a sweep of Canada in 1968; ditto for Brian
Mulroney in 1984.

Jean Chrétien enjoyed the blessing of a divided opposition, but
if he had counted on Quebec to take him to 24 Sussex Drive, he
might have finished his political days at Stornoway, the official
residence of the leader of the opposition. Without massive support from Ontario, he would certainly not have won three consecutive majorities. Not only did his opponents do more poorly in
Quebec; their candidates were also squashed in Ontario.

In the fall of 2006, Stéphane Dion became the latest Liberal
Quebecer to be propelled to victory on the shoulders of supporters from the rest of Canada. Dion beat long odds to become the
unexpected leader of the Liberal party and his victory was
achieved with little or no support from the Quebec quarters of
his party. Upon his victory, his first order of business became to
make peace with his own province. That, as Dion knew only too
well, would be crucial to his electoral success as leader.

Winning Quebec is no guarantee of winning Canada.
Trudeau demonstrated as much when he lost the 1979 election
despite securing the overwhelming support of his native
province. But the reverse proposition—that it's just about
impossible to win Canada without Quebec—has also been
demonstrated. Joe Clark, the last prime minister who did so,
came to power with a minority government that had the equivalent of a hole in its heart. It died a swift death.

Among modern Canadian politicians, none has tried as hard
to win power without Quebec, and in as propitious circumstances,
as the Reform Party's Preston Manning. With francophone Quebec

spoken for by the Bloc Québécois, with the rest of Canada still in shock over the referendum, Manning put the proposition to non-Quebec voters in the bluntest possible terms in the 1997 election. The ads his party ran, inviting voters to reject parties that were led by Quebecers, spoke for themselves—as did the instantaneous response of an overwhelming public backlash. The vision of a government run without Quebec's input is rejected by many Canadians, as the Reform Party found out the hard way.

Between 2004 and 2006, the Martinites hoped they could survive plunging numbers in Quebec, after the sponsorship scandal, by playing their cards well in Ontario. That might have worked, if the Bloc and not the Tories had picked up the Liberal slack in Quebec. Stephen Harper's emergence as the default federalist voice in Quebec deprived the Martin camp of one of its key aces outside the province; by the end of the 2006 campaign, the Liberals could no longer appeal for support in the rest of the country on the grounds that they were the only party holding the flag in Quebec.

Stephen Harper would not have had a working minority after the election if he had not secured Quebec seats and a substantial level of support in the province. More than anything, that support has sheltered him from a replay of the Joe Clark episode, and a quick return of the Liberals to power.

From the day Pierre Trudeau became Liberal leader until January 23, 2006, there had never been any solid evidence that, given a choice between one of their own and a non-Quebecer, Quebec voters would support the latter in numbers significant enough to swing victory in that direction. But over the Trudeau and Mulroney years, the feeling that a leader from Quebec was the best on offer was widely shared in the rest of Canada— the exception being Joe Clark, on whose merits Quebec and the rest of Canada begged to differ, albeit briefly.

Another surprise of the 2006 election was that Alberta's Stephen Harper did much better in Quebec than the competition from Central Canada. But since the end of the Trudeau era (and probably in reaction to it), francophone Quebec and Alberta have always been on the same side of the House of Commons. They were in power together under Brian Mulroney's successive governments; after 1993 they sat side by side in opposition; and this election brought them back together, tentatively, under Harper.

Barring secession, Canada is unlikely to have seen the last of prime ministers from Quebec. But being led by someone from that province will probably no longer be a constant feature of political life. What really died on that night in 2006 was not some mythical federal French power, but the simplistic assumption that a non-Quebec leader would automatically start from behind his Quebec competition in that province, regardless of what he or she had to offer voters.

After the Meech Lake Accord died, sovereignists came to Parliament Hill in droves, and their federalist counterparts stayed home. When he ran for the Liberal leadership, Stéphane Dion was the only top-tier federalist contender to have emerged from francophone Quebec in more than a decade. He was also the only high-profile francophone Quebec-elected recruit of the Liberal era who was not a political retread. Unlike Lucienne Robillard, Pierre Pettigrew, Liza Frulla and Jean Lapierre, Dion had not been active in the political backrooms or on the front line of elected politics before he came to Parliament Hill.

The disengagement of Quebecers from national affairs is real, but it is a federal concern, not a federalist problem. The notion that the federalist well is drying up in Quebec is not sustained by the reality of the province's politics. The days when the best and brightest of Quebec society went into public life are largely over, a by-product of the fact that the debate over Quebec's future no longer takes political centre stage there.

This is a reality that all Quebec parties have had cause to experience. As the debate has dragged on, the sovereignty movement too has run out of larger-than-life figures. Over the past decade, star candidates have been as likely to run for the provincial Liberals as for the PQ, sometimes crossing the sovereignist-federalist divide to do so.

Philippe Couillard, Jean Charest's health minister, turned out to be the top political recruit of the 2003 Quebec election, and possibly the top one of that entire period in Canada.

Benoît Pelletier, the Quebec Liberal intergovernmental affairs minister, would have been a prime catch for the PQ if only his heart had leaned towards sovereignty, and a top asset to any Liberal federal government if only he had wanted to be a federal Liberal.

Action Démocratique leader Mario Dumont supported the Yes side in the 1995 referendum, and could have gone on to take a senior seat in Lucien Bouchard's Cabinet. Instead, Dumont distanced himself and his party from sovereignty, to the point that the federal Conservatives tried hard to woo him to Parliament Hill.

In the fall of 2005, Raymond Bachand, a well-respected businessman who once served as an adviser to Premier René Lévesque, was recruited out of the sovereignist camp to become one of the top economic ministers in the Charest Cabinet.

By comparison, federal politics have operated in a vacuum in Quebec for a very long time. The federal Liberals bombed their own pipeline into the francophone reservoir of talent with the patriation of the Constitution. Their role in the Meech Lake debate then poisoned the well for all federalist parties. When the Conservatives reappeared on the Quebec map in 2006, after a decade-long absence, the prolonged Tory drought made Stephen Harper's Quebec caucus one of the weakest on record. More than six months after the Conservatives took power, none of the Quebec ministers had emerged as a major figure in the province, and most were seen as very junior players in the government.

In fact, after the realignment brought about by the 2006 election, the shortage of new Quebec blood at the federal level was more acute than it had ever been. Both the Liberals and the Conservatives had no choice but to turn their minds to replenishing their Quebec reserves.

The Conservatives could not hope to improve their standing in Quebec and bring in a majority without a more impressive lineup of candidates. At least now that they were in power, they could hope to be more attractive to political talent than they had been in a long time.

The Liberals also faced an uphill battle. The membership blitz that preceded their 2006 leadership vote left the party with only half as many members in Quebec as in Ontario. The campaign itself never had the public profile it attained in Ontario. On the eve of the leadership convention, on November 27, 2006, the party obtained a dismal 6 percent of the vote in a by-election held in the suburban Montreal riding of Repentigny, coming in 60 points behind the winning Bloc Quebecois and 12 behind the Conservatives. Moving beyond the cloud of the sponsorship scandal would not be an easy task.

Dion's election as leader stood to complicate that task. In the aftermath of his leadership victory, some of the staunchest federalists within his own party feared that his activist record on the unity front would act as a repellent in the province. There is nothing unique about the Dion paradox of a Quebec leader potentially driving support away from his party in his home province. Over the years, federal leaders from Quebec have just as often been seen as part of the federalist problem in Quebec as they have been welcomed as the agents of a solution to sovereignty in the rest of Canada.

Given the experience of the past forty years, many Canadians associate prime ministers from Quebec with the unity file. Pierre Trudeau and Jean Chrétien led the winning side in each of the referendums on sovereignty. But in the time between Pierre Trudeau and Paul Martin, support for sovereignty has gone from being a marginal phenomenon to being the option of choice for the majority of francophone Quebecers.

The monopoly of Quebec leaders on federal power has also had a dark side for the rest of Canada, curtailing its normal political conversation with Quebec, and replacing it with angry exchanges between squabbling Quebec clans. Since both sides have been entrenched in irreconcilable positions, this has been a dialogue of the deaf. Because it has been carried on at high volume and almost exclusively in French, it has spooked all but the bravest non-Quebecers away from the table. It is a rare dinner guest who voluntarily steps into the crossfire of a family feud.

During the reign of prime ministers from Quebec, the Canadian political class has become increasingly bilingual. But too often, that skill has been employed to mouth platitudes rather than to engage Quebecers—a task usually left to the Quebecers within the government. As they practised the various tenses of the subjunctive, many federal politicians from outside the province seemed to forget that communication, even in a second language, has to be a two-way street.

Quebec is not the geographical equivalent of the other side of a cereal box, a French-language translation of the rest of Canada. Understanding what makes it tick requires more than learning the rudiments of its primary language. The evidence is that Stephen Harper, for one, did more listening than talking in Quebec between his two election campaigns. That paid more dividends than he'd have gained if he'd spent those months hopping from one television appearance to another, making generic but ill-informed and off-target pronouncements.

Another consequence of the continuous presence of Quebecers at the top in Ottawa has been the exportation of Quebec polarization into every aspect of federal life. A prime minister from Quebec is by definition someone who has consciously rejected sovereignty as an option. As someone whose base is in Quebec, he or she works, eats and sleeps in the trenches of the debate.

Prime ministers who are not Quebecers are naturally expected to be federalists. From a Quebec perspective, they cannot be accused of turning on their own people, as Pierre Trudeau and Jean Chrétien so often were. There is also less risk that a non-Quebec prime minister will be accused of favouritism by other Canadians, for getting along with Quebec counterparts, or gaining a solid audience in the province.

And while no prime minister, regardless of birthplace, would want the federation to break up on his or her watch, a leader who is not from Quebec would not wake up without a political home base on the morning after a Yes vote.

A non-Quebec prime minister faces other distinct challenges, though.

For instance, except for the brief Clark interlude, the Parti Québécois has never been in power at a time when the prime minister was not a fellow Quebecer. It could be an explosive mix.

At least until the 2006 election, the sovereignty movement had always thought that a prime minister who was not from Quebec would be an asset for its side. René Lévesque would have much preferred fighting the 1980 referendum against Joe Clark rather than Pierre Trudeau. Given a choice between doing battle against Stephen Harper or Paul Martin a quarter of a century later, though, sovereignists might have been better off taking on the latter.

The sovereignists' preference for facing a non-Quebecer was at least partly based on the premise that such a prime minister would have arrived in office without much help from Quebec.

Now that premise—like other sovereignist tenets—has been over-taken by events.

But that doesn't mean that a non-Quebec prime minister doesn't herald a different Quebec–Canada dynamic. In the event of a referendum, for instance, one of the first decisions such a prime minister would have to make would be whether to even participate in the campaign. No politician from Quebec—prime minister or otherwise—would have to ponder that question; staying out of the fray would be akin to leaving one's own home undefended.

Stephen Harper won seats in Quebec on the basis of what voters felt he had to offer them. His seats were not just a consequence of the weakness of the two Quebec leaders on offer, but a result of his commitment to a more open federalism. But another federal leader whose vision was found more compelling could quite possibly sway Quebec to a different party.

For most Quebecers, where that leader came from would be a secondary consideration—and that, frankly, is not all that different from the way things have been in the past. It has simply become more obvious.

—

## CHAPTER TWENTY-TWO

## GHOST STORIES

Despite poor election-night omens, it did not take long for the Harper government to put the ghost of Joe Clark's brief minority government behind it. On election day, the Conservative Party had been all that stood between the federalist camp and the most devastating rout of its history in francophone Quebec. This time, the spirit of Canadian unity could not be invoked to justify the swift defeat of a minority Conservative government.

For any prime minister, Liberal or Conservative, putting the contrary ghosts of Pierre Trudeau and Brian Mulroney to rest is a riskier affair. And yet, if future federal governments are to fulfil the potential of their mandates, it will eventually have to be done.

In the 2006 election, Quebec and Alberta, the two pillars of the Mulroney coalition, came together again. Their last association had ended badly. As they went their separate ways in the early nineties, they had left a wrecked national party behind them.

It is impossible to have a clear sense of what Canada would be today if the Meech adventure had had a happy ending for its authors. The accord has left no trace on the country's Constitution. In time, it will not be worth more than a few paragraphs in the history books; as scores of defeated political leaders can testify, failures rarely are. Still, few non-events have changed the course of so many political lives.

Lucien Bouchard would probably be a wealthier man. He had planned, in the unlikely event that Meech passed after he abandoned the Mulroney government in the spring of 1990, to go back to private legal practice. He would not have lacked offers. He was already a darling of the Quebec business community. At his first public appearance outside Ottawa after his spectacular resignation from the government, the Quebec Chamber of Commerce had given him a standing ovation worthy of a national hero.

Given his popularity and his undeniable addiction to politics, Bouchard would probably have come back to public life at some point after Brian Mulroney's retirement, although not necessarily in the federal arena. He might well still have become Quebec premier, but it would not have been as the head of a Parti Québécois government. Over the years, it has come to be forgotten that the Bloc did not start out as a federal branch plant of the sovereignty movement. That came later, after all constitutional efforts failed in the Charlottetown round.

At first, Bouchard actually resisted PQ efforts to rein in his party under the sovereignist umbrella. He set up a coalition that was initially as close to Liberal premier Robert Bourassa as to PQ leader Jacques Parizeau. Two Liberals who had fought for the No side in the 1980 referendum, Jean Lapierre and Gilles Rocheleau, sat at Bouchard's side in the Commons. Neither was still around by the time the next referendum came along; Lapierre had retired, and Rocheleau had failed to be re-elected under the Bloc banner.

In different constitutional circumstances Lucien Bouchard might still have founded a party, but it almost certainly would have been a provincial one, closer to today's Action Démocratique than to the PQ. In time, he might have made up with his ex-protégé Jean Charest, and convinced him to make the jump to his provincial party, and eventually perhaps to succeed him.

If Meech had passed, the first non-Quebec federal leader to beat the odds and win a national mandate from Canadian voters in the post-Trudeau era might have been a woman. In 1993, Kim Campbell would certainly have faced better odds against Jean Chrétien, especially in Quebec and Ontario. Western Canada might have had a prime minister whose term lasted more than a wink, long before Stephen Harper finally made it to the top. But then, who knows whether the Tories would have turned to a female leader in 1993 if they hadn't been in such dire straits? Competition for Mulroney's job would surely have been fiercer if the party hadn't been so desperately low in the polls.

Bob Rae might never have been premier of Ontario; the Meech Lake backlash was pivotal in his surprise victory over David Peterson in 1990. Who can say whether he would be a federal Liberal today, or whether, having never had a brush with the realities of power, he would have remained a New Democrat?

The 1995 referendum would not have taken place. Even driven by the full force of the nationalist backlash that followed the failure of the Meech Lake Accord, the sovereignty movement could not raise its support to 50 percent. In time, a new party (led by Lucien Bouchard?) would have jostled the PQ off centre stage, sapping its chances of coming back to power.

The sovereignty movement would still have existed the day after Meech passed, but instead of expanding quickly into federal politics, it would have lost more of its sympathizers to federalist politics. Many sovereignists had already started to make that transition after the advent of Brian Mulroney's first government, in 1984. Lucien Bouchard was just one of them.

If Meech had passed, it is hard to imagine that it would have made the federal government any more ineffective in matters of social policy than it has proved to be without it. Prior to 1990, many opponents of the accord claimed that they wanted to preserve the capacity of future federal governments to play a leadership role in social matters. But after 1990, the federal spending power they had so fiercely sought to protect was never used to expand Canada's social safety net in any significant way.

Ottawa moved forward on the fiscal front, most notably by revamping the national child benefit—something it could just as easily have done within the Meech parameters. On the program front, though, the post-Meech years were a time of federal retrenchment, not expansion. Even after big surpluses became a norm, the Liberal government took a while to get down to the task of mending the worst tears in the social system, many of them of its own making.

By then, the provinces, which had all recently swallowed a bitter medicare pill, had become wary of grand plans. They feared that whatever structure the federal government set out to build in their backyards today would be something they would have to maintain tomorrow, and forever after.

The failure of the Meech Lake Accord did not prevent Quebec from continuing to build a progressive and different social model. Over the following decade, the province put in place a comprehensive child-care program, pioneered a pharma-care system and created a new regime of parental leave.

But even with a so-called progressive federal government in office, one that had both the unfettered power to spend and the money to do so, there was no similar progress at the national level. In matters of social policy, the post-Meech era demonstrated that "Where there's a will, there's a way" only operates when the will belongs to a provincial government. Ottawa can play a supportive role but it can't lead by sheer force of pocketbook, no matter how much social activists would like it to.

In theory, the provinces' right to opt out of federal programs within their areas of constitutional jurisdiction, with full compensation, died with the Meech Lake Accord. But in practice, in

the years that followed, every Quebec government—sovereignist
or federalist—resisted federal efforts to impose national standards
in any of its exclusive areas of jurisdiction. At times, Quebec
was joined by other provinces—particularly Ontario, under
Conservative premier Mike Harris.

The last time Jean Chrétien gathered the premiers, to discuss
health care in the winter of 2003, he emerged from the meeting
with an accord that bore no signatures. To the pleased surprise of
Bernard Landry, the Quebec premier, his provincial colleagues
had joined in refusing to formally sign the deal, although all of
them accepted the federal money.

For any prime minister, it is a given that dealing with a sovereignist premier is bound to be tough. But negotiating with a
federalist one can turn out to be even tougher.

After Meech, the dangers of isolating a federalist Quebec
leader stayed clear in the other premiers' minds. Jean Charest
benefited from some of the lessons that had been learned at the
expense of Robert Bourassa. To get a federal-provincial deal on
health care in September 2004, Paul Martin had to agree to a
side deal exempting Quebec from the federal accountability
sections of the general accord.

A year later, the Charest government patriated Quebec's share
of the federal employment-insurance monies devoted to parental
leave to fund its own separate program.

With Quebec keeping itself out of federal-provincial frame-
works, the checkerboard federalism that Meech opponents so
wanted to avoid became more, rather than less, a reality.

—

## CHAPTER TWENTY-THREE

## A DISTINCTIVELY FUTILE BATTLE

B y far the biggest windmill the Meech opponents set their quixotic sights on was the distinct-society clause. Rarely has a country inflicted so much political pain on itself for so little gain.

The Canadian Constitution may not spell out the fact that Quebec is a distinct society, but the courts don't doubt that history has already bestowed that status, and that this has some legal consequences. In the very midst of the Meech furor, the Supreme Court ruled that Quebec had special responsibilities for the protection of the French language, and that, in its efforts to live up to them, it could favour French over English. The court accordingly gave Quebec the green light to require commercial signs to be predominantly in French.

A more recent attempt to argue that the restrictions on English-language education in Quebec were no longer justified by any precarious status of the French language also failed to sway the courts. One doesn't need a graduate degree to know that maintaining a French-speaking society of less than twelve million people on a continent overwhelmingly dominated by the English language will continue to require a collective act of will, sometimes backed by legislation.

In an ironic and cruel twist a decade after Meech, it was

suggested that the Mulroney government might have been able to give Quebec the symbolic recognition it sought without going through that three-year, divisive national debate.

In 1987, Canada had no experience with the new amending formula of the Constitution, and no precedent to help it chart a course. The formula had only kicked in after Pierre Trudeau patriated the Constitution and negotiated the addition of a Charter of Rights and Freedoms to its framework.

But after the constitutional failures of the early nineties, the federal government managed to make seven amendments to the Constitution. Some of them were minor but others were significant. In every case, the federal government proceeded on a one-on-one basis with a given province.

In this fashion, the equal status of French and English in New Brunswick was enshrined by an act of that province and a matching one from the federal government.

On the same basis, the constitutional obligation placed on Quebec to run a Protestant school system alongside its Catholic one was abrogated. The province then reorganized the management of its school system along language lines.

Section 93 of the Constitution originally covered religious-education rights in six provinces. Some experts felt that it involved an element of reciprocity between Ontario and Quebec, as it imposed symmetrical obligations on Canada's two major provinces vis-à-vis their religious minorities. Yet neither Ontario's agreement nor that of any of the other four provinces covered by the section was deemed necessary to relieve Quebec of its obligation to run parallel Protestant and Catholic school systems.

Those precedents opened new avenues for amending the Constitution. In a 2002 paper prepared for the Quebec government, José Woehrling, one of Quebec's top constitutional experts, argued that Ottawa could have dealt with the distinct-society issue on a one-on-one basis, enshrining it with the agreement of only Quebec and Parliament.

As compelling as Professor Woehrling's academic arguments may have been, though, they came too late for the politicians. If there ever was a shortcut to enshrining Quebec's distinct status in the Constitution, it was blocked off once the concept became overloaded with popular mistrust and suspicion.

Back at Meech Lake in 1987, in an age of relative constitutional innocence, it was thought that securing the unanimous backing of all provinces for the accord would send a powerful symbolic message that Quebec was being reintegrated into the constitutional family, through the front door. "Canada says yes to Quebec," proclaimed the headline of *Le Devoir* on the morning after the accord was finalized. Three years later almost to the day, on June 24, 1990, the same paper printed a special Sunday edition to report the death of Meech. In the fall of 2006, the call by federal Liberals from Quebec for their party to endorse the recognition of Quebec as a nation followed by Harper's unexpected motion—one that every single Quebec MP supported—has shown that the issue still resonnates loudly in the province.

What is less obvious to many Canadians in and outside Quebec is that the failure to address the latter's place in the Constitution also reverberates through the country's federal system. It accounts for many of its failings on a host of other fronts.

After Meech died and the Charlottetown Accord foundered, the constitutional issue came to be given the wide berth usually reserved for radioactive dumpsites. All those who had been even remotely associated with the file quarantined the experience on their hard disks.

For almost a decade, between 1985 and 1993, the country's politics had been dominated by the attempt to normalize Quebec's constitutional status. It had amounted to a colossal waste of energy, and had left the federal political scene a shambles. Reformatted by these two successive failures, the makeup of the country's political establishment no longer included a constitutional reform program.

A generation of pundits suddenly discovered what it must have been like to be in the business of shoeing horses after cars hit the road. Almost overnight, the knowledge and expertise accumulated over years of constitutional rounds became obsolete. Most of it wasn't even deemed useful enough to be recycled into books—save those whose prime (and exclusive?) market is academia. Mainstream history, after all, is almost always written from the point of view of the winners, and this chapter had not produced any lasting ones. It certainly had not advanced the agenda of those who had scuppered Meech in 1990.

The aboriginal leadership had hoped the post-Meech train would deliver it to the destination of constitutional accommodation for Canada's First Nations. It woke up the morning after the Charlottetown referendum without a political venue to discuss its own historical grievances. In short order, the aboriginal issue found its way back to the inside pages of the newspapers. Some native leaders successfully brought their battles to the courts and scored significant victories. But these remained defensive, exhausting battles fought one inch at a time, rather than becoming a march forward under the banner of a comprehensive framework.

Feminist activists paid an even steeper price. Some members of their sisterhood had tried to hop on the constitutional train by derailing Meech. Their efforts had hit a low in the spring of 1990, when a group of Manitoba women argued in front of a travelling parliamentary committee that the distinct-society clause would allow future Quebec governments to invoke the greater good to force women to have more children by keeping them out of universities and well-paid jobs.

Before Meech, the feminist lobby had been a mainstream force in federal politics. No politician in his or her right mind wanted to land on the wrong side of the National Action Committee on the Status of Women (NAC). Such was the group's influence that in the 1984 election, all federal leaders complied with its demand for a debate devoted solely to so-called women's issues. But after Charlottetown, NAC became increasingly marginalized. In time, few politicians outside the NDP cared much about what (if anything) the feminist lobby had to say about them. The rift between the feminist movement in Quebec and that in the rest of Canada was never really mended.

The Senate reform train also lost its steam. Over the years, the notion of a Triple-E Senate, equal, elected and effective, so dear to the heart of the Reform Party, gradually faded from the federal landscape. The Conservative movement lost its appetite for what came to look like a lost cause. In the transition from the Canadian Alliance to the new Conservative Party, the issue of the Senate became a second-tier item on the Tory agenda, rather than a central piece of it.

In the aftermath of the 2006 election, it still remained to be seen whether the first Alberta-strong federal government in decades would manage to address the issue, or whether Stephen Harper would have to be content to pay lip service to Senate reform by tinkering with the edges of the institution. He did move to limit Senate terms and also put forward plans to turn the Senate into an elected house. But short of calling a constitutional round, he could do nothing about fixing the obsolete regional make-up of the upper house.

As for the checkerboard federalism that so many Meech and Charlottetown critics had feared would result from either accord, it actually bloomed once both of them had been nipped in the bud. Piecemeal reforms and one-on-one agreements became the norm rather than the exception. Sections of the Constitution were rewritten solely on the basis of the will of Parliament and the province concerned.

For constitutional junkies, the 1995 Quebec referendum was the last hit of an era, a near-fatal federalist overdose that convinced many that Canada would either remain on the constitutional wagon or risk fatal divisions.

Afterwards, Canada's politicians looked for other causes to pursue. In short order, the poor shape of the country's finances caught up with them. The war on the deficit would reshape the social union in ways that no constitutional reform could have achieved, and social activists found themselves watching powerlessly from the sidelines.

The NDP, their traditional voice in Parliament, was silenced by the 1993 election, and muted by its mediocre results in the elections that followed. The new opposition parties—the Bloc Québécois and the Reform Party—had no interest in going to the barricades to defend the social union. For different ideological reasons, both held similar views on decentralization. In power, the Liberals had more pressing priorities—one being to attract the small-c conservative vote left in limbo by the division of the right.

Attempts at normalizing Quebec's place in the constitutional scheme of things had failed, but the original division of powers defined by the Constitution remained intact. Quebec and, over time, other provincial governments became jealously protective of their exclusive control over social policy. It turned out to be harder for the federal government to exercise leadership than it would have been under any of the co-operative processes prescribed by the defunct accords.

Back when Meech failed, it had seemed that Quebec—and in particular the Quebecers who believed that the federation was big enough to accommodate a vibrant, self-confident French-language society—would be the biggest losers. But in the end, Canada and its institutions have ended up suffering the most.

Quebec has moved on. It is as distinct today as it ever was, possibly even more so than it would have been if the Meech or Charlottetown rounds had worked out. But it is also psychologically more disengaged from federal politics and policies than it has ever been.

With the province massively invested in opposition on Parliament Hill for the first time in its history, the National Assembly's status as the prime operative centre of Quebec politics has inevitably been consolidated. It has become an increasingly stronger magnet for the province's talent, drawing some of the best elements of their generations—people like Lucien Bouchard and Jean Charest—away from federal politics and into the Quebec arena. That too has been Canada's loss.

When Premier Bouchard set out to create a universal child-care system in Quebec, he wanted to show that the Parti Québécois had not sacrificed its social conscience on the altar of balanced budgets. His goal was to highlight the rewards attendant on his victory over the deficit, especially to the social-progressive wing of his own party. But he also achieved something else. He demonstrated that even within the current federalist context, even in the absence of substantial reform to the federation's workings, it was possible for Quebec to pursue a social model of its own.

In light of this, instead of begging for more federal leadership in social affairs, Quebecers of all political stripes came to agree that they wanted *less*. Time and again, the province's social activists found they had more leverage on the Quebec government than on the one in Ottawa. And this held just as true for fiscally conservative Quebecers.

The battle to end the fiscal imbalance was born out of that collective experience—which also created the opening that produced a Conservative breakthrough in Quebec in the 2006 election.

Under the impetus of a federalist government in Quebec that was resolved to play an activist role on the federal-provincial scene, every other province followed Jean Charest's lead and joined the fiscal-imbalance debate. New Democratic Manitoba, Progressive Conservative New Brunswick and Liberal British Columbia all joined Quebec in a bid to wrestle a bigger piece of the fiscal pie from an affluent but disoriented federal government.

As for Ontario, traditional keeper of the tenet of strong central government, under a Liberal premier it fought for its share with no less gusto than the hungriest of the have-not provinces.

Meanwhile, in the years after Meech and Charlottetown, the action moved away from Parliament Hill and its outdated institutions. Big-picture items were dealt with outside its precinct, on the international scene or at the federal-provincial table. Federal politics largely became a spectator sport, its players running on a treadmill of leadership conspiracies and election campaigns, with a lot of politics, and precious few policies, between.

If the Meech Lake Accord had passed, the Canadian Senate would already be an elected house. The accord stipulated that future nominees to the upper house be chosen from lists drawn up by the provinces. Some — starting with Alberta — would have selected their candidates through senatorial elections. In time, other provinces would have followed suit.

Chances are the Senate would have undergone an even more radical transformation, and most other federal political institutions along with it. Once Meech was passed, the reform of the upper house would have been next on the agenda, and it is unlikely that it would have been limited to electing senators.

Back in 1990, many Canadians complained bitterly that the Meech Lake Accord was Quebec-driven. But the primary goal of the process was to get Quebec formally back on board, so that the country could resume a normal constitutional dialogue and move on with reforms on a host of other crucial fronts. Beyond the addition of Pierre Trudeau's cherished Charter, the purpose of patriating the Constitution in 1982 had been to allow Canada to bring institutions conceived in colonial times into the twenty-first century.

Instead, the federation ended up with a political Chernobyl. The disaster atrophied the federal system. In the post-Meech era, co-operative national initiatives became few and far between, and many were flawed at birth—often missing one or more essential limbs. In this fashion, attempts to craft a more fluid social union never really got off the pages of a federal-provincial agreement signed shortly after the 1995 referendum.

Far from going away, the need for a different national deal has become more acute over the years. For over a decade, Canada has wilfully closed its eyes to the many institutional cracks in its structure. Over that period, they have become wider.

Every region of the country has become more vibrant in the post-Meech era, and more distant from the institutions of the federation—and none more so than Quebec and the provinces of Western Canada. The West's well-justified sense of estrangement from the running of the country's affairs is unlikely to be assuaged for very long by the fact that one of its own is prime minister. After all, a four-decade string of prime ministers from Quebec didn't mute that province's demands for different political arrangements. On the contrary, today there are fewer Quebecers than ever who find the status quo adequate, and more than ever who have stopped caring about being engaged in federal politics.

Whether the absence of a resolution of constitutional issues keeps sovereignty alive has become a secondary debate. The real question is not whether the federation will break up over its incapacity to modernize itself; it probably won't. If that ever happens, it will not be primarily because of an antiquated constitution, or a half-empty–half-full debate on fiscal arrangements.

But if Canada is to move forward as a working federation, it needs to rebalance more than its fiscal arrangements. To do one without doing the other amounts to pumping air into the tires of a car with a broken steering wheel.

As the past decade of decline in federal governance has shown, weak national political institutions cannot be offset by a financially strong federal government. They can only be further destabilized into irrelevance.

The Alberta–Quebec phoenix that rose out of the ashes of the defunct Reform and Progressive Conservative parties on January 23, 2006, was different from its predecessor in one significant way. The 1984 Mulroney coalition had come together to claim its place in Canada's institutions and make them more hospitable to its aspirations. It failed, and the fledgling Alberta–Quebec Conservative coalition was born as a result, out of a common fallback desire to keep federal institutions at bay. The Canadian federation has gone from being a divided house whose inhabitants squabbled in the parlour to a rooming house whose tenants would rather eat in their rooms and let the kitchen crumble into disrepair than attempt to agree on renovations.

Stephen Harper's Conservative Party will not be entirely whole again, and it will not succeed in becoming the natural governing party of the twenty-first century, until it has succeeded where Brian Mulroney so spectacularly failed. As his risky 2006 motion on the Quebec nation demonstrated, it is a reality he is acutely aware of.

But those who assume that the core malaise in the federation will be solved by chasing away a potentially dysfunctional Conservative coalition are once again charging at windmills. Regardless of the party in government, the federation will be increasingly less than the sum of its parts as long as its institutions operate in a way that leaves some of its most vibrant participants feeling that they are on the outside looking in.

Ending that exclusion should be more important to those who claim to speak for a more progressive Canada than just finding the quickest way to get the right out of office. For until it's done, Canada will not have a natural governing party, but just a succession of fundamentally flawed parliaments.

# PART VI

# WINNING THE WAR, LOSING THE PEACE

—

## CHAPTER TWENTY-FOUR

## JEAN CHRÉTIEN: CHESS MASTER

J ean Chrétien almost lost the 1995 referendum battle, but he made up for his near miss by winning the cold war that followed. His success in turning a near victory of historic proportions for the Quebec sovereignty movement into a debilitating stalemate is one of the less-told political stories of the past decade.

Most of us are familiar with only bits and pieces of it. We tend to remember best what we heard about last. Given the prominence of the story, it is only natural that most Canadians have come to equate Chrétien's unity battle with the tawdry details of the sponsorship affair. But a look in the rearview mirror reveals a larger picture, one that does more justice to his political skills.

Between the 1995 referendum and his 2003 retirement, Chrétien played three simultaneous games of chess. He outwitted his sovereignist foes on the international front; he co-opted the diverging federalist forces of the rest of Canada into following his game plan; and he took control of the federalist scene in Quebec. At times, he manoeuvred some of the top figures in Quebec, in the rest of Canada and on the international scene as if they were pawns on a board.

Jacques Chirac and Bill Clinton played strategic roles in this game. Preston Manning, the brainy founder of the Reform Party, and Paul Martin, Chrétien's arch rival, were both productively used to advance his domestic strategy. And Chrétien easily check-mated the Progressive Conservative Party not once but twice along the way.

In 1995, France's Jacques Chirac started off his presidency as the Parti Québécois's best international friend. In the event of a Yes vote in 1995, he was publicly committed to pursuing the cause of secession on Quebec's behalf in global circles. Yet by the time Jean Chrétien retired, President Chirac had become a personal friend who took side trips to visit the Inuit and the Acadians on his visits to North America, the better to celebrate the many nations living under the single roof of the Canadian federation.

Bill Clinton was even more direct. No foreign head of state, certainly no American president, has skated quite as close to the edge of Canadian internal affairs as Clinton did in the lead-up to and aftermath of the 1995 referendum. He only got away with this intrusion because of the immense popularity he enjoyed in Quebec, which endures to this day.

At a news conference just days before the referendum, Clinton waded into the fray by forcefully restating the United States's strong preference for a united Canada. To the dismay of the sovereignist leadership, the American president described Canada as a country that "basically works." His statement was front-page news in Quebec at a crucial time for federalist fortunes in the referendum, and it had positive consequences for the No camp.

In the name of the Parti Québécois, Bernard Landry remonstrated with the State Department, but Clinton was unrepentant. At a subsequent federal conference on federalism held in Mont-Tremblant in October 1999, the president went further, delivering on Canadian soil, and in front of a mixed federalist-sovereignist audience, an articulate but no-holds-barred defence of federalism as the ideal way to balance the aspirations of different peoples within a single state.

To be sure, Jean Chrétien's efforts to expand his pro-federalism campaign onto the international scene benefited from a favourable context—that of the ethnic wars that were devastating the Balkans. It's hard to think of a better time to be a Canadian federalist in need of international moral support than in the nineties, when so many industrialized countries were trying to come to grips with the nationalist forces unleashed by the fall of the Berlin Wall and the demise of the Soviet empire.

But given that Canada is rarely central to the preoccupations of top heads of state—after all, the country was hardly the scene of a full-fledged conflict, and few movements have been as scrupulously respectful of democracy in their pursuit of a cause as Quebec sovereignists—it took someone to bring horses the size of Chirac and Clinton to water, and Jean Chrétien had them there, and drinking, too.

The prime minister was also getting his ducks in a row at home; those he couldn't line up to his liking, he simply shot out of the pond. In this fashion, Jean Charest and later Joe Clark were both disposed of. While they endured different fates, the outcome, from Chrétien's perspective, was the same; the only two leaders who dared quack loudly at his post-referendum strategy were dead ducks in relatively short order.

As for the other federalist parties, Chrétien used their glaring weakness in Quebec to convert them into docile partners in his strategy.

After 1995, the Reform's Preston Manning could have emerged as the voice of the rest of Canada. He was arguably the only leader whose elbow room was not constrained by Quebec. A case could be made that he was best placed to draw a line in the sand of any referendum rematch. Jean Chrétien pulled that rug out from under Manning's feet by espousing the original Reform idea of establishing Canada's conditions for dealing with sovereignty. After the referendum, he made the idea his own under the name of the Clarity Act. In 1998, Chrétien headed to the Supreme Court to seek its advice on possible terms of secession of a province, and at the end of 1999 he brought down his landmark bill.

At first, Preston Manning balked at supporting the act. He argued that its timing—four years after the referendum, and at a time when sovereignty seemed to be in a lull—would ensure that it came across as a tactic to intimidate Quebecers, rather than as a way to engage them in a sober dialogue. Those reservations were short-lived. The vocal pressures of Manning's own supporters, starting with Stephen Harper, who was by then installed as president of the National Citizens Coalition, quickly turned the Reform Party leader into a compliant and co-operative partner in Jean Chrétien's unity strategy.

In the sixties, the NDP had been the first federal party to support Quebec's right to self-determination. Many experts saw the 1999 Clarity Act as a means to make that right subservient to the whims of the federal parliament of the day, and hence to a Canadian majority. In Quebec, the party's progressive allies made it clear that they would consider NDP support for Chrétien's initiative a hostile act. Those warnings found echoes within progressive circles in Ontario. Alexa McDonough hesitated, but only long enough to be read the riot act by some of her Western Canada allies. They included Jean Chrétien's brother-at-arms at the time of the patriation of the Constitution, the NDP premier of Saskatchewan, Roy Romanow.

That left only the Progressive Conservative Party to stand in Chrétien's way. The party was also the Prime Minister's only federalist competition in francophone Quebec. After the referendum, Tory leader Jean Charest enjoyed a bigger audience there than Jean Chrétien. Outside Quebec, Charest was widely considered as having offered a more articulate, more effective referendum defence of federalism than the prime minister. Jean Charest was wary of Chrétien's hardline approach, and opposed his so-called Plan B from the start. That ended when the Quebec federalist establishment made Charest an offer he could not refuse. As it happens, André Ouellet, Chrétien's Quebec lieutenant at the time of the referendum, was the first to publicly promote the idea of installing Jean Charest as leader of the Quebec Liberal Party. In an interview with *La Presse* only two months after the referendum, Ouellet suggested that Daniel Johnson should step down in the name of the greater cause of federalism, and that Charest should take his place.

With Charest on his way to the Quebec front to slaughter the sovereignist dragon, Jean Chrétien then methodically cut the legs out from under his successor, Joe Clark. On the morning after the new Tory leader secured a ticket back to Parliament in a by-election, the prime minister brought two of the remaining three Quebec Tory MPs over to the Liberals. In the general election held only a few months later, Chrétien added the bulk of the Conservative federalist vote in Quebec to his own side, and turned the total into his best score ever in the province. As a bonus, he also won votes from Clark outside Quebec, as a result of Clark's opposition to the Clarity Act.

After the referendum, Chrétien recruited Stéphane Dion out of his university classroom and put him to work to deliver the political lectures that he himself did not have the credibility or authority to give in Quebec. He absolutely needed a Quebecer in the post-referendum window, and Dion, who had spent years sharpening his debating skills by taking on all sovereignist comers in Quebec academia, fit the bill.

Prime Minister Chrétien's referendum point man would not have won a prize for congeniality, but he made up for that with nerves of steel. And it was probably lucky that Stéphane Dion did not crave affection. The mission Chrétien handed him would turn him, at least for a time, into the most disliked political figure in Quebec, a title previously held by the prime minister himself.

Launched as it was in the lead-up to the referendum, the war to eliminate the federal deficit could have had devastating consequences for the federalist cause. Over time, the deep cuts to social programs required to balance the books could have galvanized the social-democrat base of the Parti Québécois into action, and given it a compelling new rationale for promoting sovereignty. But Jean Chrétien avoided much of the backlash by putting his chief rival, Paul Martin—the friendliest face of his government in Quebec—in charge of the file, and allowing him to claim the battle as his personal crusade. The popular, congenial Martin was able to take the sting out of the cost-cutting measures.

To help matters, Lucien Bouchard, a former Conservative minister who had sat at the Cabinet table when Brian Mulroney was struggling to solve the crisis that had overtaken public finances, was more inclined to match Jean Chrétien's determination on the fiscal front than to fight it. During the referendum, sovereignists had argued time and again that Canada's finances were a mess. They could hardly allow the Chrétien-Martin team to clean them up without getting the red ink out of the provincial books. In his new capacity as premier, Bouchard pursued a zero-deficit policy with his usual stamina. He rallied the Quebec establishment behind his flag, securing support from the left as well as from the right, and promptly won his own war on deficit. But the energy and momentum required for a quick referendum rematch were both, inevitably, casualties of that battle.

In 1995, Quebec sovereignists had almost scored a historic goal into a near-empty federalist net. Afterwards, Jean Chrétien set out to move the goalposts of future referendums, and to a great extent he succeeded.

On his first foreign trip after the referendum, he had a chance to measure first-hand the world community's growing concern over the post–Berlin Wall ethnic strife. Upon his return, he used that concern to transfer the capital of international sympathy from Quebec sovereignists to Canadian federalists. Under the guise of the Clarity Act, he put a road map to Canada's eventual destruction on the federal books, without a single federalist party seriously standing in his way.

He enticed his former referendum rival, Lucien Bouchard, into matching his deficit-elimination efforts, a task that kept both governments fully occupied for the bulk of the immediate post-referendum period (and also had the virtue of keeping the federal government out of the hair of its Quebec counterpart).

Some of the debates Jean Chrétien opened—notably on the need for a clear referendum question, and a higher voting margin than a simple majority before secession could proceed— eventually percolated through the sovereignty movement.

It's hard to believe that a political leader capable of such sophisticated and often ruthless strategy would have believed, as Chrétien has repeatedly claimed he did, that an initiative as simplistic as the sponsorship program was central to his bid to preserve the unity of Canada. In a broader scheme that involved heads of states, premiers and a full set of federal party leaders, the sponsorship program was a mere detail, unworthy of prime-ministerial attention. In dollar figures, it was a relative blip on the fiscal radar screen of the federal government. It was not even an important part of the activities of the Department of Public Works, which was technically responsible for it.

Yet the Gomery commission has heard a lot of compelling testimony, none of it fundamentally contradicted by Chrétien or his associates, that the program was important to the prime minister. Civil servants and political flacks alike have testified that the sponsorship program got away with the public accounting equivalent of murder because it was known to be close to the prime minister's heart. Clearly, that status is what earned the rogue program and those who ran it immunity from the most basic scrutiny.

Both in the House of Commons and in front of the Gomery commission, Jean Chrétien himself has testified to his belief in the power of federal visibility in the struggle for Canada's unity in Quebec. Knowing that the prime minister has never been averse to killing two birds with one stone, it's not a big stretch to conclude that, from his perspective, one of the advantages of the sponsorship program was to make up for the acute absence of federal Liberals in Quebec by keeping their government as visible as possible. At that point, in Quebec, Chrétien's Liberals no longer had any federalist competition to contend with. They had little cause to see a difference between their narrow partisan interests and the larger ones of federalism.

The sponsorship program played no part one way or the other in Jean Chrétien's winning of the post-referendum war. But it was a big reason, although hardly the only one, why Paul Martin lost the peace.

The reality is that, over the years, Canada's prime ministers have been more successful at winning wars on the unity front than at securing peace. Pierre Trudeau and Jean Chrétien won the two referendums, but they also made it more difficult for their successors to move to the next logical step, reconciliation between the rest of Canada and Quebec. The last prime minister who came close to winning the peace was Brian Mulroney, and it almost killed his party. His failure also poisoned the federalist well in Quebec for more than a decade. And yet, the evidence is accumulating that the Quebec voters who supported Stephen Harper in January 2006 were looking for a prime minister who would try, once again, to win the peace.

—

## CHAPTER TWENTY-FIVE

# DAVID SUZUKI'S QUESTION

In June of 2006, David Suzuki, Canada's best-known environmentalist, travelled to Montreal and put to Quebecers the question that had been haunting the left since the January election.

"Is more powers all that Quebec wants? Is this really what will determine everything else?" Suzuki wondered, during an interview with *La Presse*. The question of whether Quebec voters would give the Conservatives a blank cheque federally in exchange for more autonomy provincially had become more pressing for him and for the environmental lobby since the election. In the wake of his victory, one of Stephen Harper's first gestures had been to indicate that Canada would not meet the commitments it had undertaken in signing the Kyoto Protocol.

Much more than Harper's vocal militancy on the need for an increasingly muscular mission in Afghanistan, the retreat from the global-warming front indicated to the international community that a substantial political realignment was in progress, and that the country was changing camps.

It also confirmed the worst post-election fears of the Canadian left, when it was already reeling from the recent campaign. For the left, the 2006 election had been a nightmare come true—a virtual replay of the 1988 free-trade election. The NDP and some of its leading activists had spent the campaign in a highly divisive public squabble over the best way to counter the Conservatives.

Early in the campaign, Buzz Hargrove, the president of the Canadian Auto Workers Union, appeared at a rally alongside Paul Martin and urged progressive voters to support the Liberals wherever they had the best chance of winning. It was a shot across the bow of the NDP and its leader, Jack Layton, that would reverberate until voting day.

While most of the NDP's traditional allies did not go quite as far as Hargrove, by the end of the campaign he was no longer alone in his frantic efforts to push NDP prospects into the Liberal camp. The other activists who had joined the chorus may have been more subtle, but their message was clear: voters should jump from Layton's raft to Martin's stranded ship, and help him row back to power.

Neither Hargrove nor his soulmates had seen the Quebec Conservative breakthrough coming until it was too late. At the tail end of the campaign, Buzz Hargrove hit the panic button — and it virtually blew his finger off, showering Paul Martin with debris in the process. With only days to go until the vote, and with the prime minister looking on, Hargrove urged Quebecers to support the sovereignist Bloc rather than the federalist Conservatives.

That piece of advice was anything but helpful to Gilles Duceppe. By then the Bloc was bleeding from its right flank, not its left. The recommendation was also highly controversial in the rest of Canada, where defeating sovereignists usually takes precedence over keeping other federalists out of office.

In the end, the NDP sailed home to its best score, seatwise, in eighteen years. But it was a true-blue conservative who won.

In the months that followed, it became apparent that there was more to the Conservative surge in Quebec than a temporary aberration. By the time David Suzuki brought his question to Quebec in June 2006, the Conservatives alone, of all four federal parties, had momentum in the province. The prospect that Stephen Harper could ride to a majority on the shoulders of Quebecers no longer seemed remote. Suzuki's question was anything but academic.

Notwithstanding some of the fears of socially progressive Canadians, the 2006 reappearance of Quebec within the Conservative coalition was essentially good news for every federal party, with the possible exception of the Bloc Québécois. The fact that it convinced Stephen Harper to try to find his way to a majority through Quebec was even better news. As for the prime minister's determination to focus on the core missions of the federal government, it created an immense opportunity for the other federalist parties, although not necessarily for the reasons some of their more short-sighted strategists imagined on election night.

Ever since the birth of the Reform Party, many progressive Canadians have feared the rise of a hard-right party along the lines of the American Republican Party. That fear almost killed the federal NDP in the nineties, as left-leaning voters flocked to the Liberals to stop the ascent of the Reform/Alliance. The Common Sense Revolution of Mike Harris and the Conservatives in Ontario aggravated those fears. If Ontario could be taken, why not all of Canada?

Even with the Tories gone from power at Queen's Park, the spectre of a Reform-style Conservative government in Ottawa remained a potent Liberal weapon against the NDP in that province in the last two federal elections.

In theory, the merger of the Canadian Alliance with the former Progressive Conservative Party should have assuaged those fears. The presence within the ranks of the new party of high-profile red Tories such as Ontario senator Hugh Segal and former federal minister John Crosbie, and the active support of a middle-of-the-road

Conservative premier such as New Brunswick's Bernard Lord, should have given the party a fresh veneer of moderation. But the fact that the Canadian Alliance imposed its leader on its Progressive Conservative partner, the pointed absence of Joe Clark from its ranks, and the early defection to the Liberals of Scott Brison, an openly gay Tory MP who had risen to national preeminence by seeking the leadership of the former Progressive Conservative Party, followed by the even more spectacular departure of Belinda Stronach a year later, all sent the message that Canadians were really dealing with the alpha-male Reform Party in a Tory skirt.

In fact, after Stephen Harper became leader, the party shed the bulk of its social-conservative baggage. Its 2006 platform clearly resulted from a concerted effort to be seen as moderate. In the past two elections, Harper even tried to argue that it was not a given that he would have sent troops to Iraq if he had been prime minister in 2003. Still, his 2006 victory amounted to a sharp departure from a past when Tories only won federal elections when they were led by a member of their progressive wing.

In 2006, a minority government was probably as far as Harper could push the Conservative envelope. Unless he blunted its edges some more before his next bid, progressive voters stood to mobilize against him under a single flag. And if that happened, his hopes for total victory would vanish.

In Canada, there are few quicker shortcuts to mellowing a right-wing party than the injection of a strong Quebec component. If Harper meant to accelerate the mainstreaming of his party, his decision to take the Quebec road to a majority was well advised. If he did not, he was in for a rocky ride.

To the eventual exasperation of many of those who turned their backs on the province to create the Reform Party, Quebec was the social conscience of the Mulroney government. The Conservative Quebec caucus was instrumental in killing the 1987 bid to restore the death penalty. It had no appetite for the politics of abortion. It disliked any tinkering with the employment-insurance system, as well as cuts to social programs. And it played a large role in keeping the environment on the Tory government to-do list for far longer than anyone expected.

Over his two mandates, Mulroney had five environment ministers. Four of them were from Quebec; Jean Charest was the last. In that capacity, Charest learned early on that few issues cut across the sovereignist-federalist divide as smoothly as the environment. He knew that when he was a federal Cabinet minister, and he has remembered it in the years since becoming a provincial politician.

Over the past few years, Quebec's influential artistic community, along with a growing number of its intellectuals, has been investing in the environment issue the fervour and passion it used to channel into the advancement of sovereignty. Over his first mandate, Charest ran into more flak on environmental files than on anything related to language or federal-provincial relations. In a province where politics is often a religion, the environment has replaced language as the iconic issue of a new generation. It has also emerged as a new meeting ground between sovereignists and federalists. As comedian Sophie Cadieux told Radio-Canada in a 2006 interview, "When it comes to the environment, there are no federalists and no sovereignists, just people who are concerned and want to do something about it."

When Stephen Harper walked away from the Kyoto Protocol, his closest provincial ally wasted no time in sending him the message that he was making a mistake. Jean Charest lamented the Conservative decision in private and in public. He also set out to implement the Quebec Kyoto targets on his own. To do so, he proposed to introduce the first carbon tax in the country, a taboo in Harper's books.

A month later, both Jean Charest and Mario Dumont, the prime minister's top political allies in Quebec, distanced themselves publicly from Stephen Harper's Middle East policy.

In June 2006, when David Suzuki went to Quebec with that question, he got the beginning of his answer from Premier Charest and Mario Dumont. In his quest for a majority, Stephen Harper would ignore the progressive realities of Quebec at his peril.

—

## CHAPTER TWENTY-SIX

# A PROGRESSIVE BATTLEFIELD

Before the 2006 election, the other federalist parties warned Canadians that a massive federal disengagement from the country's social affairs would inevitably follow a Conservative victory.

In a case of old habits dying hard, the NDP and the Liberals woke up on the morning after the vote determined to fight Harper's anticipated hands-off approach to social policy every inch of the way. Many of their MPs wanted to refight the child-care battle. Some itched to fight Alberta and Quebec by proxy, by taking on Stephen Harper on medicare. For his part, Paul Martin set out to try to keep alive the Kelowna Accord, a wide-ranging framework agreement he had negotiated with the First Nations and the provinces in the dying days of his minority government.

Few of those battles resonated loudly outside the immediate circle of Liberal and NDP supporters. They fell particularly flat in Quebec. The Conservative agenda did not put the province's child-care program at risk. The directions that Charest was taking on medicare enjoyed broad support. Quebec's First Nations had boycotted Martin's Kelowna summit. If anything, the Liberal years had demonstrated that there was little incentive for Quebecers to support federal parties that were more interested in the core missions of the provinces than in their own.

It quickly became apparent that both the NDP and the Liberals would be better advised to engage Harper on his chosen terrains—the environment, trade, foreign affairs, national defence, immigration and the gun registry—than to drag his government back into the disputed federal-provincial fields that had preoccupied the last Liberal Parliament.

Stephen Harper's determination to refocus the federal government on its core missions has been a defining trait of his political personality. His thinking has evolved on a number of issues over the years, but he has been unwavering in his belief that Canada would work better if the various levels of governments "stuck to their own knitting," as he put it during his last leadership campaign, in 2004.

In the 2006 election, that approach earned him the attention of Quebecers. In the next one, it could turn out to be his undoing.

As it happens, the core missions of the federal government are all of major interest to Quebecers these days. Most of the issues they involve have more legs in public opinion than Harper's Quebec battlehorse of fiscal imbalance. In every single case, Quebecers' instincts lean away from long-held Conservative positions.

It is no accident that the federal Liberal Party went up in the polls in Quebec over Jean Chrétien's last activist year in office. Many of the Quebecers who had spent the Chrétien era counting the days till the prime minister's retirement finally liked what they saw. But in opposition, Stephen Harper was on the wrong side of Quebec on every issue dear to Quebec. A Conservative government focused on its core missions was not only bound to have a high profile in Quebec, it would also have to win Quebecers over to views that were foreign to the province's mainstream.

In strategic terms, Harper's focus amounted to giving the NDP and the Liberals the advantage of the battlefield in the next federal election. If they really wanted to engage Quebec voters against the Conservatives, they could do a lot worse than choose grounds that are by definition federal.

As the defeated federalist parties took stock of the situation after the 2006 election, it should also have been obvious to them that, if federal governments were to play a leading role on the social front in the future, a strategic retreat was in order.

The past few years have demonstrated beyond a doubt that a federal government that continues to fail at its core missions will be unable to exercise effective national leadership. The clumsy attempts at activism during the Martin era blurred the lines of accountability between the two orders of government, leaving voters confused (and frustrated) as to whom to credit or blame for the ups and downs of the system. Predictably, the provinces and the federal government all claimed credit for what worked, but none would take the blame for what didn't.

Because of their collective insistence on keeping Ottawa out of their affairs, Quebecers were probably the least confused. When the Supreme Court ruled against Quebec's ban on private insurance for essential medical services in 2005, they didn't call for the federal government to help sort out the province's health system, or to protect it from whatever reform the Charest government brought forward. Quebec voters know that they will ultimately be the judges of their provincial government's decisions. Most of them feel no need for a federal watchdog to look over their government's shoulder.

On the morning after the 2006 election, the biggest danger to Canada's social union was not a disengaged federal government, or even one that was determined to dispose of the bulk of its surplus rather than keep money to use as leverage on its provincial partners. Over the past decade, Ottawa had had more negative influence on social policy when it was broke and cut transfer payments to make ends meet, than it had positive influence when it was rich and tried to draw the provinces into expanding the social safety net.

The real danger was that the provinces—whose governments operate on the short-term calendar of four-year mandates—would abandon longer-term investment in their social fabric, and use freed-up federal money to engage in a race to the bottom of the tax-rate ladder.

On that score, the most ominous post-election sign was not inflicted by the new Conservative government—not even when it abandoned the Liberals' early childhood education initiative, and substituted old-style family allowances for future child-care places.

Rather, it was inflicted by the provinces themselves, when not a single one of them came forward to take over some of the tax space that Ottawa was giving up. Even Quebec made no move to ensure that the parents who benefit from its generous child-care program give Stephen Harper's $1,200 yearly allowance back to the system, in whole or in part. That could have been accomplished by simply raising fees for the program by a dollar a day. But with a re-election campaign imminent, the Charest government allowed parents—even the most affluent ones—to double-dip, at the expense of both orders of government.

Over the next few years, the directions that Alberta takes may be more crucial to the future shape of Canada's social union than those of the federal government. If the province chooses to reinvest its riches in its social infrastructure, Ontario, Quebec, British Columbia and the others will at least try to follow suit. In a modern economy, competitiveness is measured partly by the quality of hospitals, daycares and universities. But if Alberta focuses on tax cuts and on turning itself into even more of a fiscal haven, that is the ground on which the next big interprovincial competition will take place—at the expense of the social programs of many provinces.

In the nineties, the Harris tax cuts had more impact on Quebec's social policies than anything the federal government did. It was not that Quebecers envied the Ontario cuts; they did at first, but the attraction wore off as some of the social trade-offs became apparent. Still, no province is immune to the pressures of fiscal geography, and no federal government, activist as it may be, can change that. But it can, by being more disciplined in its approach to federalism, ensure that voters are more able to hold the appropriate order of government accountable for its choices.

Take Canada to war and I will take you to an election, Gilles Duceppe told Stephen Harper right off the bat, on the occasion of their first meeting after the 2006 Conservative victory. The Bloc Québécois leader did not mean the ongoing deployment in Afghanistan; his party had supported Canada's peacekeeping commitment to the region in 2003, as well as Paul Martin's decision to redefine the mission's role along more militarily proactive lines.

Despite the Bloc's support, though, the mission was never popular in Quebec. A significant majority of Quebecers had opposed the deployment from the very start. A Harper visit to the Afghan front early in his mandate did more to raise the profile of the mission in Quebec than the Bloc's support ever did, and also had an impact elsewhere in Canada.

When the prime minister surprised Parliament by asking MPs to support a two-year extension of the mission, in the spring of 2006, the Bloc seized on the chance to hop off the train before the inevitable day when the military rotation delivered another Quebec regiment into harm's way, sometime in 2007. Gilles Duceppe accused Stephen Harper of jumping the gun on the extension, by giving it the go-ahead almost a year before the current mission was due to expire. His caucus voted unanimously against the government's motion.

But back in the immediate aftermath of the 2006 election, it was Iraq that was on Duceppe's mind when he first met with Harper. Alone of all the federal leaders, the new prime minister had pushed for Canada to get involved in the conflict three years earlier. Later, Harper would nuance his position, claiming that he meant Canada to offer moral support for the Americans. But that was not how it came across at the time, either in the United States or at home. With the U.S.-led coalition mired in Iraq, Gilles Duceppe was serving early notice that, as far as his party was concerned, the days of the minority government would be numbered if it set out to embark Canada on that adventure, or on another run along the same lines.

It was not an empty threat. True, the results of the 2006 election had destabilized the Bloc Québécois. Its strategists were deeply perplexed by the unexpected appeal of the Conservative Party in Quebec, and uncertain as to the longer-term prospects of their own party.

Paul Martin's minority government had provided the Bloc with the longest free ride in its short history. For eighteen months, Gilles Duceppe and his caucus had never felt any of the discomforts usually attendant on the more crowded circumstances of life in a minority Parliament. The NDP and the Conservatives had often agonized over the impact of the timing of a government defeat on their own prospects; they had worried that Canadians would find them overeager to pull the plug on Paul Martin's government if they acted precipitously; they had fretted about looking as if they were in bed with sovereignists when they tried to defeat it. The Bloc had had no such concerns.

From its perspective, the sooner Canada went back to the polls the better, before the sponsorship memories started to fade from Quebecers' minds. In an ideal world, the Bloc would have campaigned before the Gomery commission had a chance to sort things out and exonerate Paul Martin. For almost two years,

Gilles Duceppe had been able to say without bluffing that his party would welcome an election whenever the other opposition parties agreed to bring down the Liberal government.

In the interval between Paul Martin's first campaign and his final one, it had seemed that every cloud had a silver lining for the Bloc. Jean Chrétien, *in absentia*, had unexpectedly become Gilles Duceppe's fairy godmother.

After the 2004 election, the Bloc was awash with money for the first time in its history. Just prior to retiring, Chrétien had changed the rules regulating the financing of Canada's political parties. Tailored on the model introduced in Quebec in the late seventies, the new regimen banned corporate and union donations, and replaced them with generous government subsidies.

Chrétien surely hoped to be remembered for getting big money out of federal politics, rather than for presiding over the creation of one of the shadiest programs in recent federal history. For the Bloc, though, the initiative was all sweet and no sour. From its inception, the party had voluntarily complied with the more stringent Quebec rules. It had never accepted union and corporate donations. Under the new law, it would lose nothing but would gain the gift that kept on giving: a recurrent federal subsidy.

For every vote it won, the Bloc—like every other federal party—would get a fixed per capita subsidy. As a bonus, every dollar the Bloc received was bound to stretch farther than the dollars falling into the competition's pockets. For obvious geographical reasons, the costs of running a campaign in one province are immensely lower than those of a national campaign.

With the Parti Québécois out of power, Gilles Duceppe didn't spend a lot of time, at least initially, worrying that some voters would be reluctant to use his party as an outlet for their anger at the Liberals for fear of giving sovereignty a boost. With a federalist government just getting down to work in Quebec City, that issue was temporarily at rest.

The Parliament that was born after January 2006 could not have been more different from the previous one. Even before the House opened, the Bloc could no longer count on the sponsorship scandal for momentum and it was on the wrong side of the Quebec election calendar. Duceppe, who had left the previous Parliament in the fall as the leader with the best prospects, was coming back with his hands tied. From then on he would have at least as much cause to fear a quick return to the polls as any other opposition leader. In the lead-up to the election, the Bloc had spent liberally; the party had been significantly in the red, and would need months, maybe as much as a year, to restore its finances. On top of that, Duceppe had to avoid finding himself on the campaign trail at the same time as his Parti Québécois associates, as the two largely shared the same organization. But neither he nor they had any control over the provincial election clock. That was in the hands of Premier Jean Charest.

In the bed of quicksand that the House of Commons became for the Bloc Québécois after the 2006 election, Iraq—and the broader issue of the potential realignment of Canada's foreign policy with that of the Bush administration—stood out like a rare patch of rock-solid political ground. In the time between the 1995 referendum and Jean Chrétien's retirement, there had been countless federal-provincial irritants between Quebec and Ottawa, but none had seemed to change the fundamental *rapport de force* between federalists and sovereignists. And then Iraq came along. The debate galvanized Quebec in an unprecedented way.

When Chrétien decided to keep Canada out of the U.S.-led coalition that moved against Saddam Hussein, it was widely said that the prime minister didn't want to squander Jean Charest's chances in an imminent Quebec election. But the stakes were actually higher. In the lead-up to the Iraq war, Quebec had taken to the streets as it had not done since the days after the Meech Lake debacle. In fact, more people walked against the Iraq war in Montreal, on one of the most bone-chilling days of the winter of 2003, than paraded to mourn Meech on June 24, 1990.

Many of the francophone Quebecers who came out to oppose the war had pounded the same pavement in the past, to ask for tougher language laws, or to affirm their distinct identity. But this time they were walking alongside allophones and anglophones. Old Quebec and new Quebec marched together for the first time ever, standing as one against a war that was about to be fought on foreign soil.

—

## CHAPTER TWENTY-SEVEN

# A NEW PARADIGM

I n recent years, Quebec has been getting a larger proportion of its immigrants from the Muslim areas of the Middle East and North Africa than has any other Canadian province. According to a 2005 federal Department of Citizenship and Immigration survey, three out of ten very recent immigrants to Montreal were Muslims. While the immigration statistics of Toronto and Vancouver are dominated by South Asia, Algeria, Morocco and Lebanon are among the top six sources of new Quebec immigrants. The majority of newcomers to Canada from French North Africa, Syria and Lebanon settle in Montreal, with the Lebanese currently making up the fourth-largest community there.

That is no accident. By virtue of a federal-provincial agreement, Quebec has had a say in the selection of the immigrants settling in the province since the seventies. The system grants extra points to French-speaking applicants. In the natural course of things, they are also more likely than others to be drawn to a francophone environment.

This slant in the immigration mix naturally colours the province's approach to the international scene; that became apparent after 9/11. But other factors also predispose Quebec to filter global events through a different prism than the rest of Canada. By virtue of language, Quebec gets a blend of overseas information unlike that received by the rest of the country. It is much more exposed to European sources, and less so to American ones. Over time, that has led Quebecers to have a more positive view of the prospect of moving to another medicare model. They have drawn inspiration from the French experience, rather than apprehension from the American one. After 9/11, Quebec brought the same distinctive perspective to bear on the war on terrorism.

Quebec's wariness to follow the American lead has more to do with the above than with a supposedly bred-in-the-bone pacifist tradition, or some strong anti-American streak. The depiction of Quebec as a hotbed of anti-Americanism simply does not jibe with its recent history, or with the observations of some of the American officials who have been in close contact with the province over the past two decades.

In the days of Brian Mulroney, Quebec was as eager as Alberta—the province that enjoys the most pro-American reputation—to jump on the free-trade bandwagon. At the time of the referendum, U.S. president Bill Clinton was the most influential international figure in francophone Quebec. According to polls sponsored by the No committee, his referendum intervention impacted more positively on the federalist cause than the so-called love-in that brought thousands of non-Quebecers to Montreal in the immediate lead-up to the vote.

After he left his post, Paul Cellucci, George W. Bush's outspoken envoy to Canada, wrote in his 2005 memoir that he had never detected an ounce of anti-Americanism in the post–9/11 positions defended by the Bloc Québécois in the House of Commons—a comment he was not inclined to make about either the federal NDP or the Liberals. (In his memoir, appropriately titled *Unquiet Diplomacy*, he also described Gilles Duceppe as the most impressive of the federal leaders he had encountered during his tenure.)

As for the so-called pacifist streak that is supposedly inbred in Quebecers, it didn't stop them from heartily supporting the sending of Canadian troops to Haiti, the former Yugoslavia or Rwanda. None of these theatres qualified as soft duty.

In the twenty-first century, Canada is unlikely to fight over language again. And while the constitution is still a hot button issue in some quarters, the days when Quebec and the rest of Canada would throw themselves body and soul into a constitutional discussion are probably as unlikely to return as those when Quebecers quarrelled furiously over their political future at the dinner table.

But Canadians may come to miss the times when their biggest wars involved words, and were fought by proxy by pundits making dire predictions on the basis of the few lines of a parliamentary motion or some constitutional clause. The debates of the new century are lining up to be both immensely more basic, and immensely more complex for a mere national government to control. They already involve the air Canadians breathe, the energy they consume, the future of the country's tradition of civil liberties and, yes, whether their sons and daughters go to war and, if so, under what flag and in the name of what cause.

The events of 9/11 have also upped the stakes of national politics for more recent Canadians. They were mostly spectators of the divisive debates of the past, as the country's founding people, the French, English and First Nations, tried to formalize their respective places in modern Canada. But these days it is not only francophone Canadians who feel no emotional tug towards the prospect of joining an Anglo-Saxon alliance to fight global terrorism, or who see little intrinsic merit in an alignment along such lines.

On that basis old Canada might naturally have gone to Iraq in 2003, but new Canada was not so sure. Old and new Quebec, though, were on the same wavelength. The white ribbon that the three Quebec provincial leaders wore throughout the provincial campaign spoke to that reality.

One of the strengths of federalism in Quebec has always been the attachment to Canada of those who came to the province from other parts of the world. It has usually been stronger than their attachment to Quebec itself. It is difficult to know whether, in future, finding themselves on the losing side of debates on the federal government's international directions may impact on these newer communities' sense of loyalty. It is quite possible that it will.

Jean Chrétien was the first modern Quebec prime minister to find himself at the helm at a time when Canada was called upon to join its Anglo-Saxon allies in a theatre of war. (Louis Saint-Laurent and Brian Mulroney enrolled Canada in the Korean and first Gulf wars under the auspices of the United Nations.) Chrétien certainly took into account more than the traditional Quebec–Canada debate and the upcoming partisan test of a Quebec election when he declined the invitation to move into Iraq. Canada cannot pride itself on the diversity of its model and its concept of civic nationalism, and then fall back on the instincts of its white Anglo-Saxon Protestant past to chart its course in the world.

Since Pierre Trudeau, every Canadian prime minister has been more of a war prime minister than the last. Brian Mulroney took Canada into the first Gulf war. Under his leadership, Canada was the first to send peacekeepers to the former Yugoslavia. That theatre would forever change the definition of peacekeeping, a Canadian contribution to the world that is probably as close to the hearts of Quebecers as the invention of medicare has come to be to many other Canadians.

Jean Chrétien's tenure was dominated by the genocides in the Balkans and in Rwanda; his very first European mission involved a NATO discussion that resulted in air strikes against the former Yugoslavia. He agreed to have Canada participate in NATO's military operation in Kosovo, declined to join the Iraq war, but readily committed troops to Afghanistan.

In his relatively brief time in office, Paul Martin redefined the military mission in Afghanistan along more proactive lines. According to Stephen Harper, the former Liberal prime minister also considered allowing Canada to take on a role in Iraq.

For all of that, Brian Mulroney, Jean Chrétien and Paul Martin were all reluctant warriors. In sharp contrast with his predecessors, Stephen Harper embraced his status as a war prime minister with gusto. His first overseas foray as prime minister took him to a military base in one of the most intense war zones on the international scene. His first foreign policy speech was laced with militaristic rhetoric.

Over his first months in office, not a week went by without Harper showing up at some event that was associated with the military. War memorials, military cemeteries and bases have all emerged as favourite venues of this prime minister. His PMO has been dutifully prompt to issue regrets over the deaths of Canada's soldiers or police officers in the line of duty, but a lot less so to comment on Canadian civilian casualties abroad. His first hundred days in office were marked by more deaths in combat than Brian Mulroney's entire first term as prime minister. Harper's first G8 summit was dominated by a resurgence of hostilities in the Middle East, and by his willingness to pick a side in the conflict.

Throughout its history, Quebec has never supported a war prime minister. As the 2006 election demonstrated, there is a first time for everything. But Duceppe's post-election sense that Harper would court a backlash in Quebec with his foreign policy was prescient.

—

## CHAPTER TWENTY-EIGHT

## THE POLITICS OF SELF-DELUSION

After the 1995 referendum, some Canadians claimed that they no longer cared what Quebec did. They complained that the province was a drag on the rest of the country. They prayed for the day when the prime minister would no longer be a Quebecer. They anticipated the moment when a federal government would emerge that was not beholden to Quebec.

After all that, many of them ended up at the Conservative victory rally in Calgary on election night 2006, cheering the victories of ten Quebec MPs and hoping for more in the next election.

More than a few of the Quebecers who voted yes in 1995 spent the next decade raising one hand to show their undying love for sovereignty, and doing everything they could with the other to make sure they would not be asked to stand up and be counted in a referendum again. In the aftermath of the debate on the Clarity Act, they stayed home rather than support the Bloc Québécois. They told pollsters that they were as eager for another referendum as they were for the onset of winter. They abandoned the Parti Québécois in droves in the 2003 Quebec election.

In response to a poll conducted for the Centre for Research and Information on Canada in September 2004, 55 percent of Quebecers refused to describe themselves as either federalists or sovereignists. A good number of those quietly voted for Stephen Harper two years later.

The morning after the 1995 referendum, the sovereignist leadership put itself on a collective prescription of Prozac. It obsessed over the fifteen thousand votes that could have made the difference between defeat and victory, but not over the hundreds of thousands of voices that were missing from a solid pro-sovereignty consensus.

Leading sovereignist activists dismissed every counter-argument to their prediction of a smooth transition to statehood as specious federalist rhetoric. When their own research came up with many of the same findings, they put it out of their minds. The government-financed Quebec studies on the conditions for the province's accession to sovereignty remain unchallenged, only a few Google clicks away from resurfacing.

In Ottawa, top-tier Liberal Cabinet ministers went selectively blind. They did not seem to notice that their party was a shadow of its former self in Quebec—or if they did, they were too polite to talk about it in public, or they simply didn't care. For the most part, they looked the other way, happy to be kept out of the often messy Quebec loop. They stayed out of the post-referendum fray and cultivated their leadership ambitions. They kept a low profile on Quebec-related issues. In the end, one of them had such a lead in the succession sweepstakes that most of the others didn't even run for Jean Chrétien's job.

Quebec's politically astute federal ministers temporarily lost their sense of smell. They didn't pick up any bad odour as their government sprinkled sponsorship money on the province like manure in springtime.

Many Liberals from Quebec had spent years in Jean Chrétien's Cabinet and caucus waiting for a different era of federalism under Paul Martin. But they apparently never suspected that they would be in for less of the same policies towards Quebec. It could be that they never asked — or that they read what they wanted into his self-imposed silence on the Quebec–Canada issue. Silence is sometimes camouflage for an empty mind.

Some Liberals made themselves believe that being in the party of official bilingualism earned them an exemption from being bilingual themselves. They put a lot of time into nurturing leadership ambitions, and very little into practising French verbs. So many of those ran for the leadership of the party after Paul Martin quit in 2006 that the party that had given birth to official bilingualism was unable to hold a cogent leadership debate entirely in French.

Other Liberals treated the Charter like a pull-down menu from which they were free to choose the rights that jibed with their personal views. Gay and abortion rights did not fit their beliefs. Many of those were MPs. On election podium after election podium in 2006, they stood alongside Paul Martin as he pleaded with Canadians not to put Charter rights in Conservative hands.

As for the Bloc Québécois, it developed a bad case of amnesia. Early on, Lucien Bouchard had predicted that if the Bloc lingered on Parliament Hill after a referendum defeat, it risked becoming a federal security blanket for Quebecers. The forward post of the sovereignty movement, its founder had correctly forecast, would morph into a reassuring backup for those who wanted to take a chance on federalism.

In 2006, the party advertised itself along lines eerily similar to those of a home-insurance sales pitch, the kind vaunting the peace of mind that comes from having a paid-up policy against fire and theft. With the sponsorship disaster still fresh in every mind, the Bloc slogan invited Quebecers to count their blessings for having the sovereignist party on watch on Parliament Hill.

On January 23, 2006, twelve Bloc MPs were elected for the fifth time — a happy dozen federal lifers.

The New Democratic Party continued to see itself as the conscience of Parliament, but it never seemed to worry about examining its own conscience. It preached a dogma that some of its own provincial governments would not practise. Its culture of innovation turned into a culture of resistance to change, and its thinking became a prisoner in the box of its orthodoxy.

The NDP pretended that it could on one hand sell a new generation of activists on the merits of electoral politics, and on the other be content as impotent paragons of virtue in the House of Commons. In 2006, 308 New Democrats tried to win seats but only 29 were elected. The sound of one hand clapping should have greeted the best NDP score in almost two decades.

The Liberals and the NDP presumed to proudly call themselves national parties, even though they couldn't find enough common ground with Alberta or francophone Quebec to be a real presence in either place. The Liberals came to see the Bloc as a blessing in disguise, and they seized on it as an insurance policy against an alternative national coalition. The Conservative government of Alberta became the whipping boy of federal NDP leaders.

Many MPs believed themselves that they could call each other unethical and dishonest and not collectively lose the respect of Canadians. The Liberals commended Jean Chrétien to voters in 2000 and then promptly turned around and got down to the business of deposing a sitting prime minister. The Martinites let Sheila Copps, their best-known female MP, get run out of her riding, and then assured Canadian women that the Liberal Party had their political advancement at heart.

The federal government neglected its programs. It turned the gun registry into a billion-dollar white elephant, and tried to stifle questions about its runaway costs. The party in power confused its interests with those of the country, and then presumed to give the provinces lessons in accountability and transparency.

MPs were handed the opportunity of two consecutive minority parliaments to show their mettle, and both times played politics rather than produce co-operative policies. The Opposition spent Martin's minority Parliament trying to force the government to go to the polls, and the Harper government quickly used its relative control of a minority Parliament to dare the Opposition to drag it into an election.

The 2006 election was a fitting end to a decade of political self-delusion. Or was it just a pause? In the winter of 2006, Stephen Harper's promise of a more open federalism opened Quebec doors that had previously been locked to his party. But the new prime minister wasn't handed the keys to the house just yet.

Alone of all Canadians, Quebecers have twice had occasion to say yes to Canada in recent years. They did so in the face of the best efforts of René Lévesque and Lucien Bouchard, two of the most compelling and articulate leaders this country has produced. Between the two referendums, the list of Canadian features that would be guaranteed to become features of a sovereign Quebec got longer. Its nationalism today is as civic as that on offer in the rest of Canada or in the United States. In its values and its approach to the world, a sovereign Quebec would not be very different from Canada as it was when Stephen Harper became prime minister.

It would be delusional to believe that Quebec would for very long offer blind support for federal policies that go against the grain of its collective convictions, in exchange for a bit more provincial autonomy.

But then, Stephen Harper would hardly be the first man to read too much promise into a first-date kiss.

Within the space of four years, Stephen Harper brought the Canadian Alliance back from the dead. He put an end to the feud that had divided the Conservative movement for more than ten years. He became the diffident leader of a new party, and brought it to power in less than two years. In the process, he emerged as a new federalist voice in Quebec at a time when it seemed that most Quebecers were well past listening.

For all the misgivings that the Conservative leader inspires in so many quarters, all of this is good news, for it has restored competitiveness to the federal system. And that did not happen a moment too soon.

Many of the ailments that have rendered federal politics so dysfunctional over the past decade have been by-products of the unhealthy monopoly of the Liberal Party. As a result of its dominance, the party often saw itself as bigger than the country. Its petty battles became national wars. Without the monopoly of the Liberal Party as the default federalist option in Quebec, the sponsorship scandal might have been nipped in the bud.

Over those years, the Liberal caucus came to replace the House of Commons as the venue where issues were thrashed out and where compromises were reached. Most of this happened behind closed doors, rendering the system even more opaque to average Canadians. Too often, it involved trade-offs that could not have been negotiated in broad daylight, for they would have failed the test of sound public policy. Even when ethics are not at stake, it is against the public interest to have caucus dynamics and a culture of mutual back-patting determine the course of a national government.

This disproportionate importance of internal Liberal dynamics produced the Martin PMO, a nest of sharp political operators whose wings turned out to be too short to soar to the heights of statesmanship. Martin's dithering on same-sex marriage and missile defence—to name just two issues—resulted from those dynamics rather than from clear policy vision, with consequences for both his and Canada's credibility.

If Stockwell Day had turned out to be a stronger leader of the Canadian Alliance in 2000, the Chrétienites and Martinites might not have felt that they had the luxury of allowing civil war to serve as a substitute for an orderly transition between leaders. Over the years, many observers have remarked on the uncommon loyalty that Brian Mulroney always inspired in his caucus. For much of his last mandate, his Tory government was sinking in the polls, and yet most of Mulroney's MPs remained ready to walk to hell and back with him. But then, it's rarely in a storm—when all hands are required on board—that mutinies occur.

Only an incredible (and false) sense of comfort can account for the fact that a governing party turned against a leader who had delivered three consecutive majorities, as the Liberals turned against Jean Chrétien. As subsequent events revealed, Chrétien may have made winning elections look easy, but a campaign is never a cakewalk.

With the real action taking place elsewhere, the House of Commons sank to new lows of pettiness and futility. As Ed

Broadbent wistfully noted in his 2005 farewell speech, it was hard for young question-period watchers to believe that Parliament Hill was the place where some of the most crucial pages of the history of Canada had been written. The flag debate, the Charter discussion, the free-trade battle—all these echo very faintly in a chamber whose current members devote so much energy to the pursuit of the superficial to the detriment of the essential.

But Ed Broadbent could also have noted his own party's descent into irrelevance. After the 1993 election, the NDP lost its ambition and its edge. It gave up trying to preen itself as a contender for government, and became content with permanent opposition status. It let itself go, as far as policy was concerned.

Today, the federal NDP has more elder statesmen and stateswomen than rising stars, and more rigid memories than fresh ideas. Even its wish for a more proportional electoral system involves a dose of copping out of the divisive but essential task of squaring the twenty-first-century circle of party policies.

Jack Layton and his predecessors are not primarily to blame for this state of affairs; the federal NDP's malaise is rooted in its spirit, not its leadership. It has become a party suspicious of success. Having lived for so long on the consolation of moral victories, it has come to find its validation in defeat.

In those circumstances, it's no wonder that after 1993 the intellectual energy in federal politics transferred from the left to the right, as the Reform Party rather than the NDP provided the Liberals with the policy inspiration for so many of their accomplishments.

The Bloc Québécois's enduring presence on Parliament Hill is part of a larger malaise within the sovereignty movement. It amounts to a waste of talent, as most of the Bloc's members—including the many able ones—will never know any other life than that of opposition MP. Up to a point, Gilles Duceppe and his caucus have been hostages to the narrow results of the 1995 referendum. If the defeat had been more decisive, the party might have been more inclined to question its continued existence.

But the Bloc's enduring success is also a symptom of the federalist parties' post-Meech failure to engage francophone Quebec. The 2006 federal election demonstrated that there are voters out there waiting to be re-engaged. There is no reason why Stephen Harper should have a monopoly on them.

That election took place at a time of great flux in Quebec. The search for a life in politics outside the sovereignist/federalist box has become a strong undercurrent of Quebec politics. The end result could be a society polarized along different but more traditional ideological lines. In that scenario, the province would become just another front in the battle between progressives and conservatives. But the outcome could also be a society that moves beyond its historical divisions to build a new consensus around reconfigured stakes.

Connecting with Quebec—as Stephen Harper did in 2006—was one thing. Keeping the connection alive is another matter. There have been times since his victory when it has not been obvious that he fully grasped that, for his contact with Quebec to amount to more than a spark, the current has to flow both ways.

It is difficult to predict the future of a relationship on the basis of a single kiss—and for the Conservatives, that is all the 2006 election results amounted to. That being said, blind dates are among the rare romantic encounters that both parties enter with their eyes wide open. Expectations on both sides are mercifully low.

Quebecers are not sentimental voters; just ask Lucien Bouchard. For all his charisma, he found that there were clear limits to his appeal. Quebec voters have never followed a leader blindly, and many of those who appealed to them in vain were more compelling than Stephen Harper.

For his part, the Conservative leader has had inspired flashes of pragmatism in the past. He has also displayed a clear understanding that in this game, gains will not be achieved without taking some substantial risks. That combination has brought him to power. But as Brian Mulroney's experience demonstrated, there are limits to how far his party can bend without breaking.

Whether Quebec and Stephen Harper confirm their union in a future election, produce a majority and live happily ever after will be a topic for another book.

# ACKNOWLEDGMENTS

Until Diane Martin sent me an email to probe my interest in writing a book for Knopf Canada, in the dying days of the 2006 federal election, I had always thought that if I ever wrote anything longer than a column, it would be a French-language work of fiction—an escape from writing daily in English on politics. In the end, though, I could not resist trying to match the entrails of the election to the disjointed parts of the Canadian body politic.

No one was asked to bare his or her soul for this book. And none of the people listed below was consulted on its conclusions. But journalists are by definition voyeurs, and over the years, the willingness of so many people to allow me to see the political world through their spyglass has been particularly helpful.

I first met Hugh Segal when I was a young reporter covering Queen's Park. For better or for worse, the way Premier Bill Davis shepherded his party through two minority spells in the seventies very much shaped my sense of what a responsive government coalition should be like. Senator Segal's contrary faith in a Conservative Canada—albeit a progressive one—continues to intrigue me, possibly because it keeps failing to materialize.

Patrick Parisot lived under my roof for many of the years when he served as press secretary to Jean Chrétien, including the referendum period. It has been a long time since our paths have crossed, but his sense of his prime minister has left a trace, surfacing in this book in spite of the accumulated grime of the sponsorship affair.

Over the past five years, I have watched with some trepidation and much fascination as Jean Lapierre and then Michael Fortier — two people I have come to know well — have hitched their respective stars to comets they believed in. Catching glimpses of Paul Martin and Stephen Harper through the eyes of these two Quebecers who changed their lives to serve a leader who inspired them has provided me with unique insights into the meaning and the consequences of political loyalty.

I have a well-deserved reputation as a professional loner, but I have always been blessed with a cohort of supportive colleagues. Among them: Daniel Heureux, who has put up with my lunchtime rants for the best part of two decades; Patrice Roy, Michel C. Auger and Vincent Marrissal, who double as friends and sounding boards; my bureau chief, Susan Delacourt, who already knows more about book-writing than I can possibly hope to learn; my column-mate, James Travers, who will be the one least surprised to learn that I did not share a line of my manuscript with anyone before I handed it in to Knopf; and *The Star* itself, for encouraging me in this project.

For as long as I have covered politics, I have also been raising a family. As life would have it, in the summer of 2006 I temporarily found myself living in an empty nest, for the very first time. To Bruno and Antoine I want to say that writing this book, as satisfying as it has been, did not really make up for their absence.

CHANTAL HÉBERT is a national political affairs columnist for the *Toronto Star* and a weekly guest columnist in *Le Devoir*. She is regular guest on the "At Issue" political panel on CBC Television's *The National*. A graduate of York University's Glendon College, Hébert is a senior fellow of Massey College, University of Toronto, and the 2006 recipient of the Hyman Soloman Award for Excellence in Public Policy Journalism. She lives in Montreal.